To Jane ~ Richard Levy

I hope you believe this,

Bob Welsh
Oct 14, 2023

Bob's Theology

R. BROWNLEE WELSH

Dedicated to Marlis Welsh, my wife of 73 years, and my son, Robert Brownlee Welsh, Jr., who passed away too soon

Copyright © 2023 R. Brownlee Welsh.

All rights reserved. No part of this book may be used or reproduced by any means, graphic, electronic, or mechanical, including photocopying, recording, taping or by any information storage retrieval system without the written permission of the author except in the case of brief quotations embodied in critical articles and reviews.

LifeRich Publishing is a registered trademark of The Reader's Digest Association, Inc.

LifeRich Publishing books may be ordered through booksellers or by contacting:

LifeRich Publishing
1663 Liberty Drive
Bloomington, IN 47403
www.liferichpublishing.com
844-686-9607

Because of the dynamic nature of the Internet, any web addresses or links contained in this book may have changed since publication and may no longer be valid. The views expressed in this work are solely those of the author and do not necessarily reflect the views of the publisher, and the publisher hereby disclaims any responsibility for them.

Any people depicted in stock imagery provided by Getty Images are models, and such images are being used for illustrative purposes only.
Certain stock imagery © Getty Images.

Original cover art by the author

ISBN: 978-1-4897-4899-7 (sc)
ISBN: 978-1-4897-4898-0 (hc)
ISBN: 978-1-4897-4900-0 (e)

Library of Congress Control Number: 2023915656

Print information available on the last page.

LifeRich Publishing rev. date: 09/08/2023

CONTENTS

CRUCIFIED	1
THE JESUS DREAM	3
REVELATION POEM	4
THE MESSIAH	6
GOD'S JUDGEMENT	7
EXILE	8
CHRIST'S COMING	9
A MIRACULOUS BIRTH OF A CHILD AT EIGHTY-NINE	10
PREDESTINATION	11
THE PENTECOST	13
WRATH OF GOD	14
JESUS SECOND COMING AT PENTECOST	15
FAITH AND WISDOM	17
TRINITARIAN FORMULATION	18
SECOND COMING AT PENTECOST	20
GOD AS JESUS	22
COMPLACENCY	23
HOLY SPIRIT	24
NUTSHELL	28
SOPHIA AS MESSIAH	29
WHY GOD BECAME MAN	30
CREATION AND CREATURE	31
COMING AGAIN SOON II	33
JOHN'S JESUS	34
BELIEVE IN MY NAME	35
GOD AS THE MESSIAH SAYS	36
DIVINE INTERVENTION	39
NAME DROPPING: ELOHIM	40
CHRISTMAS TIME	41
MIRACLE	43
BROWN MOUNTAIN LIGHTS	44
HEAVEN	45
LOVE YOUR ENEMY	47
RULER OF THE WORLD JN 14:30	48
CONSCIENCE	49

BIBLICAL ANALYSIS	50
FROZEN CHOSEN	52
THE WELLSPRING OF LIFE (SAMARITAN WELL)	53
MARY MAGDALENE	55
DIVINE INTERVENTION	57
A VALENTINE	58
CREATION	59
ELIJAH	60
JESUS	62
JESUS ORDERS JUDAS TO DISCLOSE HIM	63
THE LAST WILL	64
SECOND ADAM	65
ELOJIM	67
JUDAS	68
CRUCIFIXION	71
HAPPY EASTER	73
EZRA	74
LAMENTING	76
ORIGINS OF JESUS	77
MICAIAH	79
HIS COMING – 2ND OR 1ST	80
JESUS ORDERS JUDAS TO DISCLOSE HIM	81
BABYLON IS HELL	82
THE HOLY GRAIL	83
ENOCH	84
NEHEMIAH'S RETURN	85
ANTINOMIANISM	86
NEHEMIAH	87
SON OF MAN	89
GOD'S STRUGGLES	91
THE PROPHET ISAIAH	95
THE SUFFERING SERVANT	99
ISAAC, SON OF GOD	100
JEREMIAH	101
HUNCH	104
GOD SAYS TO JEREMIAH	105
SYNAGOGUE	106
ONE OF THREE	107
EZEKIEL	110

IS THERE A TRINITY	111
MORE EZEKIEL	113
PENTECOST SUNDAY	114
FORGIVENESS	115
JONAH	116
PETER'S FAITH	117
DANIEL	118
THE MACCABEES	119
JONAH PREDICTION	121
TRINITY VIEW	122
NATURE	124
TRUTH	126
JOSEPH'S VERSION	127
CURE	129
JOSEPH'S VERSION	130
THAT'S HIS JOB	132
TO BE OR NOT TO BE	134
STORM AT SEA	136
QUANDARY	137
CONVERSION OF SAUL	138
JESUS SAID	140
BIZARRE	141
JUSTIFICATION	142
THE PATRIARCHS	143
HERITAGE	148
THE NEW COVENANT AND CIRCUMCISION	149
THE HIERARCHY	152
THE ARK OF THE COVENANT	154
PRAISE	156
THE HOLY SPIRIT AND THE LIGHT	157
DELIVERANCE	158
KING OF THE UNIVERSE	159
JUSTICE AND RIGHTEOUSNESS	160
EXODUS	161
CHRIST THE KING	162
THE SONS OF GOD	163
CHRISTMAS LESSONS	164
THE TALMUD	165
SON OF MAN	166

REBIRTH	169
TRINITY	171
THE RHYTHMIC UNIVERSE	172
ONE AS THREE	174
CHRISTMAS EVE	176
HAPPY BIRTHDAY JESUS	177
TODAY'S LESSON	178
UNIVERSAL SALVATION	180
WHY HAST THOU	181
OPPOSITES	182
THE COVENANT	183
TRUTH	184
BOB'S CREED	185
SACRIFICE	186
THIS EARTH	187
CREATION	188
WE	189
GOD'S LIGHT	190
OUR GOD, THEIR GOD	191
IT WAS GOD	193
GOD:	194
ONE GOD	195
SUBSTITUTE	197
GROUNDS FOR INCRIMINATION	198
A TRINITY	199
JOHN THE BAPTIST	201
THE FIG TREE	202
CIRCUMCISION	204
THE WORD IS GOD	205
COMMUNION	206
THE LOST ARK	208
CHRIST'S SPIRIT (PAUL TO GALATIANS)	209
OPPOSITES	211
REBIRTH	212
SALVATION	213
IN EXILE	214
MESSIANIC SECRET	215
THE WORD	216
LAZARUS	217

THE HOLY SPIRIT	219
FAITH	221
THE GRAIN OF WHEAT	222
REBIRTH	223
PORTENT OF ISRAEL	224
THE PEARLY GATES	225
THE BIRTHRIGHT	227
LOVE	228
ATON	229
MOSES	230
COMMANDER IN CHIEF	231
ZARUBBABBLE	233
HATE ONE'S PARENTS?	234
FAVORITE BIBLICAL CHARACTER	236
QUMRAN	238
WHY ANOTHER GOD	239
THE GREAT EXPERIMENT	241
WONDER	243
SAVIORS	244
THOMAS	245
TEASE	246
CREATION	247
TRUTH	249
ACKNOWLEDGEMENTS	251

CRUCIFIED

WE ARE THE ONES NOW BEING TRIED
WE ARE THE ONES BEING CRUCIFIED
I WAS TRIED AND FOUND GUILTY AS HELL
WHATEVER WE HAD ITS BEEN LOST AS WELL

WE ARE GETTING A TASTE OF THE ROMANS' LASH
ENGULFED LIKE JESUS IN THIS MORASS
THE TAUNTING SARCASM AND CROWN OF THORNS
WE RUE THE DAY THAT WE WERE BORN

IS THIS ANOTHER STORY OF JOB?
THE FAITHFUL ONE WHO SATAN PROBED
HERE THE WHOLE WORLD IS UNDER THE LASH
FROM RICHES TO RAGS IS JUST A FLASH

BUT JOB IS THE ONE WHO WAS NEVER FOUND WANTING
HIS FAITH WAS EVER MORE SURMOUNTING
THERE'S NOT ONE PERSON IN THE WHOLE WIDE WORLD
WHO'S NOT BEEN AFFECTED BY COVID'S ONGOING SCOURGE

IT'S NOW OUR TURN TO BE CRUCIFIED
TO FIND OUT WHAT IT IS LIKE TO BE THRASHED AND DIE
THE TORTURE OF WEARING A CROWN OF THORNS FOR
CONFINEMENT IN THIS JAIL FOR A MONTH, MAYBE MORE

SO NOW WE STILL DON'T KNOW HOW JESUS FELT
BEING TAUNTED, DEFILED, LASHED WITH THE WHIP
WE'RE JUST CONFINED TO OUR HOMES TO REPENT
EXAMINE OUR SINS TO SEE WHAT EXTENT

A NEW ERA HAS JUST BEGUN
WE HAVE NO JOBS; WE HAVE NO FUN
THE GOVERNMENT SENDS OUT CHECKS
FROM A DEPLETED TREASURY, IT DOESN'T MAKE SENSE.

ISAAC AS A SON OF GOD, WAS ALSO TO BE SACRIFICED
BUT INSTEAD OF SAVING, HE WAS SAVED BY A RAM THAT DIED
THIS WAS SYMBOLIZED AS THE END OF FIRSTBORN HUMAN SACRIFICE,
BUT THINK OF THE NUMBER OF EGYPTIAN FIRSTBORNS WHO DIED.

IS JESUS' DEATH THE ATONEMENT FOR THAT PASSOVER
AS WELL AS IS CLAIMED SALVATION FOR BELIEVERS
AT ANY RATE, WE KNOW HE WAS CRUCIFIED
FOR PIECES OF SILVER BY THE ONE, HE WAS IDENTIFIED

IT'S TIME FOR YOU TO LEAVE THE LAST SUPPER
HIS IDENTITY THE SOLDIERS WILL NOW DISCOVER
AS SET UP AND REVEALED BY THE ONE JESUS LOVED MOST
BY THE TREASURER DISCIPLE NAMED JUDAS WAS KISSED

IN THE GARDEN OF GETHSEMANE, LIKE THAT OF EDEN,
WHETHER A SERPENT OR CONSPIRATOR, THE SAME DEED WAS DONE.
ALL SINS COMMITTED SINCE ADAM AND EVE
ARE ALL RELINQUISHED NOW FOR THOSE WHO BELIEVE

WHILE WE ARE SUFFERING FOR OUR LIES AND OUR SINS
NAILED TO OUR HOMES AND MUCH TO OUR CHAGRIN
PERHAPS WE'LL CONFESS, REPENT AND BEGIN
AS UNBLEMISHED BABES IN THIS WORLD ALL OVER AGAIN

RB WELSH, 4 10 20

THE JESUS DREAM

THE ROBOT MUST HAVE BEEN A DREAM,
FOR JESUS IS A HUMAN BEING.
HE EATS WITH THE PHARISEES
AND SLEEPS ON THE SEA OF GALILEE.

JESUS WAS SAID TO BE THE SECOND ADAM.
CREATED IN THE VIRGIN WOMB, AND MARY HAD HIM.
THAT HE'S A ROBOT. I WAS WRONG,
GOD WAS JESUS ALL ALONG.

MARK, WHO WROTE ABOUT IT FIRST, SAYS
IT'S GOD AS MAN STARTING HIS CHURCH.

THE GOSPEL WRITERS DISAGREE,
MATTHEW AND LUKE SAY THAT HE
WAS OF A VIRGIN EVEN BORN,
IN A MANGER WITH THE COWS AND CORN.

THEN JOHN IN C.E. 90 SAYS THEY'RE WRONG,
THE WORD IS GOD HIMSELF AS SON.

RB WELSH, 12 7 22

REVELATION POEM

THEN THE NEW HEAVEN AND EARTH CAME INTO VIEW, (REV 21:1)
THE ALPHA AND OMEGA BEGAN TO START THINGS ANEW.
"I WILL BE THE WATER OF LIFE,
TO ALL THOSE WHO CONQUER, THERE'LL BE NO MORE STRIFE."

THE ONE WHO WAS TRIED AND CONVICTED ONE TIME,
WHO DIED FOR YOU HAVE COMMITTED NO CRIME.
BUT NO ONE UNCLEAN WHO COMMITTED AN ABOMINATION, (REV 21:27)
OR LIARS WILL BE ADMITTED INTO THIS NEW NATION.

THEN INTO THE CITY OF THE STREETS FILLED WITH GOLD AND GEMS, (REV 21:27)
THE EAGLE DEPOSITED THE MOTHER INTO "NEW JERUSALEM."
THE CHRIST REBORN "ISRAEL" CAN BEGIN AGAIN "TO BE,"
WITH THE DEATH OF THE DRAGON, ITS MOTHER IS FREE.

ONLY THOSE WRITTEN IN THE LAMB'S BOOK OF LIFE, (REV 21:27)
CAN ENTER THE GATES WHERE THERE IS NO STRIFE.
THE RIVER LINED WITH TREES OF LIFE THROUGH THE CITY DOES FLOW,
NOW ALL CAN SEE GOD; HIS FACE IS AGLOW. (REV 22:4)

IT'S LIKE ADAM AND EVE HAVE RETURNED TO THE GARDEN
OF EDEN, WHERE JESUS AND JUDAS, THE SATAN OF GETHSEMANE
HAS BEEN DEFEATED, HIS TEMPTATION REJECTED,
SO NOW, THE SYMBOL OF ETERNAL LIFE CAN BE ACCEPTED.

NO RICH ARE ALLOWED; ONLY THE PURE NOW SERENE. (MK 10:25)
THE MANSIONS ARE MANY, NO TEMPLE IS SEEN. (JN 14:2)
THE GATES ARE OF PEARL, THE WALLS CRYSTALLITE, (REV 21:22)
WITH THE LAMP OF JESUS HOLDING GOD'S GLORIOUS LIGHT.

AFTER ALL OF THIS WICKED AND BLUSTERING THUNDER,
THAT I HAD WITNESSED AND HAD BEEN CONSTANTLY UNDER,
THERE MUST BE A POINT THAT I'D SEEN, OR I'D HEARD,
THAT SHOULD NOW BE HEEDED AS NOT BEING ABSURD.

AH! IT IS THIS THAT EACH SHOULD PASS ON:
THAT WITH ONE'S TOUCH AND CONCENTRATED PRAYER,
EACH ONE OF US HAS RECEIVED THIS SAME IDEAL POWER.
TO FLY THEIR FRIEND FAR AWAY FROM A DRAGONS STINGS,
TO SAVE ONE ANOTHER ON FAITHFUL SOLID WINGS.

"TO COME AGAIN" MEANS HE'S NOT COMING ON CLOUDS,
BUT WILL BE VISITING US IN A LIGHT THAT ENSHROUDS
EACH ONE INDIVIDUALLY, LIKE A SPIRIT FROM AFAR,
THAT'S WHY THEY CALL HIM THE MORNING STAR.

SO IF I'M RETURNED TO THE PRISON OF MY CAVE,
I WANT TO BYPASS ALL THIS MEANT FOR A KNAVE.
THE HOLY SPIRIT HAS ITS OWN HEAVEN FOR SURE,
I'LL PRAY WHEN I DIE; I'LL GO WHERE IT'S PURE.

WITH THAT, JESUS PROMISES TO COME TO YOU SOON.
AS ISRAEL WAS REBORN FROM THE LADY ON THE MOON,
THE TREE OF IMMORTALITY FLOURISHES FOR THOSE SACRIFICED,
FOR THAT TREE OF EDEN IS JESUS THE CHRIST. (REV 22:15)

RB WELSH, 4 12 20

THE MESSIAH

THIS IS THE INCIDENT TO MAKE BELIEVERS OF ALL MEN,
BUT IT'S THE ONE THAT MADE THE JEWS CRUCIFY HIM.
THEY THOUGHT HE HAD COME TO GET RID OF THE ROMANS.
ALL THEY WANTED TO DO NOW WAS TAKE HIM OUT AND STONE HIM.

JESUS HAD ALREADY ADVISED THE PHARISEES TO PAY CAESAR WHAT WAS DUE
NOW HERE IS THE MIRACLE OF PUTTING THEM IN A STEW.
JESUS WAS SUPPOSED TO RID ISRAEL OF THE ROMANS,
BUT HERE HE WAS CURING THEM WITH HIS SPIRIT, NOT TOUCHING THEM.

YES, THEY HAD HEARD ABOUT RAISING LAZARUS FROM THE DEAD,
SO HE SHOULD NOW BE ABLE TO TAKE CARE OF HIMSELF.
JESUS WAS NOW BEING TRIED WITH OTHER ROBBERS AND THIEVES,
LET HIM SAVE HIMSELF. WE'VE BEEN DECEIVED.

ST. PAUL COULD HAVE CONVINCED GENTILE CITIZENS OF ROME,
IF HE HAD ONLY TOLD THEM ABOUT THIS INCIDENT OF RENOWN.
AND COULD HAVE PORTRAYED IT AS THE SPIRIT OF CHRIST,
THAT WE NOW DEPEND UPON IN TODAY'S PRAYERS OF CRISES.

I DIDN'T HEAR THE CENTURION THANK JESUS FOR THE CURE,
HE DIDN'T BELIEVE IT TILL HE GOT HOME AND WAS ASSURED.
SO WHAT HAPPENED TO THE MESSIANIC MISSION?
THE HEBREWS HAD BEEN DENIED, SO HE COULD NOT BE THE CHRIST.

RB WELSH, 7 6 22

GOD'S JUDGEMENT

THE THIRD WOE FROM HEAVEN HAS BEGUN ITS FINALE,
FOR GOD IN HIS ARK WILL JUDGE HOW THEY PLEA.

LOVE OR WRATH? MAN'S DESTINY IS ALL ON THE LINE.
THESE SOULS STAND BEFORE YOU IN THE COURT OF THE DIVINE.
YOUR SERVANTS, PROPHETS, AND SAINTS, WAIT TILL YOU TELL
OF THEIR DESTINY AT LAST, IS IT HEAVEN OR HELL?

THE 7TH TRUMPET BRINGS THE THIRD WOE INTO THE SEVEN BOWLS, (REV 11:15-19)
THE TEMPLE OF GOD WITH ITS COVENANT UNFOLDS,
WITH THE USUAL ACCOMPANIMENT OF FLASHES OF LIGHTNING, THUNDERSTORMS, AND NOISE,
ALL BEING PRIED LOOSE FROM THEIR BEARING AND POISE.

EXILE

WHILE THE JEWS WERE EXILED AND IN BONDAGE,
GOD HAD TAKEN HIS LIBERTIES AND WAS FOUND GONE AGAIN.
TURNING THE TRIBE OVER TO HIS "SERVANT" NEBUCHADNEZZAR.
THE SON OF MAN APPEARED AS THE PROMISED MESSIAH.

THE TRIBE'S SAVIOR HAD COME TO EARTH AS THE SON OF MAN, (JER 23:5)
RIDING ON CLOUDS TO READ THE KING'S MESSAGE ON THE WALL.
TO GO INTO THE LION'S DEN, THE EXTRA MAN IN THE FIERY FURNACE.
HAVING CYRUS INVADE BABYLONIA TO FREE THE JUDEANS.

GETTING ZERUBBABEL TO WEAR GOD'S SIGNET RING (HAG 2:23)
EZRA AND NEHEMIAH ORGANIZED THE RETURNING.
TO JERUSALEM TO REBUILD AND WORSHIP IN GOD'S TEMPLE,
THE ARK WAS NOW MISSING, AND OTHER PROBLEMS WERE SEVERAL.

IT WOULD BE 400 MORE YEARS DURING THE APOCRYPHA,
OF HISTORY REMOVED OF THE GALLANT MACCABEANS,
TILL THE MESSIAH REAPPEARS AS THE SON OF GOD,
MIRACULOUSLY BORN OF A VIRGINS WOMB.

RB WELSH, 6 3 23

CHRIST'S COMING

THIS SEASON IS THE SEASON OF JOY AND MIRTH
AS WE CELEBRATE THE DAY OF CHRIST'S BIRTH.
THERE'S PLENTY OF EXCITEMENT IN THE AIR,
FESTIVITIES WILL BE GRAND WITH LOVE TO SHARE.

A DRIFTING SNOW FALLS ON THE STREET LIGHT
AS CAROLERS SING PRAISES TO GOD WITH DELIGHT.
THE SALVATION ARMY BELL RINGS IN TUNE WITH THE ANGELS,
THE SAVIOR AND KING IS TO BE BORN IN A MANGER,

WE CALL HIM KRIS KRINGLE, BUT WE KNOW IT IS GOD
WHO COMES DOWN THE CHIMNEY LIKE SANTA CLAUS;
FILLING THE STOCKINGS, BRINGING THE GIFTS,
THANKING US ALL FOR ALL OUR DEVOTION TO HIM.

IT'S WITH AGAPE LOVE THAT GOD CELEBRATES
THE BIRTH OF HIS SON WITH LOVE AND GRACE.
IN THE BACK OF OUR MINDS, WE THINK IT'S THE CHRIST,
A SECOND COMING ON THE CLOUDS DURING THE NIGHT.

BUT I OFTEN WONDER WHY MAN NEEDS THREE GODS?
LIKE, ONE IS GOOD FOR THIS, THE OTHER FOR THAT, BEATING THE ODDS.
BUT THEN, WE KNOW IT'S HIS SPIRIT THAT'S ALWAYS THERE
GIVING ADVICE, HELPING OUT; HE'S JUST A BABE AND EVERYWHERE.

RB WELSH, 12 21 21

A MIRACULOUS BIRTH OF A CHILD AT EIGHTY-NINE

IS JUST AS MIRACULOUS AS ONE BY A VIRGIN BRIDE.
PAUL'S ANALOGY TO THE GALATIANS OF THE TWO WOMEN IS NOW CLEAR
FOR THE CHILD OF HAGAR IS REPRESENTED IN THEIR EARTHLY TERMS OF THE
JERUSALEM OF THIS EARTH, WHILE THE CHILD OF SARAH IS
REPRESENTED IN THE JERUSALEM HEAVEN ABOVE.
MEANING THAT GOD'S LAW IS NOT BEING REPLACED BY CHRIST'S SPIRIT, BUT
THE LAW BY GOD'S SON ISAAC IS UPHELD.

RB WELSH
GAL 4:21-5:7

PREDESTINATION

WITH A WORLD OF NATURE AND ALL ITS DELIGHTS
AND ADAM PURSUING EVE ALL DAY AND ALL NIGHT
WHY WOULD GOD EVER CREATE JUST ONLY ONE TREE
IN HIS NEW WORLD, UNCOMPLICATED AND FREE

GOD, OF COURSE, KNEW MAN WOULD ALWAYS RESIST
THEY WERE PREDESTINED TO REBEL; THIS WOULD ALWAYS PERSIST
GOD'S AMBITIOUS PLAN IN THE MAKING OF MAN
RELIED UPON MAN'S FREEDOM TO UNDERSTAND

IN ITS INCEPTION, GOD HAD GRANDIOSE IDEAS
OF A BEAUTIFUL WORLD OF NATURE AND ITS BLESSINGS
BUT A MAN LESSER THAN A GOD WAS BOUND TO FAIL
ESPECIALLY WHEN THE PROMISE RAN INTO ANOTHER GOD BAAL

TO KEEP THE RACE PURE, MARRIAGE WAS ALWAYS WITH JEWS
WITH THE EXCEPTIONS OF JOSEPH AND MOSES OF NON-HEBREWS
WITH ALL THE EXTERMINATIONS ON THE WAY TO CANAAN
NO COMMANDMENT ON THIS POINT, SO VIRGINS WERE THE EXCEPTION

THE ONLY REASON FOR SETTING UP ANY COMMANDMENTS
GOD MUST HAVE KNOWN THEY WERE PREDESTINED TO BE BROKEN
THAT'S THE REASON WHY PAUL SAID THE SPIRIT OF CHRIST
WAS INSTITUTED TO SUPERSEDE FOR GODS LAWS WERE TOO PRECISE

IF THE HOLY SPIRIT COULDN'T CONTROL ALL ITS GODS
THEY WOULD CONSTANTLY BE WARRING WITH EACH OTHER LIKE KIDS
SO EACH GOD ENDED UP WITH A CASE OF JEALOUSY
IN COMPETITION FOR WORSHIPERS TO PRAISE THEM AND BELIEVE

GOD HAD LOST ALL CONTROL OF HIS PRECIOUS MAN
THERE WAS JUST NO WAY THAT THEY WOULD UNDERSTAND
SO INSTEAD OF A FLOOD TO RID HIMSELF OF MAN AGAIN
HE INVOKED THE ASSYRIANS AND BABYLONIANS TO TAKE THEM

GOD WILL SEND A MEDIATOR TO RESOLVE MEN TO HIM
FOR ALL AXIAL NATIONS HAVE A KRISHNA OR BUDDHA
WITH A HUMAN MINDSET THAT UNDERSTANDS STRIFE
AND A PERPETUAL REBIRTH OR AN AFTERLIFE

SO NOW THAT THE CHRIST HAS APPEARED AND THEN DIED
IT LOOKS LIKE THE HEALINGS WOULD BE MULTIPLIED
BUT THERE'S ONLY BEEN PROGRESS IN MEDICINE AND SURGERY
THERE'S NO INSTANT HEALING AS THERE WAS WHEN HE WAS HERE

THE HEBREW NATION IS STILL WAITING ON THEIRS
WILL IT BE OF A VIRGIN OR COME OUF OF THIN AIR
THE WORSHIP OF CHRIST IS NOW EXPECTED OF ALL MEN
BUT GOD MADE NO EFFORT TO CONVERT CANAANITES OR EGYPTIANS

HE WOULDN'T HAVE ALL HIS PROBLEMS LIKE THIS WITH BAAL
NOW WE HAVE CHURCHES AND LOCAL TEMPLES AS WELL
HOWEVER, FOR BELIEVERS IN THE HOLY SPIRIT FOR WORSHIPING
THERE'S ONLY ONE, AND THAT'S IN HEIDELBERG GERMANY

THERE ONCE WAS A CHURCH TO MELCHIZEDEK, WHO PORTRAYED
HIMSELF AS GOD TO ABRAHAM IN A PROTEAN WAY
TELLING US HOW TO TITHE AND CONDUCT COMMUNION
IN WORSHIPING HIM WITH BREAD AND WINE TO OBTAIN UNION

WITH NOTHING SAID ABOUT EATING FLESH OR BLOOD
FOR ANY CIVILIZED PERSON THAT IS UNDERSTOOD
IN THESE THOUSANDS OF YEARS HAS GOD MADE AN IMPACT
OR IS MAN STILL WORSHIPING A BAAL BEHIND GOD'S BACK

IS GOD BEING DUPLICITOUS I'M ALWAYS IN WONDER
FOR I THINK IT'S MY FAULT WHENEVER I BLUNDER
WHENEVER GOOD THINGS HAPPEN, I THANK GOD HIMSELF
IT'S ONLY FOR DISASTERS THAT I INVOKE JESUS' NAME
NEVER CALLING ON THE SPIRIT IN ANY CASE

RB WELSH, 5 5 21

THE PENTECOST

JESUS WAS SUPPOSED TO SOON RETURN
THAT IS WHAT: PAUL TAUGHT, AND EVERYONE LEARNED
CITIES OF ASIA RESUMED WORSHIPING TO ASHERAH
FOR JESUS DIDN'T RETURN AS PROMISED BY PAUL

WITH GOD SENDING HIS ANGEL GABRIEL OF THIS EARTH'S HEAVENS
TO A VIRGIN IN ISRAEL TO SAVE MANKIND FROM ITS TRANSGRESSIONS
BORN OF THE BETROTHED JOSEPH AND MARY, JESUS WAS OF THIS EARTH
WITH THE HOLY SPIRIT COMING UPON HER, HE WAS HUMAN BY BIRTH

FLEEING TO EGYPT, WHERE OMNIAN WAS A TEMPLE OF GOD
ESTABLISHED IN ISAIAH'S DAY OF WHICH HE HAD FORETOLD
FOR JESUS TO RECEIVE POWER AND GLORY WHERE HE HAD GONE
THAT WAS CLAIMED, OR THE "EGYPT" COULD HAVE BEEN AT QUMRAN

WHERE STUDENTS WERE, CAMELS WERE GOING THRU "THE EYES OF A NEEDLE."
TO GRADUATE IN THREE YEARS TO SPREAD GOD'S WORD TO THE PEOPLE
RETURNING TO THEN BE BAPTIZED BY THE HOLY SPIRIT AND THE DOVE
THEN AFTER BEING TEMPTED, GO OUT SPREADING HIS MESSAGE OF LOVE

BUT MAN, IN HIS PERNICIOUS WAY ON THE SURFACE, CLAIMS TO BE SAVED
BUT HIS INNER-SELF THINKS THAT NO MATTER WHAT, JESUS WILL SAY, "IT'S OKAY."
BUT YOU WILL NOT KNOW WHEN OR WHERE I WILL BE
JESUS HAD SAID TO THE BRIDEGROOM, SO IT WAS STILL A MYSTERY

THEN IT WAS AT PENTECOST WHEN FULFILLED AS PROPHESIED BY JOHN THE BAPTIZER
THAT WHEN JESUS CAME, MEN WOULD BE BAPTIZED BY THE HOLY SPIRIT AND FIRE
SO WHEN GATHERED TOGETHER, FINGERS OF FIRE BAPTIZED THE MEN NOW
SPEAKING IN TONGUES
THIS WAS JESUS' RETURN. THEY COULD SPEAK IN MANY LANGUAGES, NOW BECOMING
GOD'S SONS

WHY THIS ISN'T' A NATIONAL HOLIDAY IS A MYSTERY
FOR IT WOULD BE AS GREAT AS CHRISTMAS OR EASTER
IF REALIZED, MERCHANTS WOULD THEN REALLY POUNCE ON
NEXT WEEKEND TO SELL OUT THEIR STORES EVEN WITH NO COUPONS

RB WELSH, 05 08 20

WRATH OF GOD

TO YOUR TENTS, OH ZION
THE WRATH OF THE LORD IS NIGH ON
A DEADLY PLAGUE IS SWEEPING THE WORLD-
MEN ARE DYING; THEIR BLOOD HAS BEEN CURDLED.

ERADICATING THOSE WHOSE SIN IS LYING
THE WORLD HAS STOPPED NO SELLING OR BUYING
THE SUN MAY AS WELL STAND STILL AGAIN
FOR PROGRESS IS HALTED TILL GOD KNOWS WHEN

YOU AND I ARE THE INNOCENT ONES WHO NEVER HEARD
TO EVER THINK, LET ALONE SPEAK A WRATHFUL WORD
IT'S ONLY THOSE OTHERS THAT PRINT FALSEHOODS
THEY GET ON TV WITH THEIR WRATHFUL WORDS

DESIGNED DOWN BELOW. MADE UP IN THE CELLS
EXTREME ACCUSATIONS RIGHT OUT OF THEIR HELL
DEATH WILL CONTINUE. THAT'S CERTAIN TILL WE
UNIFY AS ONE PEOPLE ACTING RESPONSIBLY

WE GREW UP UNITED AND WERE TILL WE
PAID ENORMOUS SUMS TO GO TO A UNIVERSITY
THAT TAUGHT COURSES AS LEFTIST AS SOCIALISM
THE NATION WOULD SUCCUMB TO EVEN COMMUNISM

WHERE ALL THESE IDEAS EVER EMANATED
THEY CERTAINLY HAVE BEEN EXACERBATED
SO TO GET RID OF THE DISEASE THAT CONFINES US ALL
WE MUST SELF-INSPECT OR GET READY TO FALL

RB WELSH, 5 1 20

JESUS SECOND COMING AT PENTECOST

THERE'S A SANTA AT CHRISTMAS TO CELEBRATE THE BIRTH OF THE LORD
REMINISCENT OF THE WISE MEN BRINGING GIFTS WHEN JESUS WAS BORN
PREPARATION IS OBSERVED EACH SUNDAY IN DECEMBER FOR THIS EVENT
WITH SOMBER RELIGIOUS SERVICES, THAT ARE CALLED THE ADVENT

FAMILIES ARE IN READINESS FOR FEASTING AND EXCHANGING OF GIFTS
THERE'S BEEN SUSPENSE AND EXCITEMENT THAT ONE CAN'T RESIST
FOR MONTHS NOW, THE MERCHANTS HAVE BEEN SELLING GIFTS AND THE TOYS
TO BALANCE THEIR BOOKS AS WELL AS THE BRINGING OF LOVE AND JOY

THEN AT EASTER, THERE ARE PRELIMINARIES TO THE CHURCH PAGEANTS
WITH SALES OF EASTER BONNETS, CHOCOLATES, AND RABBITS
WHILE CELEBRATING CHRIST'S RISING FROM THE GRAVE
CHILDREN SCOUR THE YARD FOR THE GOLDEN EGG

JOHN HAD BEEN BAPTIZING, SAVING MEN FROM THEIR SINS
A WILD AND WOOLLY MAN WEARING CAMEL HAIR SKINS
IMMERSING MEN IN THE JORDAN FOR THEIR SALVATION
OF THESE GALILEANS FROM THEIR SINFUL DEGRADATION

WHEN ASKED ABOUT THE SAVIOR, HE REPLIED
ONE IS COMING WHO IS MIGHTIER THAN I
THE THONGS OF HIS SANDALS I'M NOT FIT TO UNTIE
FOR HE WILL BAPTIZE YOU WITH THE HOLY SPIRIT AND FIRE

IT WAS THE ASSEMBLAGE OF BELIEVERS AT PENTECOST
AWAITING THE RETURN OF JESUS AS PROMISED
WHEN A RUSHING OF WIND SPIRIT AND FINGERS OF FIRE
WAS JESUS RETURNING AS PROCLAIMED BY JOHN THE BAPTIZER

WITH ALL THIS EXCITEMENT, ONE MIGHT SAY
THIS TO BE A MEETING OF TRIUMVIRATE
FOR GOD IS HERE, AND GOD IS THERE
WE KNOW THAT GOD IS EVERYWHERE

BUT JESUS COMING ON CLOUDS WOULD ONLY BE SEEN LOCALLY
THOUGH SURVIVORS AT PENTECOST THE WORLD OVER BE MANY
A RAPTURE WHERE ALL BELIEVERS BOTH LIVING AND DEAD
WILL MEET CHRIST IN THE SKY AT ONLY ONE PLACE INSTEAD (1 THES 4:13)

PEOPLE HAD FLOCKED BY THE SCORE TO THE JORDAN
FOR BAPTISM BY JOHN FOR THE FORGIVENESS OF SIN
JESUS HAD RETURNED FROM THE CROSS AS A SURVIVOR
AND WAS SAVING THEM NOW BY BAPTISM WITH FIRE

BEING BAPTIZED WITH FIRE IS LIKENED TO DESCENT INTO HELL
RETURNING ALL SIN NOW STERILIZED TO ITS SOURCE IN THE CABAL
SO WITH THIS BAPTISM, MEN RETURN TO THE GARDEN OF EDEN
EATING FROM THE TREES OF LIFE AND KNOWLEDGE LIKE EVE DID

MEN BAPTIZED WITH FIRE BECOME NEW BEINGS
LIFE SUDDENLY HAS NEW MEANINGS
WE HAVE NOW RECEIVED THE LIGHT OF JESUS
FROM THOSE FEELINGS OF GUILT, HE HAS FREED US
THIS DAY SHOULD BE CALLED THE DAY OF REPENT-ECOST
FOR IT CELEBRATES CHRIST SAVING ALL THOSE WHO ARE LOST

WITH THIS BAPTISM WITH THE HOLY SPIRIT AND FIRE
JESUS RETURNED "REAL SOON" AFTER BEING CRUCIFIED
TO SAVE MEN NOW, NOT WAITING FOR THEM TO DIE
ALL THIS WAS FORETOLD BY JOHN THE BAPTIZER ABOUT OUR KING (LK 3:16)
AND THIS IS THE SCRIPTURE READING OF JESUS' SECOND COMING

SO INSTEAD OF SANTA AND THE BUNNY FOR THE MERCHANT SALES TO RING
PERHAPS THE FIGURE OF JESUS ON SOME FLYING KITES TO BRING
EXCITEMENT FOR GIRLS AND BOYS AS A FAD OF THE PENTECOST
TO BE SAVED AND DELIVERED FROM THE LOST

RB WELSH, 5 20 20

FAITH AND WISDOM

THE POSSESSION OF FAITH IS LIKE A TREASURE
FAITH AS VALUABLE IS BEYOND MEASURE
ONE CAN BE A GENIUS OR DUMB AS A STUMP
THE POSSESSION OF FAITH DEPENDS NOT ON WISDOM

FAITH IS PRODUCED BY SIGNS AND POSTS
ON ONE'S WAY THRU LIFE THAT HE NEEDS THE MOST
IT'S MAINLY RECEIVED BY REVELATION
RECEIVING THE "CALL" OF ILLUMINATION

ONLY WITH THE GUIDANCE OF THIS HOLY SPIRIT
WHO CAN FORESEE ONE'S WAY WITH SURE CONVICTION
INSPIRING THE WAY THROUGH UNSEEN PITFALLS GALORE
ONE'S FAITHFUL RECEPTORS REACH THE FINAL GOAL

RB WELSH, 8 2 20

TRINITARIAN FORMULATION

JESUS SAID HE'D FORGIVE EVEN IF IMPROPER
IF ONE BLASPHEMED HIM OR THE FATHER
BUT NOT IF ONE USED THE SPIRIT'S NAME
AS ANY EXPLICATIVE OATH IN VAIN

THIS SEEMS TO SEPARATE THE THREE
AS NOT BEING ONE, NOT AN ENTITY.
SO WHERE DID TRINITY COME FROM
WAS IT DIVINE OR FROM A HUMAN?

VOTED ON NOT BY GOD BUT PRIESTS AND MEN AT NICEA
INSTIGATED BY CONSTANTINE AND ATHANASIUS
TO BRING ORDER FROM THE CHAOS
OF THE EMPIRES' SEPARATE RELIGIOUS BELIEFS

CONSTANTINE SAID:

MY NAME IS CONSTANTINE THE GREAT,
I RULE THIS EMPIRE AND ITS FATE.
HUNS AND GOTHS, GREEK AND JEW,
AS SLAVES, ALL WORK WITH ZEAL FOR FOOD.

THEY SERVE THEIR MASTERS LOYALLY,
IT'S BETTER THAN IF THEY'RE FREE.
THIS GREAT EMPIRE IS SO VAST,
I NEED A SYMBOL THAT WILL LAST,
SO WE CAN UNDERSTAND EACH OTHER,
AND BE LIKE ONE ANOTHER'S BROTHER.

LANGUAGE DRESS AND CUSTOMS NEW,
RABBLE, BARBARIANS, EGYPTIAN TOO,
WORSHIP IDOLS, NOT A FEW.
I BEAUTIFIED THEIR LAND, BUILT ROADS,
AQUEDUCTS BY THE MILE,
IN ALL THE WORLD CAME QUITE THE STYLE.
FAR AND WIDE, THIS EMPIRE GROWS,
SEA TO SEA, SHIPS SAIL TO AND FRO.

AS I WAS PONDERING THIS DILEMMA,
TO UNIFY THE WORLD FROM CAIRO TO BRITANNICA

THE LANGUAGE, DRESS, AND CUSTOMS TOO,
THE HUNS, EGYPTIANS, GOTHS, AND JEW,
WILL ALL BELIEVE; WORSHIP AS ONE,
WE'RE ONENESS NOW, UNDER THE SUN.

I'LL CALL A COUNCIL OF THEIR PRIESTS,
CONVENE FROM GREATEST TO THE LEAST.
TO SETTLE ON ONE THEORY,
AND SCUTTLE OTHERS AS HERESY,
BURN THEIR BOOKS, EXILE THEIR AUTHOR,
DON'T ASK JESUS; DON'T BOTHER.

JUST TAKE THE CREED OF SOCRATES,
THAT MANY ARE ONE, EVERYBODY SEES.
WE HOPE THAT GOD DOESN'T CARE,
HIS MONOTHEISM HE MUST SHARE,
WITH HIS SON, JESUS, AND HOLY SPIRIT,
JUST MAKE THEM EQUAL SO THEY'LL FIT,
IN MY CONCEPTION OF UNITY,
SO WE CAN CALL IT, THE TRINITY.

SO WITH THIS ELABORATE EXPLETIVE
ONE CAN READILY SEE THE REALITY
THAT MAN FORMED THE TRINITY
NOT BY GOD OR JESUS OR SPIRIT ALONE
SO GOD CREATED ISLAM TO BE ONE AGAIN

THE CONNOTATION OF TRINITY TO ME MEANS THREE
TO BE THREE IN ONE, IT SHOULD BE NAMED TRI-ENTITY

BUT WE'LL CARRY ON WITH OUR FINGERS CROSSED
IT'S LIKE DRINKING BLOOD THOUGH, STARTED BY PAUL
IN HIS LETTER TO CORINTH, PICKED UP BY THE GOSPELS
SUBSTITUTING CHRIST FOR THE DIONYSIAN BLOOD BULLS.

RB WELSH

SECOND COMING AT PENTECOST

JOHN WAS BAPTIZING MEN IN THE RIVER JORDAN
IN REPLYING ABOUT JESUS, FOR THEY HAD IMPLORED HIM
TO THIS, HE ANSWERED ONE IS COMING WHO IS GREATER THAN I
FOR HE WILL BAPTIZE YOU WITH THE HOLY SPIRIT AND FIRE

AFTER THE CRUCIFIXION, HIS DISCIPLES IN THE UPPER ROOM,
JESUS HAD PROMISED THAT HE WOULD COME AGAIN SOON
JESUS CAME AGAIN AT THE PENTECOST AS PROPHESIED
TO BAPTIZE THEM AS JOHN SAID WITH THE HOLY SPIRIT AND FIRE

HE HAD DESCENDED INTO HELL FOR THE BRANDING IRON
THE PEOPLE SPOKE IN TONGUES BY BEING SO INSPIRED
SO WHY IS IT THAT WE STILL WONDER
WHEN HE'LL COME AGAIN TO TEAR SATAN ASUNDER

THE CHURCH HAS ITS BIG BOOK OF ORDER
CONTAINING LISTS OF RITUALS THAT WE USE AS FOLLOWERS
THE GENERAL ASSEMBLY SHOULD MEET TO BECOME MORE FACTUAL
TO CHANGE SOME RULES AS THEY DID TO ORDAIN HOMOSEXUALS

BY COMING ON THE CLOUDS TO SAVE YOU AND ME
THE RAPTURE COULD HAPPEN ONLY LOCALLY
HOW WILL THIS HELP US TO BELIEVE THERE'S A TRINITY
AT PENTECOST, THE THREE WERE ACTING INDEPENDENTLY.

AND TO SHOW THREE ARE NOT ALL THE SAME
PAUL RE-BAPTIZED SAMARITANS IN THE HOLY SPIRIT'S NAME (ACTS 8: 16)
WE ARE NO LONGER CHILDREN BUT SEASONED ADULTS
WE'RE OLD ENOUGH TO RECOGNIZE TRUTH AND BE TAUGHT AS SUCH

ALL WE HEARD ALL OUR LIVES ABOUT NOAH'S FLOOD
WAS A COVENANT ABOUT A RAINBOW, NOT THE ONE AGAINST EATING BLOOD (GEN 9:4)
THEN AT JERICHO, WE'RE TAUGHT ABOUT WALLS TUMBLING DOWN
BUT NOTHING ABOUT GOD AS A SOLDIER THREATENING JOSHUA (JOS 5:13)

MELCHIZEDEK WAS GOD AS A HUMAN AGAIN
EXPLAINING TO ABRAHAM ABOUT THE COMMUNION
SIMPLY TO HAVE THE BREAD AND THE WINE (GEN 14:18)
WITH COLLECTIONS FOR THE POOR AS A TOLL, HE ASSIGNED

WE ALL ADMIT GOD WAS HUMAN AT MAMRE
AT A PICNIC WITH ABRAHAM AND TWO MORE IN HIS PARTY
SO GOD CAN BE ANYONE ANYWHERE
YOU MIGHT MEET HIM TOMORROW SO TAKE CARE

WHY IS IT THAT WE HAVE TO HAVE SOME DEGREE
TO BECOME A PROFESSOR OR PREACHER WITH A PHD
TO QUALIFY AS ONE TO PRONOUNCE THE FAITH
TO BE RIGHT OR WRONG IN EXPRESSING WHAT WE THINK

MOST PEOPLE POOH-POOH EXTRATERRESTRIALS AND UFOS
BUT GOD WAS HOVERING OVER EZEKIEL'S YARD OF BONES
HIS WHIRLWIND FLYING SAUCER PICKED UP ELIJAH
AND MAY HAVE RAISED JESUS FROM THE DEAD

NOTHING WAS SAID ABOUT DRINKING BLOOD
OR TO EAT FLESH, MOST PEOPLE NEVER UNDERSTOOD
THERE ARE SOME TIMES THAT WE HAVE TO FACE IT
WE HAVE BEEN BRAINWASHED AND, IF WE WISH, CAN CORRECT IT

I'M JUST TELLING YOU WHAT BOB BELIEVES
EACH ONE OF US CAN THINK WHATEVER HE PLEASES
SO IF YOU ARE WAITING FOR JESUS TO COME AGAIN, AS SUNG BY THE CHOIR
HE DID AS HE PROMISED AT PENTECOST BY BAPTIZING WITH TONGUES OF FIRE

THIS PENTECOST IS THE MOST PROMINENT BIBLICAL EVENT
OF CELEBRATORY RELIGIOUS SERVICES HEAVEN EVER SENT
BUT IS MAINLY IGNORED BY THE CHURCH EVERYWHERE
AND FOR NO REASON WILL BE CASUALLY MENTIONED FOREVER

BUT WHERE ELSE ARE ALL THREE THAT WE PRAY TO THE MOST
EVER SEEN TOGETHER AT ONE TIME EXCEPT AT THE PENTECOST

RB WELSH, 5 30 20

GOD AS JESUS

YES, GOD IS HERE AS JESUS CHRIST
THROUGH JESUS, WE CAN ATTAIN THE HIGHEST
WE ONLY HAVE TO BELIEVE IN HIM
TO BE IN HEAVEN RELIEVED OF SIN

THOUGH GOD IS ONE, HE DID ASSERT
"LET US MAKE MAN," GOD SAID AT FIRST
JOHN ASSERTS THAT JESUS IS THE *LOGOS*
THAT HE WAS THERE TO ASSIST YOU KNOW

INSTEAD OF THE HOLY SPIRIT, WHICH MAKES MORE SENSE
SINCE JESUS WASN'T EVEN BORN TILL THOUSANDS OF YEARS HENCE

THE HOLY SPIRIT'S ALL AROUND
IN ALL THE UNIVERSE, IT DOES ABOUND
THAT'S ALL THAT CONSTANTINE DID NEED
AT NICEA FOR, HIS PRIESTS VOTE FOR A TRINITY

SO MAN INVENTED THIS TRINITY
IT'S NOT A BIBLICAL RECIPE
ISHMAEL'S PROMISE BECAME THE PHENOM
THAT FORMED GOD'S ONENESS AGAIN IN ISLAM

GOD CAN BE ANYONE OR ANYTHING
A BURNING BUSH OR GARDNER TO MARY MAGDALEN
SO GOD BECAME A MAN AT THE GATES OF TOWN
LIKE THE SOLDIER CONFRONTING JOSHUA WHERE THE WALLS FELL (JOS 5:13)

GOD CAN'T SEEM TO COMMUNICATE WITH HIS CREATION,
FOR MAN IS IGNORANT OF WHAT HE SAYS IN THIS RELATION.
SO THEREFORE, GOD BECAME JESUS AS A MAN
TO FACILITATE THE WAY AGAIN.

THOUGH HE HAD NO SIGNET RING
MARY MAGDALENE KNEW JESUS WAS THE KING,
INSTEAD OF ANOINTING HIM ON HIS HEAD,
SHE POURED PRECIOUS OIL ON HIS FEET INSTEAD. (JN 12:1-8; LK 7:36-8)

RB WELSH, 5 4 20

COMPLACENCY

THE ISRAELITE NATION HAD ALREADY BEEN SPLIT
SINCE THE SONS OF DAVID WERE ALWAYS IN CONFLICT
THE PROPHET AHIJAH TOLD JEREBOAM, A BUILDING CONTRACTOR
THE NATION WOULD BE SPLIT, AND HE WOULD BE NORTH'S KING BENEFACTOR.

BUT HE PLACED GOD'S TEMPLES ON THE NORTH'S EXTREME BORDERS
WITH GOLDEN BULLS TO WORSHIP, THAT LED TO DISORDER
THE ASSYRIANS REMOVED THE TEN TRIBES TO THE NORTH
NEVER TO BE SEEN AGAIN FOR WHAT IT IS WORTH

WAS THIS EVEN A HINT TO THE JUDAEANS OF THE SOUTH
WHICH WAS ALWAYS THE BATTLEFIELD RIGHT ON THE ROUTE
BETWEEN ASSYRIA AND EGYPT, PEACE NEVER BEING INSTILLED
WHERE THE ONLY GOOD KING JOSIAH SHOT WITH AN ARROW AND KILLED

WITH JERUSALEM HAVING THE ONLY TEMPLE IN WHICH TO PRAY
BUT WITH BAAL ALTARS EVERYWHERE, JUDEAN PEOPLES WERE TEMPTED TO STRAY
AND COMMERCE BEING GOOD EVEN SOME POOR BEING FED
THIS LAX INDIFFERENCE CAUSED JEREMIAH TO DREAD

SINCE HE COULD FORETELL THE UPCOMING EXILE
HE SOLD ALL HIS LANDS IN STOCK, BREAKING STYLE
HE EVEN DEPARTED WITH THE PUZZLED JUDEANS
TO SET UP THE WRITING OF THE TALMUD BY LEVITE HISTORIANS

DANIEL SEEMED TO BE THE HEBREW PROMISED MESSIAH
CYRUS OF PERSIA ATTACKED THRU CISTERNS FOR THEIR SURVIVAL
ESTHER BECOMES THE WIFE OF KING AHASUERUS, A PERSIAN,
SAVING THE JEWS AGAIN FROM MORDECAI AND EXTINCTION.

FINALLY, A REMNANT OF THE PEOPLE COME HOME
TO FIND THE DISASTER JERSULEM FACED WHILE THEY WERE GONE
ZARRSBBABLE, A PRINCE, RECEIVED GOD'S SIGNET RING
NOTHING WAS SETTLED. IT'S STILL HAPPENING.

RB WELSH, 5 16 20

HOLY SPIRIT

WHENEVER ONE LOOKS UP AT THE STARS
HE IS FILLED WITH WONDER ABOUT THOSE THINGS AFAR
WONDERING ABOUT THE UNIVERSE
ABOUT ONE'S LIFE AND WHY WE ARE HERE

THEY MUST HAVE BEEN SET IN MOTION
BY A POWERFUL ONE WITH PERFECT PRECISION
SET OFF BY LIGHT IN A PERFECT ROTATION
GATHERING PARTICLES OF DUST BY GRAVITATION

SPINNING AND WHIRLING IN A DANCE HARMONIC
STARS WERE EXPLODING LIKE DRUMS, SYMPHONIC
ALL THIS WAS PERFECTED BY A POWERFUL SPIRIT
BILLIONS OF LIGHTS BUT WITH NO ONE TO SEE IT

THE SPIRIT ASSIGNED GODS TO THEIR OWN CONSTELLATIONS
IT WAS THEN SUBDIVIDED INTO GALAXIES WITH THEIR OWN SUNS
NOW THE PLANETS WERE ORBITING IN RHYTHMIC ROTATION
OUR GOD AND SPIRIT CREATED MAN TO VIEW THIS GALAXY'S PERFECTION

GOD SELECTED THIS PLANET SAYING, "LET US MAKE MAN IN OUR IMAGE."
SO THE SPIRIT WHO MADE CHRIST HELPED MAKE MAN BEGIN IT
WHILE MOTHER NATURE CONTINUED WITH THIS EVOLUTIONARY TREND
SHE KEPT ON CREATING EARTHQUAKES AND TORNADIC WINDS

SO THE GODS PICKED OUT PLANETS IN THEIR CONSTELLATION
PERFORMING MORE MIRACLES IN MAN'S INCUBATION
GOD IS JEALOUS OF THESE OTHER GODS
HE'S JEALOUS OF BAAL, THE CANAANITE GOD

A GOD OF THE HARVEST WITH TEMPLE PROSTITUTES
WITH ALTARS IN TOWN SQUARES FOR ALL TO USE
AND AS I LOOK UP AT THIS MAGNIFICENT WONDER
I SOMETIMES THINK ABOUT WHY WE BLUNDER

OTHER GODS MADE MEN IN THEIR OWN IMAGE
HOW ELSE COULD THERE BE SO MANY RACES
AS ENGLAND DEPORTED CRIMINALS TO AUSTRALIA
OTHER PLANETS SENT OUTCASTS TO EARTH AS WELL

SOME WERE GIANTS LIKE GOLIATH
OTHER ORIENTALS SETTLING IN ASIA
THESE ARE CALLED THE AXIAL NATIONS
BRINGING THE KARMA, THE CHARISMA, THE PREDESTINATION

SO THE HEBREWS HAD THE EARTH'S ORIGINAL MEN
OTHERS CAME FROM OUTER SPACE PLANETS BEFORE THEY EXPLODED
ARRIVING IN THEIR CHARIOTS LIKE SAUCERS OF ZARATHUSTRA
SETTLING IN ASIA AND INDIA WITH TRANSCENDENCE AND KARMA

THE GREEKS HAD THEIR SOCRATES SO ALL IN ALL
THE WORLD FILLED WITH PHILOSOPHIES OF OTHER RACES
WE WONDER ABOUT STONEHENGE AND THE PYRAMIDS BUILT BY EGYPTIANS
IF THEY ARE TRANSMITTERS TO HEAVENLY GODS OF MAGICIANS

SO THE MANTRA AROUND MANY SPIRITUAL WORLDS DO ABOUND
TO TRADE SECRETS AND RITUALS BUT CAUSE WARS ALL AROUND
THESE ARE THE GODS THAT FOUND EARTH'S WOMEN DESIRABLE
BRINGING IN THEIR GODS WAS CAUSING MUCH TROUBLE

SOME RELIGIONS ARE VERY NAIVE
ALL ONE HAS TO DO IS BELIEVE
BUT IT TAKES A LOT MORE THAN JUST THAT
IT'S DEEPER AND TAKES TWO THE GOD AND RECIPIENT

WITH ALL THESE RACES AND RELIGIONS
THERE'S ONLY ONE THAT HAS SALVATION
IT REQUIRES A LOT OF IMAGINATION
TO SEE HOW DEATH COULD SAVE MEN FOR HEAVEN

ALL THIS UNDER THE AUSPICES OF THE HOLY SPIRIT
WHO WAS THE "US" IN GOD'S CREATING EARTH AND ALL THAT IS IN IT
THE NEXT TIME THE SPIRIT WAS CALLED UPON
WAS ITS POWER IN CREATING THE NEWBORN JESUS?

SOME RELIGIONS THINK THAT BEING REBORN
IT MEANS YOU GET A SECOND CHANCE IN THE SKIN OF YOUR OWN.
WHILE OTHERS ONE HAS HAD PREVIOUS LIVES,
AS BLACK OR YELLOW AND NOW'S WHITE AND SURVIVED.

THE GOLDEN CALF AND THE INDIAN BULL
BEING HELD IN REVERENCE IS HARD TO BE UNDERSTOOD

THIS HAD TO BE THE ENDING OF THE REDEMPTION OF SIN
BY SACRIFICE OF AN UNBLEMISHED ANIMAL OR IN THIS CASE GOD'S SON
FOR HE WAS TEMPTED BY SATAN IN THE DESERT FORTY DAYS
AND STILL HAD MERCY FOR THE SICK AND DEPRAVED

THERE MUST BE BETTER WAYS TO SAVE MEN FROM SIN
THAN, TO HAVE ONE'S SON DIE TO BELIEVE IN HIM
NOTHING WAS SAID ABOUT THE SALVATION OF ISAAC THE PROMISED CHILD
OR ATONEMENT FOR KILLING EGYPT'S FIRSTBORN DURING THE EXILE

SO WHERE WAS THE HOLY SPIRIT ALL THIS TIME
IT WAS THERE FOR HIS BIRTH AND WHEN BAPTIZED
ALL THIS WAS TO PROVE THAT MEN ARE SAVED FROM SIN
BY JUST BELIEVING IN HIM AND THAT ALL OF THIS HAPPENED

THE SYMBOL OF THE DOVE ON TOP OF HIS HEAD
WAS THAT OF THE LIGHT OF THE SPIRIT BEING EMBEDDED,
LIKE THE SENSATION OF A BEAM OR RAY DOWN INTO THE CRANIUM
PENETRATING JESUS' BRAIN WITH PURITY AND LOVE TO ALL MEN.

JESUS'S MOTIVE FOR HIS EXISTENCE ON EARTH
WAS POINTING THE WAY FOR MAN'S REBIRTH.
IF ONLY THEY BELIEVED THEN THESE ESTRANGED MEN
COULD BE SAVED AND RAISED INTO GOD'S HEAVEN.

IT WAS A STRANGE WAY FOR JESUS TO SAVE ALL MEN.
HE HAD TO BE CRUCIFIED AS A MAN AND DIE FOR THEIR SINS,
BY POINTING OUT THE ERRORS OF PHARISEES, THE MOST RELIGIOUS OF MEN,
WHO THEN BROUGHT CHARGES OF SIN AGAINST HIM.

INSTEAD OF HIS BLOOD BEING SPLAYED ON THE ALTAR
HE WAS TRIED AND THEN TORTURED ON A CROSS TO BE THE SAVIOR

THENCE INTO HELL RAISING THOSE WHO HAD ERRED
JESUS WAS FINALLY RAISED BY CHARIOT FROM THE DEAD
JOHN WHO WROTE HIS GOSPEL AFTER SEVENTY YEARS
PROCLAIMED A COMING AGAIN TO MEET BELIEVERS IN THE AIR

BUT IT HAD ALREADY BEEN PROCLAIMED BY JOHN THE BAPTIZER
THAT JESUS WOULD BAPTIZE MEN WITH THE HOLY SPIRIT AND FIRE
SO AT PENTECOST JESUS' SPIRIT RETURNED MEN WERE THOUGHT TO BE DRUNK
AFTER BEING BAPTIZED AS PREDICTED THEY WERE TALKING IN TONGUES

NOW YOU'VE HAD YOUR HEART CIRCUMCISED GOD'S LAW WRITTEN ON YOUR BRAIN
YOU'LL CONTINUE IN LIFE HERE ON EARTH AND FROM SIN YOU CAN EASILY ABSTAIN
SO IF YOU GO AROUND SUDDENLY SMARTER THAN EVER-
YOU MAY BE SPEAKING IN TONGUES SOLVING PROBLEMS MUCH BETTER

THEY WERE HOPING TO MEET JESUS FLYING UP IN THE AIR
BUT THIS RAPTURE IS DANIEL'S FIGMENT OF IMAGINATION
FOR HOW CAN JESUS COME IN THE CLOUDS TO ME
AND BE SEEN FROM WHERE YOU ARE IN ANOTHER COUNTRY

THE BOOKS OF THE BIBLE ARE NOT ARRANGED CHRONOLOGICALLY
BUT BY LENGTH SO ROMANS BEING FIRST THOUGH WAS WRITTEN LASTLY
PAUL'S LETTERS PRECEDED THE GOSPELS BY YEARS
SO WITH TONGUE IN CHEEK LOOK OUT FOR WHAT'S WEIRD

THE SPIRIT IS IN REALITY NOTHING BUT LIGHT
A LIGHT BEYOND THE HUMAN SPECTRUM IT'S SO BRIGHT
BEING THE RAY PERFORATING THE WOMB OF MARY
BRINGING HOLINESS INTO THE BABE OF JOSEPH SHE CARRIED

THIS SAME RAY IS THE ONE CALLED COSMIC CONSCIOUSNESS
THE LIGHT OF THE WORLD THAT JESUS PROMISED US
INSTALLING ONE'S BRAIN WITH CHRISTLIKE POWERS
LIKE HEALING OR EVEN MAKING HEROES OUT OF COWARDS

RB WELSH, 6 2 20

NUTSHELL

PAUL AND SILAS HAVE JOURNEYED TO THE GENTILES,
INCITING RIOTS BY PREACHING JESUS IN THE TEMPLES.
PAUL IS RECALLED TO THE COUNCIL OF JERUSALEM,
TO STAND TRIAL FOR THE RIOTING BY JAMES, ITS HEAD

THE HEBREWS HAD LEARNED THEIR LESSONS IN EXILE,
GOD IS ONLY ONE, EVEN IF YOU'RE A GENTILE.
THE ROMANS TOOK A DIM VIEW OF THIS,
THE EMPEROR IS KING, THIS IS A CRISIS.

SENDING A LEGION, THEY SAVED PAUL FROM DEATH
LEARNED HE WAS A TARSUS CITIZEN, A MAKER OF TENTS.
SOME OF THE GENTILES CONVERTED TO CHRIST,
PAUL WROTE THE SPIRIT OF CHRIST HAD LESSENED GOD'S LIGHT. (2 COR 3:12)

SO THERE IS CONTINUAL CONTROVERSY.
A VOTE INSTITUTED BY MAN AT NICEA WON'T SOLVE IT.
IF YOU EVER SEE GOD, IT'S IN A PROTEAN WAY,
ARE WE SO BAD WE NEED THREE TO BE SAVED?

RB WELSH, 4 29 23

SOPHIA AS MESSIAH

WE THINK SOPHIA IS THE MESSIAH
FOR IN ALL THE WORLD, NO ONE IS WISER
SHE'S SITTING ON HER PINNACLE,
HER SAGE ADVICE IS INIMITABLE.

AT ONE TIME, WE THOUGHT THAT DEBORAH.
THE PROPHETESS. WAS WHO KILLED SISERA
THE CANAANITE'S ARMY COMMANDER
WHOM ISRAEL FOUGHT FOR THE PROMISED LAND.

BUT SOPHIA IS WISEST OF ALL OWLS OF THE KINGDOM.
IN HER HOUSE OF SEVEN PILLARS OF WISDOM,
SOPHIA BECKONS THE PEOPLE TO JOIN AT HER REQUEST
PARTAKING THE BODY AND SOUL AT THE LORD'S BANQUET.

HAVING BEEN HERE BEFORE THE WORLD BEGAN,
SOPHIA'S RIVALED SIN FOR THE SOULS OF MAN.
CHIDING POOR SOULS WHO FLIT AWAY THEIR LIVES
IN LYING, DISTORTIONS, AND OTHER CRIMES

THE HOUSES OF TOWN HAVE NO PILLARS
TO WARD OFF THOSE SEVEN DEADLY SINS
PORTRAYING THE EXAMPLE OF A MESSIAH
SHE TURNS LIVES ABOUT MAN'S SIGHTS BECOME HIGHER

SO COME UNTO ME YE WHO ARE HEAVY LADEN
AND I WILL RELIEVE YOU OF ALL YOUR BURDENS.
THE MEAL IS READY. THE WINE IS POURED.
DEPART FROM HITHER, AND ALL WILL BE YOURS.

RB WELSH, 6 23 20

WHY GOD BECAME MAN

UNTIL I BECOME A MAN
I NEVER WILL UNDERSTAND
WHAT IT TAKES TO MAKE US CLICK
I'LL DO THIS SO WE'LL BE IN CINQ

WE'RE JUST NOT EVER ON THE SAME PAGE
THAT'S WHY I GET INTO SUCH A RAGE
MAKING YOU SAY I'M ALWAYS UNFAIR
WHEN IT'S ONLY A MATTER OF JUST A HAIR

MEN DON'T EVEN UNDERSTAND EACH OTHER
MOST TIMES, THEY CAN'T EVEN GET TOGETHER
THEY DON'T OBEY ME, ACTING JUST LIKE THE DEVIL
SO I'LL JUST BECOME HUMAN, GETTING DOWN TO THEIR LEVEL

I WAS ONCE A HUMAN SOLDIER AT JERICHO
CHALLENGED BY JOSHUA AS FRIEND OR FOE
SOON I'LL BE ABLE TO UNDERSTAND
JUST WHAT MOTIVATES THE MINDS OF MY HUMANS.

I'LL JUST START OFF AS A NEWBORN BABE,
WITH HUMAN PARENTS BUT NONE OF MY TRAITS.
HE'LL STILL BE ONE OF LIFE'S HUMANITY.
THE SPIRIT WILL THEN GRANT HIM DIVINITY.

RB WELSH, 6 28 20

CREATION AND CREATURE

IN THE VACUITY AND WEIGHTLESSNESS OF SPACE AND LIGHT
THE HOLY SPIRIT CREATED A UNIVERSE UNLIMITED IN SIZE
WITH WAVES IN MOTION OF ROTATING MOLECULAR AIR
WINDS TRANSPOSED PARTICLES INTO MICROMETERS

OUT OF THIS FORMATION, THE UNIVERSE WAS BORN
WITH GODS OVERLOOKING CONSTELLATIONS OUT OF THIS STORM
WITH THEIR SINGULAR RACES, MEN ABOUNDED TO EVOLVE
WITH MOTHER NATURE CONTINUING CREATION FROM ABOVE

WITH EACH SUN'S SUPERNOVA, MEN SOUGHT OTHER STARS
THESE EXTRATERRESTRIALS INVADED THE EARTH AND MARS
LANDING HERE, THEY MULTIPLIED WITH GOD'S CHOSEN RACE
BEING JEALOUS, HE SCATTERED THEM WITH ALL OF TER FAITHS

WITH HIS CHOSEN RACE AND THEIR PROBLEMS OF SIN
GOD CHASTISED THEIR TRANSGRESSIONS WHEN THEY BEGAN
FOR THEY PRAYED TO THOSE OTHER GODS IF NEEDING RAIN
SO HE CIRCUMCISED THEIR HEARTS, WRITINGLAW ON THEIR BRAINS

SO GOD, IN HIS QUANDARY, DECIDED TO BECOME MAN
TO LIVE AMONGST THEM SO HE COULD POSSIBLY UNDERSTAND
THEN IN BAPTIZING JESUS, WHO RECEIVED THE HOLY SPIRIT
TO BECOME DIVINE LIKE HIMSELF AS A HUMAN AS A BEGINNING

ASSOCIATE WITH SINNERS CURE THE LAME AND THE BLIND
HIS MISSION WAS TO PERFORM MIRACLES OF ALL KINDS
CONVERSE WITH THE PHARISEES, EXPLAIN MOSAIC LAW
ATONE FOR ANY SINS OF GOD BY GOING ON THE CROSS

GOD'S PLAGUES AND THE KILLING OF THE EGYPTIAN FIRSTBORN
THE SLAUGHTERING OF CANAANITES STEALING CATTLE AND CORN
AS PRINCE OF PEACE, BRINGING HEAVEN TO EARTH
IT MAY BE FORTHCOMING WHEN MEN HAVE A REBIRTH

OTHER RACES THAN THE CHOSEN ONE CAME HERE FROM AFAR
THIS PLANET IS THE SAFETY VALVE FOR EXPLODED STARS
THE EARTH SHOULD BE PAMPERED INSTEAD OF EXPLOITED
FOR IN THIS CONSTELLATION, THERE HASN'T BEEN A SUPERNOVA

WHY SHOULD GOD GIVE ANY MAN A PLACE UP IN HEAVEN
IF MAN WITTINGLY SINS BY KEEPING UP HIS OBSESSIONS
WHY JUST SAYING HE 'BELIEVES' WILL SAVE HIM FROM HELL
WHEN HIS FINGERS ARE CROSSED WHILE CONTINUING THIS SPELL

ALL MEN SUFFER AND DIE
SOME, TO ONE EXTENT, OTHERS GET BY
THIS IS THEIR CROSS TO CARRY IN LIFE
THOSE IN HEAVEN SHOULD GIVE RELIEF AND HELP THEM SURVIVE

IF JESUS DEATH ON A CROSS ATONED FOR MAN'S SINS
MAN CAN KEEP SINNING AGAIN AND AGAIN
WHICH SEEMS THAT IS HAPPENING IN THIS DAY AND AGE
THERE IS NO ATTEMPT TO REPENT, SO MAN'S STILL ESTRANGED

THE CROSS IS REDUNDANT, FOR MAN WAS BAPTIZED
TO SAVE HIM FROM SINS COMMITTED DURING HIS LIFE
HIS ACTIONS ARE ONE IN THE MAIN PROBLEM HE ESPOUSES
FOR IT'S NOT WHAT GOES IN BUT WHAT COMES FROM HIS MOUTH

RB WELSH, 7 11 20

COMING AGAIN SOON II

JOHN THE BAPTIST WAS IMMERSING MEN IN THE JORDAN
DELIVERING FOR SALVATION THE DESPICABLE AND WANTON
WHEN ASKED ABOUT HIS COUSIN, JESUS JOHN HAD REPLIED
HE IS GREATER THAN I AM BAPTIZING MEN WITH THE HOLY SPIRIT AND FIRE

JESUS HAD BEEN TRIED AND CRUCIFIED BUT PROMISED TO RETURN
THEN AT THE PENTECOST, PEOPLE THOUGHT THAT THEY HAD BEEN SPURNED
BUT SUDDENLY, THERE APPEARED THE HOLY SPIRIT AND TONGUES OF FIRE
IT WAS JESUS RETURNING TO BAPTIZE PREDICTED MONTHS PRIOR

SO AFTER TWO CENTURIES, WE CAN NOW LOOK BACK
TO CELEBRATE THE PENTECOST AND JESUS' SECOND COMING AS FACT
HE IS HERE HE IS THERE
THE CHRIST AS LORD IS EVERYWHERE

JESUS HAS COME AGAIN. CAN'T YOU SEE
HE'S LIGHT IN YOU, AND HE'S THE LIGHT IN ME
REMOVE YOUR SANDALS AND FALL ON YOUR FACE

RB WELSH, 5 26 20

JOHN'S JESUS

THE LOGOS IS THE LIGHT OF THE WORLD
BEYOND THE SUN IN BRILLIANCE OBSERVED
AS THE SON OF GOD CREATED THE MAN
DYING FOR HIM WITHOUT REPRIMAND

MEN ARE TO LIVE IN FELLOWSHIP AND TRUTH
SET AS AN EXAMPLE BY JESUS WIN COMING TO EARTH
AS A PERSONAL LIAISON TO GOD FOR EACH MAN
A PERFECT LIFE BOTH COULD UNDERSTAND

IT'S JUST LIKE A MARRIAGE, FOR BETTER OR WORSE
WE DON'T UNDERSTAND A THING ABOUT THE UNIVERSE
YOU AND I ARE ON A DIFFERENT WAVELENGTH
IT'S TOO MUCH FOR ME; IT IS JUST TOO COMPLEX

I AM THE VINE, AND HE IS THE BRANCH
I NEED HIS SUPPORT TO CLIMB
BEING THE GOOD SHEPHERD, HE SHOWS ME THE WAY
BUT SOMEHOW, I ALWAYS AM GOING ASTRAY

MAINLY HE'S THE TRUTH, SO I'D BETTER TAKE HEED
NOT BE DISTRACTED; ALWAYS DOING GOOD DEEDS
SO I MAY BE BLESSED LIKE THOSE OF THE POOR
THE LAME AND THE BLIND SO THAT I MAY BE CURED

I MAY INDEED BE WAITING TILL I'M IN HEAVEN
BY THEN, I'LL FORGET ALL THIS ARMAGEDDON
PATIENCE SEEMS TO BE THE NAME OF THE GAME
GOOD SPORTSMANSHIP IN ALL FACETS, OR IT'S ALL IN VAIN

SO IT'S WISE FOR ME TO FOLLOW THAT LIGHT
IF I GET OFF TRACK CHRIST WILL CARRY ME BACK
TO CONTINUE SEEKING THE ULTIMATE GOAL
AT ONENESS WITH GOD SAVING MY SOUL

R B WELSH, 7 21 20

BELIEVE IN MY NAME

OH YES! THERE ARE SOME THINGS WE BELIEVE
WE BELIEVE YOU ARE THE CHRIST INDEED
THAT YOU COULD PERFORM AND PUT AT REST
BUT NOT THINGS THAT PUT YOU TO THE TEST

SOMETIMES MAN NEEDS A MIRACLE
ESPECIALLY WHEN IT IS MEDICAL
MAN SEEM TO THINK THERE'S MORE POWER IN PRAYER
if DONE IN GROUPS THE SAME TIME EVERYWHERE

WHILE WE WERE TOLD, "GO IN YOUR CLOSET"
BE STILL THE HEART AND PRAY IN EARNEST
BUT IF THERE IS ANY DOUBT OR WAVER
THE PROBLEM WON'T BE SOLVED IN YOUR FAVOR

SO I KNOW THERE MUST HAVE BEEN
THOUSANDS OF PRAYERS TO STOP COVID
AND PLENTY MORE ABOUT POLITICS
SO WHAT'S THE USE? NOTHING STICKS

THERE YOU GO; YOU DON'T HAVE FAITH
IT'S IN THE AIR; ALL YOU DO IS COMPLAIN
GET A LIFE; IT'S NOT LIKE WAR
NOW THERE IS SOMETHING TO ABHOR

SO IF YOU'RE SERIOUS AND ILL AT EASE
JUST GET DOWN ON YOUR KNEES
OR PROSTRATE YOURSELF ON THE GROUND
BE SURPRISED AN ANSWER IS FOUND

RB WELSH, 7 25 20

GOD AS THE MESSIAH SAYS

I COULD SEE I COULD NOT HANDLE THE MAN
FOR HE HAS BEEN STUBBORN SINCE THE WORLD BEGAN
SO I PROMISED I WOULD RAISE A PROPHET LIKE ME
AS AN INTERMEDIARY FOR COMPATIBILITY

THE MAIN THING FOR MAN TO UNDERSTAND AND BEHOLD
IS THAT THIS IS A UNIVERSE OF OPPOSITES TO CONTROL
PLUSES AND MINUSES TO UNDERMINE
AND SATAN IS ONE I HAVE IN MIND

TO MAKE THIS A MIRACLE, I'LL BE BORN OF A VIRGIN
IN A CAVE OR A MANGER BUT NOT IN AN INN
ALL THE WISE MEN, SHEPHERDS, AND KINGS
WILL FOLLOW JACOB'S STAR TO WORSHIP AND SING

THERE HAVE BEEN MANY MEN THROUGHOUT HISTORY
WHO HAVE QUALIFIED MIRACULOUSLY
WITH READING DREAMS AND WRITINGS ON THE WALL
OR TAMING LIONS ESCAPING FIRE AND OTHER PITFALLS

THERE WAS ESPECIALLY A MAN WHO GAVE HIS LIFE TO SAVE
THE NATION OF ISRAEL FROM BECOMING SLAVES
HIS NAME WAS ELEAZAR ARAVAN A MACCABEAN JEW
DYING UNDER THE SELEUCID KING'S ELEPHANT, HE SLEW

AFTERWARDS, THE CANDELABRA NEVER GAVE OUT OF OIL
THUS THE JEWISH FEAST OF HANUKKAH WAS BORN
SO NOW, WITH ALL THESE SIGNS AND MIRACLES
IT WAS TIME TO MAKE MY MOVE TO SAVE ALL SINNERS

ISAIAH PROPHESIED A VIRGIN BIRTH
THE HOLY SPIRIT CAN ANNOUNCE AND CONFIRM
TO HER OF MY PLAN FOR HER TO CONCEIVE
AND BEAR MY SON TO SAVE THOSE WHO BELIEVE

THERE COMES A TIME FOR US TO SIT DOWN AND THINK
THERE'S NOTHING NEW UNDER THE SUN. ALL IS MAGNIFIQUE
FOR EVERYTHING IS A MIRACLE THE STARS ON THIS PLANET
YOU AND YOUR SOUL, YOUR VERY BEING IS NOT PERFECT

REMEMBER I VISITED SARAH IN HER TENT
SHE BORE A SON AND NAMED HIM ISAAC
I MEANT TO SACRIFICE HIM AND SAVE
SOULS AFTER THAT FROM THE GRAVE

JESUS WILL COMPLETE HIS MESSIANIC MISSION
IN THWARTING SATAN OF MAN'S DESTRUCTION
ALL MAN HAS TO DO IS THAT WHICH HE'S ENJOINED
IS NO MORE THAN TO "BELIEVE" AND SATAN'S DESTROYED

WAS JESUS THE VICTIM OF ORIGINAL SIN
WHEN HE WAS BORN, LIFE BEGINS
IF IT'S A SIN OF ALL MANKIND
WHY WAS HE NOT IMMEDIATELY BAPTIZED?

WHEN A BABY POPS OUT LIKE A CORK
HE COULDN'T HAVE SINNED, BEING NEVER AT FAULT
SO HOW COULD THE SIN OF ADAM AND EVE
EVER BE TRANSFERRED JUST TO YOU AND ME

OH, THIS IS REALLY A CAN OF WORMS
A PROBLEM THAT REALLY MAKES ME SQUIRM
I AM SATISFIED THAT THERE REALLY IS NO SUCH THING
IT'S ANOTHER THEOLOGICAL HOAX. THIS ORIGINAL SIN

LIKE ISAAC WHEN HE WAS CONCEIVED
BOTH SARAH AND MARY MUST HAVE JUST BELIEVED
SOMEHOW IT WAS A DIVINE INTERVENTION
PROMISED OR PROPHESIED A PHYSIOLOGICAL CIRCUMVENTION

JESUS WAS RATIONAL AND WENT TO THE RIVER
WAS BAPTIZED BY THE DOVE FROM ALL SIN DELIVERED
HE WASN'T BAPTIZED TILL HE WAS TWENTY-EIGHT
TO BEGIN HIS MINISTRY FREE FROM SINS AS A BRAT

BOB SAYS I REMEMBER IT WAS A THURSDAY AFTERNOON
I HAVE NO CERTIFICATE AND STILL NEED PROOF
BUT WE ALL DRESSED UP AND DROVE TO THE CHURCH
TO BE SAVED FROM ALL SINS SINCE FROM OUR BIRTH

MARLIS SAID I WAS NEVER BAPTIZED
THAT I'M JUST A NICE GUY IN DISGUISE
SHE WENT THROUGH ALL THE CONFIRMATION
THAT I'M THE BIGGEST SINNER IN THIS CONGREGATION

I SAY WE SHOULD BE BAPTIZED LIKE CONSTANTINE
WAIT TILL WE CAN BE SAVED FROM ALL OF OUR SIN
CONFESS TO THE LORD ALL THAT WE CAN RECALL
AND HAVE BOTH ORIGINAL AND ALL GUILT RESOLVED

WE ARE CELEBRATING HIS BIRTH THIS VERY WEEK
THE LAME, THE STRONG, THE BLIND, AND THE MEEK
HE EVEN GAVE UP FOR US HIS LIFE AND DIED
BUT UPON HIM, REGARDLESS, WE CAN ALWAYS RELY

MERRY CHRISTMAS, Bob Welsh, 12/28/2020

DIVINE INTERVENTION

THERE ARE TIMES IN THE LIVES OF MEN
THAT GOD FINDS IT NECESSARY TO INTERVENE.
IT WAS OBVIOUS WHEN VISITING ABRAHAM,
PICNICKING UNDER THE TREES AT MAMRE.

TAKING HIM ALONG TO SODOM AND GOMORRAH,
WHERE THEY ARGUED ABOUT THEIR DESTRUCTION AND MORALS.
THENCE A RETURN TO SARAH'S TENT,
WHERE GOD BECAME ABRAHAM FOR ISAAC'S DESCENT.

IT WAS OBVIOUS THAT GOD WAS MELCHIZEDEK,
INFORMING MAN HOW TO WORSHIP WITH PROPER RESPECT.
THAT WAS CERTAINLY GOD AT THE GATES OF JERICHO
CHALLENGING JOSHUA LIKE THE BURNING BUSH SCENARIO (JOS 5:13)

OF COURSE, THAT WAS GOD CHASING JONAH DOWN,
ACTING AS A WHALE TO GET HIM TO NINEVEH.
SO NOW HERE GOD IS AS A GARDENER TO MARY,
WHO WAS ASKING HIM WHERE JESUS WAS BURIED.

IT'S BEEN GOD ALL ALONG AS SOMEBODY ELSE,
SO BE NICE TO STRANGERS, IT MAY BE GOD HIMSELF.

RB WELSH, 7 21 22

NAME DROPPING: ELOHIM

ELOHIM IS JUST ONE NAME OF GOD
ONE OF THEM WE KNOW IS THAT OF ALLAH
WHO TOOK HIMSELF OUT OF THE TRINITY
WHEN HE WAS VOTED ONLY AS ONE OUT OF THREE

HE SEEMS TO HAVE MANY NAMES
IN MANY COUNTRIES AND EVERY PLACE
HE IS THE MAKER OF ALL MANKIND
ROMANS AND PERSIANS, BLACKS AND WHITES

HE HAS MANY SONS FROM ROME TO THE ORIENT
IN EGYPT, ASSYRIA, PERSIA, AND FROM SARAH'S TENT
ALL OF THEM WERE BORN ON DECEMBER TWENTY-FIFTH
CHRISTMAS IS THE WORLD OVER SEEMS THEIR NAMES WOULD BE SMITH

RB WELSH, 1 29 22

CHRISTMAS TIME

IT'S NOW DECEMBER TWENTY-FIFTH
IN DAYS OF OBSERVING WINTER SOLSTICE
BY CELEBRATING JESUS' BIRTH
THE NEWBORN KING O'ER ALL THE EARTH

TWAS IN DIREST OF CIRCUMSTANCE
OE A CRITICAL ISSUE BY CHANCE
THE COUPLE WENT TO BETHLEHEM
FOR CAESAR ORDERED A CENSUS TO BE TAKEN

WHEN DAVID ORDERED SUCH A THING
NOT COMMANDED BY GOD AS A CENSUS TO BE TAKEN
HE WAS CENSURED FOR IT WAS FORBIDDEN
AND 70 THOUSAND LIVES WERE KILLED THEN (2 SAM 24)

NOW WITH HEROD BEING PARANOID
HE SENT OUT WORD AND AVOWED
LIKE GOD OF ALL EGYPTIAN FIRSTBORN
TO DESTROY ALL INFANTS NEWLY BORN

WITH JACOB'S STAR HOVERING OVER THEM (NUM 24:17)
POINTING THE WAY TO THE KINGS AND WISE MEN
THE BABE WAS PLACED INTO A MANGER
WITH HIS LIFE SUDDENLY IN DANGER

WAS JESUS BORN JUST TO BE
ONE IN THREE OF A TRINITY
NO, WE BELIEVE HE IS OUR GUIDE
ON OUR WAY THROUGH A TREACHEROUS LIFE

IF WE RECEIVE AN A' *KAORI*
GREEK AS "ONENESS WITH THE SPIRIT
SAYING THE PROMISE OF ETERNAL LOVE
BY PEACE OF BAPTISM BY THE DOVE

GOD IS REBORN AS A NEW BABE
AS WE MUST BE TO BE SAVED
IS JUST BE SO NAIVE AS JUST TO BELIEVE
THAT CHRIST WAS BORN AND DIED TO REPRIEVE

EVEN THOUGH THIS MAKES NO SENSE
IT IS THE EPITOME OF HOLINESS
LIVING A LIFE IN THE MIDST OF SIN
AND STILL, BE TAKEN BY CHRIST TO HEAVEN

RB WELSH, 12 24 20

MIRACLE

YES, IT WAS MOST DRAMATIC
WHEN JESUS CURED THE PARALYTIC
THE ONE THEY LET DOWN THROUGH THE ROOF
JUST TO GIVE US THE PROOF

THAT JESUS IS GOD'S ONLY SON
THE ONE BORN OF A VIRGIN
BUT WASN'T THAT JUST A MESS
THE DIRT AND STRAW AND ALL THE REST

FALLING INTO THE ROOM
LIKE THEY JUST LOWERED THE BOOM
I GUESS JESUS JUST SNAPPED HIS FINGERS
SUDDENLY THE ROOF HAD NEW SHINGLES

OH GOD I WONDER DO WE HAVE TO JUST "BELIEVE"
TO BE SAVED BY WHAT WE HAVE JUST SEEN
DOES IT MEAN TO FORGET THE OLD LAW OF GOD
TO POUR THIS NEW WINE INTO SKINS WE JUST DONNED

WERE THE POOR AIDED WHEN EXPENSIVE WINE
AT A WEDDING WHEN THERE WAS NONE MATERIALIZED
WHAT WE JUST NEED IS FRESH AIR TO BREATHE
AND MEN'S WORDS TO PREVAIL THAT DON'T DECEIVE

MIRACLES HAVE BEEN ALSO BEEN PERFORMED
BY MOSES ELIJAH ELISHA AND MORE
AT TRANSFIGURATION THEY WERE THERE
ALIVE AND WELL WITH THE SAVIOR

RB WELSH, 1 16 21

BROWN MOUNTAIN LIGHTS

PAUL WAS ALWAYS VOCIFEROUS
IN MAKING CLAIMS ABOUT JESUS
BUT WHEN HE TALKED ABOUT HEAVEN
VAGUE AS IF IT NEEDED LEAVEN

HE WAS NO ANGEL WHEN HE ROSE
INTO THE THIRD LEVEL WE SUPPOSE
IN A TRAUMATIC SCENE
UNREPEATABLE IT SEEMS

THEN JACOB SLEEPING ON THE WAY
TO GET A BRIDE IT SEEMS HE PRAYED
AFTER VISUALIZING ANGELS TO ASCEND
AND DESCEND ON A LADDER FROM HEAVEN

I ONCE HAD A FRIEND WHO TOOK ME
TO THE BROWN MOUNTAINS OVERLOOK TO SEE
EXTRA TERRESTRIALS BEING RESUPPLIED
FROM A FLYING SAUCER'S LADDER OVERHEAD

LIKE A LIGHTED TUBE OF LIFESAVERS
NOT ANGELS BUT OUT OF SPACERS
SLIDING COLORED PACKAGES DESCENDING
DOWN A SHAFT LIKE AS IF TRANSCENDIG

SO SITTING ON A ROCK ALL NIGHT
NEAR DAWN WE SAW SOME COLORED LIGHTS
BLINKING ROUND ABOUT SOME LOFTY CRAFT
BUT NEVER MOVING TO MAKE CONTACT

WITH THE BREAKING OF THE DAWN
WE WERE SHOCKED AND FORLORN
FOR OUR TRIP'S ONLY ENCOUNTER
WAS WITH THE MORGANTON WATER TOWER

RB WELSH, 1 18 21

HEAVEN

"HEAVEN AND EARTH WILL PASS AWAY
BUT MY WORDS WILL LIVE FOREVER" (MT 24:35)
IT IS NOT *MAY, COULD,* OR *MIGHT* BUT WILL
AND THAT IS WHAT REALLY KILLS

TWELFTH-CENTURY THEOLOGIANS MUST HAVE MISSED THAT
WHEN THEY REWROTE THE PASSAGES THAT CONFLICT
WITH THEIR NOTIONS OF WHAT PEOPLE SAID
TO MAKE IT PLAUSIBLE FOR BELIEVERS INSTEAD

THIS MEANS WE'LL STILL HAVE CHRISTIANITY
EVEN THOUGH WE DON'T LIVE IN PERPETUITY
YES, WE WILL STILL HAVE GOD'S WORDS
BUT OF WHAT USE NOW GIVES US CONCERN

YES, WE KNOW OUR STAR WILL BURN OUT
LIKE OTHER RACES HERE, WE'LL SEEK ANOTHER REDOUBT
SOMEWHERE IN ANOTHER CONSTELLATION
OUR SPACESHIPS WILL TAKE US TO OUR DESIGNATION

WAS THIS JUST ANOTHER FAIRY TALE
GOING THROUGH LIFE WITH ALL ITS TRAVAILS
TO JUST HAVE HEAVEN FADE AWAY
WHERE WE EXPECT TO GO ONE DAY

IS THIS JUST ANOTHER SANTA CLAUS,
EASTER BUNNY OR PENTECOST KITE?
WILL THIS BE IN THE ETERNAL HISTORY BOOK?
IT IS JUST A JOKE FOR GODS TO LAUGH AND LOOK

WELL, I NEVER HEARD SERMONS ON THIS
IT'S SOMETHING SUNDAY SCHOOLS OMIT
ALL WE EVER HEARD AGAIN AND AGAIN
BEHAVE BE GOOD; JUST BELIEVE AND DON'T SIN

MAYBE ONLY THE FIRST HEAVEN PASSED AWAY
FOR PAUL WAS CARRIED TO THE THIRD, HE SAYS
GOD SAYS HIS HEAVEN HAS MANY MANSIONS
ARE WE STILL OF MANY RACES AS I IMAGINE

THIS COUNTERS THE REST OF THE BIBLICAL SAYINGS
THE ONES THAT WE ARE CONTINUALLY EXPLAINING
OR JOHN 14:28, WHERE HE SAYS THE FATHER IS GREATER
GIVING EVIDENCE OF A TRINITARIAN FAILURE

RB WELSH, 1 22 21

LOVE YOUR ENEMY

GOD GAVE MANKIND THE TEN COMMANDMENTS
TO LOVE ONE ANOTHER IS NOT DEMANDED
FROM ENEMIES OBTAIN AN EYE FOR AN EYE
IT'S LUCKY IF WE CAN JUST LOVE ONE ANOTHER

BUT JESUS SAID FOR ME TO LOVE MINE ENEMY
HE REALLY MEANS THAT IN ALL SINCERETY
IT'S REALLY THE DOING AND NOT THE SAYING
THAT PROJECTS THE EMOTION ONE'S PORTRAYING

HE'S OUT THERE TO CHANGE THE THINKING OF THE WORLD
TO STOP MEN'S MADNESS OF WARS AND HATE AS ABSURD
TO BRING PEACE E AND HAPPINESS BETWEEN ONE ANOTHER
TO UNITE ALL NATIONS RACES AND HIS BROTHER

SPONTANEOUS LOVE IS EVIDENT
IT'S SO OBVIOUS IT CAN'T BE HID
IT'S BLURTED OUT SUBCONSCIOUSLY
GENUINE LOVE IS LASTING IN PERPETUITY

MANUFACTURED LOVE MAY BE COMMANDED
BUT IT'S SO FAKE THAT IT'S JUST LAUGHABLE
WHAT IS REAL IS LOVE OF ANOTHER'S VERY SOUL
LIKE MAGNETS ATTRACTION IT JUST UNFOLDS

LOVE IS SOMETHING THAT CAN'T BE HELPED
YOU CAN'T JUST BUY IT RIGHT OFF THE SHELF

IT'S STRANGE THEN WHY JESUS SAYS
TO HATE OUR PARENTS OR WE CAN'T BE HIS DISCIPLES
FOR THEY ARE THE ONE'S CLOSET TO US
THIS IS CONTRADICTORY TO HIS USUAL PULSE

SO I'LL LOVE MY ENEMY JUST AS SOON
AS JESUS SAYS, HE LOVES SATAN TOO

FOR IF MY ENEMY SAYS HE LOVES ME
HE'S JUST SETTING ME UP FOR SOME DEVILTRY

RB WELSH, 1 24 21

RULER OF THE WORLD JN 14:30

AH, SO IT'S THE RULER OF THE WORLD THAT WE ARE CONTENDING WITH
NO WONDER SOMETIMES WE FEEL SOMETHING IS AMISS
AND YOU HAVE LEFT US TO GO INTO HEAVEN
THAT SANCTUARY OF SOULS THAT HAVE MADE IT

SO WHEREIN JUST WHERE DOES OUR FUTURE LIE
WE'RE FLOUNDERING AROUND IN FISHIN THE SKY
WONDERING JUST WHY, FROM ONE DAY TO THE NEXT
WHAT IRRATIONAL THING IS TO MAKE LIFE MORE COMPLEX?

ALL WE'VE SEEN LATELY IS NOTHING BUT CHAOS
RESULTING FROM SOME SIN, IS THIS THE PAYOFF
WE FEEL LIKE MONKEYS IN A CAGE
FLOUNDERING ABOUT BUILDING UP RAGE

IF JESUS WERE HERE FEELING TOO THIS IMPASSE
INSTEAD OF SITTING AT THE WINE TABLE SIPPING A GLASS
WITH HIS DISCIPLES AT ONENESS WITH GOD
WHILE WE STILL FLOUNDER ABOUT LIKE SOME FROGS

ALL BECAUSE GOD LETS SATAN HAVE HIS WAY
LIKE HE DID WITH A POOR JOB TEMPTING HIM EVERY DAY
SO JESUS, YOU RAISED THE DEAD FROM HELL
TILL WE CAN JOIN YOU, GIVE SOME RELIEF FOR A SPELL

RB WELSH, 1 23 21

CONSCIENCE

AS HE WAS THE GARDENER AT THE TOMB TO MARY
UNRECOGNIZABLE IN FEATURES BUT THE VOICE DIDN'T VARY
SO HE CAN BE OUR VERY OWN CONSCIENCE
TELLING US WHAT TO DO IF WE BUT JUST LISTEN

YOU KNOW THERE WERE TIMES
YOU BRUSHED HIM ASIDE
AND SAID IT 'S TOO STRONG AN IMPULSE
SO I'LL DO IT ANYWAY IN SPITE OF RESULTS

IT'S JUST ANOTHER WHIP MARK ON JESUS' BACK
I 'M JUST ANOTHER ROMAN SOLDIER TAKING A WHACK
FOR HE WILL FORGIVE ME I KNOW NOT WHY
WILLINGLY GOING TO JERUSALEM TO DIE

JESUS HAS TAKEN ON THE SUFFERING I SHOULD DO
THE STRIPES ON HIS BACK THE CRUCIFIX TOO
ALL THIS HE DID QUITE VOLUNTARILY
HIS MESSIANIC SECRET WAS A RANSOM FOR MANY

SO INDEED HE HAS ALREADY COME AGAIN
TO EACH ONE AND ALL SO DON'T TRY TO SPIN
OUR DEEDS ARE ALL STACKED UP IN OUR SOULS
TO BE FORGIVEN FOR THEM IS OUR ULTIMATE GOAL

RB WELSH, 1 26 21

BIBLICAL ANALYSIS

THERE ARE QUALIFIED WOMEN IN THE MINISTRY
LIKE PRISCILLA WITH HER HUSBAND MAKING HISTORY
HE WAS A TENT MAKER LIKE SAINT PAUL, MAKING HOMES
FOR THE MANY CHRISTIANS KICKED OUT OF ROME

SHE WAS A SELF-MADE THEOLOGIAN
CORRECTING NEW BELIEVERS ON A PARTICULAR POINT

WHY AM I COMPELLED TO BELIEVE?
WHAT THEOLOGIANS OF THE FIRST CENTURY CONCEIVED?
MAY I NOT DEVELOP MY OWN THEOLOGY
LIKE PRISCILLA FROM INSPIRATION AND BEING GODLY?

POLITICIANS DISTORT FACTS AS TO WHAT WE SHOULD KNOW
THEOLOGIANS ARE POLITICIANS JUST DRESSED UP IN ROBES
THE BIBLE IS INERRANT BUT EDITED BY MEN
GIVING FALSE ILLUSIONS AS TO WHAT GOD HAS SAID

PAUL'S LETTERS WERE WRITTEN SOME FORTY YEARS
BEFORE THE GOSPEL, WRITERS TOOK UP PEN TO INSTILL
THEIR OWN VERSIONS OF JESUS AND HIS MINISTRY
FOR US TO DEVELOP OUR OWN THEOLOGY

IT'S USUALLY A JUMBLE OF FACTS FROM THEM ALL
SUPPLANTED BY GUIDANCE FROM THOSE RECEIVING THE CALL
DID GOD OR JESUS OR THE HOLY SPIRIT
ANNOUNCE THEIR ONENESS, OR WAS IT

A GODHEAD UNIFIED AS A TRINITY
INSTIGATED FOR POLITICAL UNITY
ADOPTED BY THE POPES OF CONSTANTINE
AT THE COUNCIL OF NICEA

FROM A MISSIONARY LIKE SAINT PAUL
WHO DECLARED HE WOULD DO ANYTHING AT ALL
TO CONVERT BELIEVERS, LIKE IN CORINTH,
WHERE WORSHIPERS DRANK THE BLOOD OF BULLS MEAT?

SO HE CLAIMED TO THE CORINTHIANS HE RECEIVED FROM JESUS
AN EDICT THAT IT WAS THE CHRIST INSTEAD OF DIONYSUS
WHOSE BLOOD SHOULD WE DRINK AND EAT HIS BODY
DESPITE GOD'S COVENANT WITH NOAH AFTER THE FLOOD

WHY SHOULD WE NOT WORK UP A MITHRA
THAT A SAVIOR WAS BORN IN PERSIA ON DECEMBER TWENTY-FIFTH
OR KRISHNA, WHO WAS ALSO HUNG ON A TREE
LIKE BUDDHA, WHO SITS CROSS-LEGGED IN REVERIE
IN COMMUNION WITH THE SAME GOD
JUST NOT EATING HIS BODY OR BLOOD

JUST DON'T GO AROUND WITH YOUR THEOLOGY
UNLESS YOU HAVE A DOCTORATE DEGREE
JUST DON'T TELL ME WHAT THE ESSENES SAY
OR WHAT'S IN THE GNOSTICS POTS OF CLAY

YES, WOMEN HAVE BRAINS EVEN MORE THAN MEN
PREJUDICE MUST CEASE IF THERE'S EVER TO COMMENCE
EQUALITY OF MINDSET AND RACIAL DISSENT
FOR JESUS LOVED WOMEN A LOT MORE THAN MEN

JUST THINK THAT THIS YEAR A WOMAN OF COLOR
IS NOW VICE PRESIDENT OF THE UNITED STATES OF AMERICA,
SO WHERE IS THE BEEF NOW ABOUT FEMALES
THE ISSUE IS CLOSED; THERE IS NO CASE

RB WELSH, 2 17 21

FROZEN CHOSEN

JUST WHO ARE THE BELIEVERS THAT RECEIVED GOD'S CALL?
IS IT THE WISE AND THE BELIEVERS WHO PREACH TO US ALL?
WE HAVE OUR PRAYER SESSIONS TO HEAL AND SAVE,
PRAYING THAT ALL MEN WILL BE LIKE US, CHRIST'S SLAVES.

MANY ARE CALLED, BUT FEW ARE CHOSEN,
IT IS AN EXPRESSION LABELING THOSE WHO ARE FROZEN.
BUT THE "CHOSEN RACE," THE HEBREWS,
HAVE REJECTED JESUS; HE IS JUST A PREVIEW.

FOR BELIEF IN OTHER GODS, THEY HAVE BEEN EXILED,
THE ISRAELIS' EXTINCTION IS STILL ON THEIR MINDS.
THEY BELIEVE NOW IN ONE GOD THAT HE IS NOT THREE,
THEY WILL TAKE THEIR CHANCES OF AN ETERNITY.

WE MIGHT AS WELL SAY WE ARE BELIEVERS,
IN JESUSOLOGY, FOR HE IS OUR LEADER,
WE HAVE SEEN THE LIGHT, RECEIVED THE CALL,
FOR GOD, HIMSELF IS REALLY JESUS, ONE AND ALL.

RB WELSH, 2 5 23

THE WELLSPRING OF LIFE
(SAMARITAN WELL)

IT SEEMS THAT A TOWN'S WELL IS THE CENTER OF LIFE
IT'S WHERE ISAAC AND JACOB FOUND THEIR FUTURE WIVES
THE WELL IS USUALLY IN THE CENTER OF TOWN
BUT JACOB'S WELL IS A SPRING THAT IS NOW QUITE RENOWN

JACOB'S WELL IS LOCATED OUT IN THE HEAT OF THE DESERT
MEANT FOR WATERING SHEEP NEARBY THE CITY OF SHECHEM
JESUS HAD SENT HIS DISCIPLES TO BUY FOOD IN THE TOWN
IT'S SURPRISING HE DIDN'T FEED THEM LIKE HE DID THE FIVE THOUSAND

IT WAS AMAZING THAT A SAMARITAN TOOK CARE OF A JEW
ASSAILED BY ROBBERS AND LEFT IN THE DITCH FOR DEAD
PASSED BY ON THE ROAD BY THE PRIEST AND THE LEVITE
BUT CARE TAKEN BY A SAMARITAN NEIGHBOR WHO DID RIGHT

SO WHAT IS THE MISSION CALLED SAMARITANS PURSE
IT SAVES THOUSANDS IN THE WORLD OVER FROM DISASTERS AND WORSE
IT'S CHRIST'S LOVING TOUCH FOR HEALING ALL WOUNDS
HERE JESUS IS SAVING AND UNITING SAMARITANS AND JEWS

SO IT IS STRANGE THAT A JEW WOULD EVER TALK TO THIS GIRL
IT SEEMS HE WAS WAITING TO UNITE TWO NATIONS
RIPPED APART YEARS AGO BEFORE BOTH WERE DEPORTED
FOR WORSHIPING OTHER GODS, NOT THE GOD OF JACOB

THE CHRIST HAD NO NEED FOR WATER FROM THIS WELL
FOR HE IS THE SOURCE OF LIFE AND LIVING WATER HIMSELF
BUT WHEN A WOMAN CAME WITH HER JAR TO DRAW WATER
HE REQUESTS A DRINK THOUGH HE KNEW ALL ABOUT HER

SO THE WHOLE POINT HERE IS THAT JESUS KNOWS
WHAT'S IN OUR HEARTS AND EVERYTHING IN OUR SOULS
SO WE WONDER WHY HE SPEAKS IN PARABLES
JUST FOR THE BENEFIT OF ONLY HIS DISCIPLES

BUT HIS REPUTATION HAD PRECEDED HIM AND SHE ALREADY KNEW
THAT HE WAS THE MESSIAH AND KING OF THE JEWS
AND AS KING OF ALL HE COULD BE THE ONE TO HAVE TO DIE
INSTEAD OF ALL PEOPLES IN THE NATION BEING CRUCIFIED

PERHAPS HE WOULD RID US WITH ONE OF HIS MIRACLES
OF THE ROMANS WHO OPPRESS US AND JUST MAKE THEM INVISIBLE
SHE WAS SO IMPRESSED SHE SPREAD THE WORD AROUND TOWN
SHE WAS SAVED AS MANY OTHERS WERE WHEN WORD GOT AROUND

RB WELSH, 2 3 21

MARY MAGDALENE

WE WONDER HOW A PROSTITUTE COULD GET PAST THE GUARDS
TO JOIN A PHARISEE DINNER CREATING A SCENE SO BIZARRE
UNLESS SHE WAS WELL KNOW TO CREATE SUCH A SCENE
AS WRAPPING HER HAIR AROUND JESUS'S FEET

THEN ANOINTING THEM WITH PRECIOUS OIL AT THIS FEAST
ALL OTHER KINGS BEING ANOINTED BY PROPHETS OR PRIESTS
BUT THIS IS MARY MAGDALENE WELL KNOWN TO ALL
FOR SHE HAS BEEN SAVED FROM A NOTORIOUS FALL

FOR MARY HAD AN EVIL SPIRIT THAT JESUS EXORCISED
HER SOUL NOW IN GOOD ORDER SHE STAYED BY HIS SIDE
SO BY BEING WITH JESUS SHE COULD ENSURE
THAT SEVEN MORE DEADLY SPIRITS WOULD NOT RETURN

WHEN JESUS WAS IN GALILEE STAYING WITH MARY AND MARTHA
WHILE MARTHA WAS LABORING AT THE HEARTH AND
MARY WAS AGAIN ANOINTING JESUS'S FEET WITH HER HERBS
JESUS ANNOUNCED MARY'S FAITH WAS BETTER THAN MARTHA'S WORKS

THUS AGREEING WITH PAUL VERSUS JAMES WHO SAID
IN HIS ARGUMENT THAT "WORKS WITHOUT FAITH IS DEAD"
WE KNOW THAT EACH MIRACLE TAKES A LOT OF WORK
THAT POWER IS LOST AS HEALING THE WOMAN WITH ISSUE OBSERVES

WE SEE GOD AT WORK IN MANY WAYS
SOMETIMES IT IS ONLY PERFORMED IN STAGES
THE END RESULT IS PERHAPS SURPRISING AT LEAST
FOR IT SEEMINGLY STARTED QUESTIONABLY

FOR WE KNOW THAT BEING CRUCIFIED JESUS IS REALLY DEAD
BUT HERE AS THE GARDENER HE APPEARS ALIVE AS A HUMAN AGAIN
IT IS LIKE GOD APPEARING WITH ABRAHAM AND SARAH
OR AS A SOLDIER AT JERICHO TO JOSHUA

IS IT TRUE THAT THEY ACTUALLY GOT MARRIED?
UP WITH THE ESSENES AT QUMRAN JESUS AND MARY
FOR WE'LL NEVER BE ABLE TO CLOSE JESUS'S BOOK
UNTIL HIS SEXUALITY IS SHOWN AND UNDERSTOOD

FOR JESUS BIRTH ITSELF HAS SEXUAL OVERTONES
BEING CONCEIVED OUT OF WEDLOCK HAS BEEN SHOWN
KNOWN ALL HIS LIFE AS SON OF MARY INSTEAD OF JOSEPH
A VIRGINAL BIRTH BEING AN ABNORMAL PROCESS

AS IT WAS IN DAVID'S TIME WITH MEN IT IS GIRLS
IT'S NOT MONEY OR POWER BUT SEX THAT RULES THE WORLD
JESUS AS FULLY GOD AND FULLY MAN IS SUBJUGATE
TO THAT SECRET UNDERLYING POWER TO PROLIFERATE

THIS ALL JUST SHOWS THE EQUALITY OF PERSONS AND RACES
THAT ARE IN GOD'S EYES AND THEIR PERSONAL RELATIONS
BUT WHEN IT COMES TO SENSATIONS OR FEELINGS THAT OCCUR
FOR US TO GIVE EACH PERSON THE LOVE OR RESPECT THEY DESERVE

RB WELSH, 2 9 21

DIVINE INTERVENTION

THERE ARE TIMES IN THE LIVES OF MEN
THAT GOD FINDS IT NECESSARY TO INTERVENE.
IT WAS OBVIOUS WHEN VISITING ABRAHAM,
PICNICKING UNDER THE TREES AT MAMRE.

TAKING HIM ALONG TO SODOM AND GOMORRAH,
WHERE THEY ARGUED ABOUT THEIR DESTRUCTION AND MORALS.
THENCE A RETURN TO SARAH'S TENT,
WHERE GOD BECAME ABRAHAM FOR ISAAC'S DESCENT.

IT WAS OBVIOUS THAT GOD WAS MELCHIZEDEK,
INFORMING MAN HOW TO WORSHIP WITH PROPER RESPECT.
THAT WAS CERTAINLY GOD AT THE GATES OF JERICHO
CHALLENGING JOSHUA LIKE THE BURNING BUSH SCENARIO. (JOS 5:13)

OF COURSE, THAT WAS GOD CHASING JONAH DOWN,
ACTING AS A WHALE TO GET HIM TO NINEVEH.
SO NOW HERE GOD IS AS A GARDENER TO MARY,
WHO WAS ASKING HIM WHERE JESUS WAS BURIED.

IT'S BEEN GOD ALL ALONG AS SOMEBODY ELSE,
SO BE NICE TO STRANGERS, IT MAY BE GOD HIMSELF.

RB WELSH, 7 21 22

A VALENTINE

MARY MAGDALENE SHOT AN ARROW
INTO THE HEART OF THE LORD HER SAVIOR
SAYING I AM YOURS WILL YOU BE MINE
THIS WAS THE VERY FIRST VALENTINE

EXPRESSING LOVE BY WASHING HIS FEET
WITH HER TEARS BEING NOT TOO DISCREET
AND DRYING THEM SOFTLY WITH HER HAIR
NO GREATER LOVE WAS FOUND ANYWHERE

NOWADAYS TO GAIN THE OBJECT OF ONE'S AFFECTION
IS MADE BY SENDING A BOX OF CONFECTION
FORMED IN THE SHAPE OF A BIG RED HEART
SAYING THIS IS MORE THAN JUST A LARK

PRINCE CHARLES THE DUKE OF ORLEANS WAS IMPRISONED
IN THE TOWER OF LONDON FOR TWENTY YEARS SO IN THIS POSITION
SENT A POEM OF LOVE TO ISABELLA HIS WIFE
CALLING HER *"MY GENTLE VALENTINE"*

SO CUPID IS LURKING JUST AROUND THE CORNER
ARROWS FLYING FROM HIS BOW AT HIM AND HER
PERHAPS CONNECTING MEN WITH A SECRET LOVE
JUST MADE BY GOD IN HEAV'N ABOVE

JESUS IS MAN'S SYMBOL TO BE
ONE OF *AGAPE'* LOVE AND PEACE FOR ETERNITY
SO JUST AS SOON AS EACH ONE ACCEPTS HIS CALL
THE WORLD WILL BE A PLACE OF LOVE FOR ALL

HAPPY VALENTINE!! YA'LL
Bob, 2 14 21

CREATION

THE HOLY SPIRIT IN THE VACUITY OF SPACE WITHOUT FORM,
WITH AN INVISIBLE LIGHT EMANATED WAVES INTO A SWARM
OF ROTATING MYRIADS OF CONSTELLATIONS INTO A STORM,
SHOWERING SUPER-NOVAS INTO THIS SWIRLING MORASS,
LEAVING IN THEIR WAKES, GALAXIES, PLANETS, AND GAS.

EINSTEIN THEN CALCULATED THAT THIS ROTATING LIGHT,
CREATED ENERGY SUFFICIENT TO CREATE GRANULITE,
WITH SOLAR WINDS AND GRAVITY, DUST PARTICULATES COULD GROW,
INTO ROTATING PLANETS AROUND SUNS, LIKE ORBITING GYROS.

BY SENDING OUT GODS EACH TO ITS CONSTELLATION,
THEY CREATED EACH RACE TO WORSHIP IT AS ONE.
WHEN EARTH'S GOD DECIDED TO CREATE MAN INDEED,
SOPHIA, SPIT AND DUST WERE ALL HE WOULD NEED.

NATURE THEN ENDOWED THE EARTH WITH ANIMALS AND PLANTS,
RAINBOWS OF UNIMAGINABLE COLORS FORMED IN THIS GREAT EXPANSE.
NATURE STILL CONTINUES THIS CREATION AND SPECIES STILL EVOLVE,
MANKIND WITH INTELLIGENCE PROGRESSES, INVENTS AND SOLVES.

SO FROM THE NOTHINGNESS OF ONLY STARLIGHT,
PLANETS WHILE SPINNING AROUND SUNS IN ORBIT,
ARE HASTENING DIRECTLY, RAPIDLY AND INEXORABLY,
STRAIGHT OUT OF THE UNIVERSE TO BEGIN MAN'S STORY.

OF ADAM AND EVE FIRST AND THEN A NEW BEGINNING
OF JESUS THE CHILD OF THE HOLY SPIRIT AND A VIRGINAL MARY.
WHERE HE SHOWS THE WAY FOR ALL MANKIND
TO BELIEVE THEY BE WITH GOD ON THEIR DEMISE.

RB WELSH, 3 29 21

ELIJAH

AFTER TAKING OVER CANAAN GOD WAS ISRAEL'S KING
BUT THE PEOPLE CRIED OUT THAT OTHER NATIONS HAD SOMEONE TO REIGN
SO WITH THE TABERNACLE AND ARK AT SHILOH AS CAPITOL
GOD FINALLY GAVE IN AND HAD SAUL ANOINTED BY SAMUEL

KING SAUL WAS CONTINUALLY USING HIS OWN INITIATIVE
WHEN GOD ORDERED HIM TO KILL ALL ANIMALS AND HUMAN BEINGS
SAUL SAVED THE BEST CATTLE FOR THE PRIESTS IN THE TEMPLE
TO GO THROUGH THE RITUALS OF SACRIFICE BEING REVERENTIAL

HE ALSO ALLOWED THE MIDIANITES TO RETURN
FOR THE WIFE OF MOSES WAS A MIDIANITE AS I LEARNED
THOUGH THE ISRAELITES NOW THEIR KING
GOD REMAINED IN ABSOLUTE AUTHORITY

BEFORE THE SHEPARD BOY SLAYER OF GOLIATH ASCENDED TO THE THRONE
GOD SPLIT THE KINGDOM IN TWO COMPOUNDING THE PROBLEM
THE PEOPLE WERE WORSHIPING THE OTHER GOD BAAL
AS WELL AS THE KINGS SEEKING MORE POWER TO PREVAIL

KING AHAB WAS ONE OF ISRAEL'S MOST TREACHEROUS KINGS
HE BROUGHT FROM TYRE HIS WIFE JEZEBEL AS HIS QUEEN
TOGETHER THEY INSTITUTED THE WORSHIP OF BAAL AND ASHERAH
BRINGING ON A MULTI-YEAR DROUGHT BY GOD THRUOUT SAMARIA

THOUGH KNOWING HE SHOULDN'T BRING GOD TO THE TEST
ELIJAH CHALLENGED THE PRIESTS OF BAAL TO A CONTEST
TO SEE WHICHEVER GOD COULD BRING ON A FIRE
TO BARBECUE A BULL WITH ONLY A PRAYER

THE PRIESTS BUILT AN ALTAR OF STONES AND WOOD THEN PRAYED
LAID THEIR BULL ON THE STONES AND DANCED AROUND IT ALL DAY
THOUGH EVEN SLICING THEIR CHESTS NO FIRE FROM HEAVEN WAS SENT
WHEN THEY GAVE UP IT BECAME ELIJAH'S TURN HIS BULL WAS EVEN DRENCHED

HE CALLED UPON THE GOD OF ABRAHAM TO BRING DOWN FIRE
SO IMMEDIATELY A SHEET OF LIGHTNING STRUCK AS ELIJAH DESIRED
THE ROCKS MUST HAVE BEEN OF PHOSPHOROUS FOR THEY BURNED AS WELL
ELIJAH WINNING IN THIS CONTEST HAD THE BAAL PROPHETS ALL KILLED

INSTEAD OF THEN TURNING TO GOD JEZEBEL WAS FURIOUS
THREATENING THE LIFE OF ELIJAH WHICH WAS NOW PRECARIOUS
SO TAKING OFF TO THE DESERT TOOK REFUGE IN A CAVE
ON THE MOUNTAIN OF GOD WHERE HE FELT LIKE A KNAVE

THE ANGELS AND GOD TOOK CARE OF HIS NEEDS
SENDING HIM TO DAMASCUS TO ANOINT HAZAEL AS KING
WHILE AHAB IN HIS WEAK MINDSET THOUGHT THAT HE OUGHT
TO BUY NABOTH'S VINEYARD FOR A GARDEN DURING THIS DROUGHT

NABOTH DECLINED TELLING HIM IT BELONGED TO THE FAMILY
SO AHAB IN A POUT WOULDN'T EAT OR FACE UP TO REALITY
BUT JEZEBEL WITH HER NEFARIOUS MIND HAD NABOTH SET UP
TO BE KILLED BY A RUSE SO LITTLE AHAB WOULD CHEER UP

ELIJAH PREDICTED THAT GOING INTO BATTLE AHAB WOULD BE KILLED
THAT HIS BLOOD WOULD BE LICKED UP BY DOGS AND THIS WAS FULFILLED
EUNUCHS THEN THREW JEZEBEL OFF OF HER BALCONY
WITH HORSES THEN RUNNING OVER HER TRAMPLING HER BODY

THE LORD TOLD ELIJAH TO VISIT THE WIDOW OF ZARAPATH
IN EXERCISING HIS POWERS LIKE A MESSIAH IN HER BEHALF
HE CREATED SOME PERPETUAL FLOUR AND OIL
AND BROUGHT BACK TO LIFE HER SON'S DEAD BODY AND SOUL

IN ONE RESPECT ELIJAH 'S MANTLE WAS LIKE GOD'S ARK
HE THREW IT OVER THE JORDAN AND THE WATERS WERE STOPPED
THEN AS GOD RAISED ELIJAH ALIVE TO HEAVEN IN A WHIRLWIND
IT SEEMED TO MANY THAT HE WAS THE PROMISED PROPHET AND KING

STILL I DON'T THINK THE ISREALITES GAVE UP
THEY CONTINUED TO WORSHIP BAAL AND ASHERAH
ELIJAH THEN TURNED OVER HIS MANTLE AND SIXTH SENSE
TO ELISHA WHO FOLLOWED IN HIS FOOTSTEPS

SO WITH MOSES ELIJAH RETURNED AT THE TRANSFIGURATION
PROVING TO JAMES JOHN AND PETER THAT THERE WAS A RESURRECTION
SO WHEN JESUS APPEARED AND THE PEOPLE HAD LEARNED
WAS IT SOMEONE ELSE OR HAD ELIJAH RETURNED

THE THING ABOUT BEING TAKEN UP AND RESURRECTED LIKE JESUS
IS THAT GOD CAN RESURRECT JESUS OR ELIJA OR ENOCH OR US
SO THE QUESTION IS HOW CAN WE QUALIFY
WHAT'S THE PROCEDURE FOR US WHEN WE DIE?

RB WELSH, 3 29 21

JESUS

WE CAN ARGUE TILL DOOMSDAY ABOUT JESUS'S ORIGIN
WAS HE GOD HIMSELF OR BORN OF A VIRGIN
WAS HE SON OF A VIRGIN IN BETHLEHEM
OR COME IN FROM OUTER SPACE LIKE SUPERMAN

LIKE IN CREATION OF THE UNIVERSE BY THE HOLY SPIRIT
ENTERING THE WOMB OF THE VIRGINAL MARY ITS VISIT
BROUGHT FORTH THE SON OF GOD AS PROPHESIED BY ISAIAH
THEN CIRCUMCISED BAPTIZED PERFORMED MIRACLES NOW PAYS UP

FOR THE CRIMES COMMITTED OF HEALING THE BLIND
FEEDING THE FAMISHED AND CURING ILLS OF ALL KINDS
BEING GUILTY OF RAISING THE DEAD THE ROMANS KNEW
HE COULD JUST AS EASILY GET RID OF THEM TOO

BRINGING PEACE TO THE EARTH WI TH NO MORE WAR
HONESTY WI TH INTEGRITY IN DEALINGS FOREVER MORE
SO WITH A MOCK TRIAL HE WAS FOUND GUILTY SO HE
COULD BE LEGALLY T CONVICTED AS ISRAEL'S KING

GOD HERE SHOWS THAT MAN COULD SUFFER THROUGH TRIBULATIONS
TELLING THEM NOT TO PANIC WHEN DEATH TAKES THEIR RELATIONS
FOR JESUS CALMLY ORDERED JUDAS TO GO DO WHAT HE WAS TOLD
GO TO THE AUTHORITIES TO ARREST HIM HIS IDENTITY DISCLOSED (JN 13:21-27)

THIS HAPPENED WHILE ALL WERE CELEBRATING THE PASSOVER
JESUS PURPORTED REPEATED WHAT PAUL WROTE IN A LETTER
TO EAT HIS BODY, DRINK HIS BLOOD TO STILL HAVE COMMUNION
THOUGH HE IS DEAD AND GONE THERE WILL STILL BE A UNION

SO GOD HAD THIS ALL SET UP TO GIVE MAN HOPE
THAT THERE IS AN AFTERLIFE WITH ALL SINS REVOKED
HE WENT TO A PLACE WHERE THERE IS NO CRIME
WHAT'S MINE IS YOURS AND WHAT'S YOURS IS MINE

ALL MAN SIMPLY DOES IS TO JUST "BELIEVE"
OR HE WILL BE STRUNG OUT LIKE A STRING BEAN
IN A BLACK HOLE FOREVER AND A DAY
SO LET'S ALL BELIEVE AND GO TO HEAVEN WE PRAY

RB WELSH, 3 30 21

JESUS ORDERS JUDAS TO DISCLOSE HIM

THE POINT OF ALL THIS THAT THE APOSTLE'S DISAGREE
THAT SATAN ENTER INTO HIM TO GO TO THE AUTHORITIES
BUT JUDAS WAS ORDERED BY JESUS TO DISCLOSE HIS IDENTITY
"WHAT YOU ARE ABOUT TO DO GO DO IT QUICKLY" (JN 13:27)

SO THE MESSIANIC SECRET THAT JESUS SAID HE MUST DIE
IS CULMINATED IN A FINAL ORDER TO JUDAS TO DO IT QUICKLY
IT TOOK JOHN FIFTY YEARS TO REALIZE ALL THIS
THAT EARLIER GOSPEL WRITINGS WERE SIMPLY AMISS

RB WELSH, 4 1 21

THE LAST WILL

THIS IS THE LAST WILL AND TESTAMENT OF JESUS THE CHRIST,
I HEREBY LEAVE TO MANKIND ON MY DEMISE,
ALL MY EARTHLY GOODS AND POSSESSIONS
AND IF THEY BELIEVE, PERPETUITY IN HEAVEN.

1. IS LOVE OF ALL MANKIND.
THIS IS MEANT TO BE SPREAD AROUND.
2. IS HEAL THE SICK AND THE BLIND.
INVENT PROSTHETICS OF ALL KINDS.

3. CONTRIBUTE REGULARLY FOR CANCER CURE.
4. LOVE ALL MEN SO THERE WILL BE NO MORE WAR.
5. I LEAVE YOU ALL OF MY EARTHLY THINGS,
ALL YOU HAVE DO IS BE REBORN AS NEW BEINGS.

ALL I CAN DO NOW IS HEAL THE INDIVIDUAL,
IF HE'S BLIND, HAS LEPROSY, AND HEAL HIS SOUL.
I BEQUEATH TO YOU THAT WHEN YOU DIE,
THAT YOU WILL BE WITH ME IN PARADISE.

RB WELSH, 2 16 22

SECOND ADAM

WITH SOPHIA SPIT AND MUD GOD CREATED THE FIRST MAN
WITH THE HOLY SPIRIT AND VIRGIN MARY HE WAS BORN AGAIN
IF GOD CAN CREATE BOTH HEAVEN AND EARTH
HE CAN SURELY IMPREGNATE A VIRGIN TO GIVE BIRTH

BY MERELY BLOWING ITS SPIRIT INSUFFLATING HER WOMB
JESUS WAS BORN TO SUFFER FOR OUR SINS THEN GO TO THE TOMB
HIS MISSION ON EARTH WAS NOT TO DESTROY THE ROMANS
AS ISRAEL CONTINUALLY PRAYED BUT TO BRING GOD'S GLORY

HE HEALED MANY BUT NOT ALL OF THOSE BLIND OR THOSE MAD
HIS MOTHER HAD HIM CREATE WINE WHERE NONE WAS TO BE HAD
BUT ONE TIME HE ASKED WHO IS MY MOTHER AND WHO ARE MY BROTHERS
ONE SHOULD HATE HIS PARENTS INSTEAD OF GOD'S COMMANDMENT TO HONOR

PAUL WAS FERVENT IN THAT THE SPIRIT OF CHRIST
SUPERSEDES THAT OF GOD'S LAW WAS HIS ADVICE
JESUS WAS PURPORTED TO BE THE PRINCE OF PEACE
BUT WARS HAVE INCREASED IN VIOLENCE AND NEVER CEASE

THAT HE WOULD GO TO JERUSALEM ONLY TO DIE
WAS THE MESSIANIC SECRET THAT WAS PROPHESIED
SOMEONE HAD TO ATONE FOR ALL OF MAN'S SINS
SO THE SON OF GOD WAS THE ONE CONDEMNED

SO IF WE JUST BELIEVE IN ALL OF THIS
WE WILL NOT BE THROWN INTO THE ABYSS
ALL THOSE WHO BELIEVE THAT HE IS THE WAY
WILL JOIN HIM FOR ETERNITY IN HEAVEN SOME DAY

SO HERE WE ARE WITH OUR TONGUE IN CHEEK
CELEBRATING HIS DEATH AND RISING THIS WEEK
IF WE ARE WEALTHY WE'LL NOT MAKE IT TO HEAVEN
TO SEE OUR RELATIONS SO I'M IN A DEPRESSION

HOW MANY MEN HAVE I KILLED OR MAIMED?
I CONFESS I SKIMMED ON MY TAXES I AM ASHAMED
I MUST HAVE GOTTEN BY WITH OVERCHARGING
FOR A LIFE STYLE LIKE MINE ALL THIS IS ALARMING

AND WHAT ABOUT WOMEN
THIS HAS ME SQUIRMING
I KNOW THAT HE KNOWS
SO I HOPE HE WILL LET THAT GO

I DON'T THINK I WOULD VOLUNTEER
TO GO TO JERUSALEM WITHOUT ANY FEAR
THROW OVER TABLES OF MONEY CHANGERS AS PREDICTED
WITHOUT A GOOD LAWYER TO BE TRIED AND CONVICTED

IT IS SAID THAT JESUS DESCENDED INTO HELL
IT TOOK THREE WHOLE DAYS TO RAISE THE DEAD
POLITICIANS AND CROOKS WERE INCLUDED IN THIS
LIKE THE ROMAN SOLDIER AND THIEF ON THE CROSS NEXT TO HIM

SO I GAVE UP COKES DURING THE LENTEN SEASON
AS THE SYMBOL OF SACRIFICE JESUS WAS THE SUFFERING SERVANT
I'M AFRAID JESUS NOW HAS TO OPEN MY EYES
INSUFLATE MY SOUL WITH A NEW BEING AND BE BAPTIZED

RB WELSH, 3 31 21

ELOJIM

GOD WAS JESUS FROM THE VERY FIRST.
JOHN'S GOSPEL SAYS JESUS WAS THE WORD.
CREATING THE UNIVERSE AND MAN,
GOD WAS JESUS HIMSELF WITHOUT A VIRGIN.

EVEN THOUGH GOD IS PROTEAN AND CAN BE
ANYONE, ANYTIME ANYWHERE ANYTHING.
WHY WOULD HE EVER BE LIKE THE NEPHILIM,
COMING IN TO HAVE SEX WITH THE DAUGHTERS OF MEN?

SO IF GOD IS NOT THE FATHER OF CHRIST,
HE MUST BE JESUS HIMSELF WITHOUT A WIFE.
IT WAS GOD HIMSELF WHO WAS CRUCIFIED,
INSTEAD OF YOU, FOR YOUR SINS, SO YOU NEVER DIE.

RB WELSH, 4 29 23

JUDAS

JUDAS THE DISCIPLE WAS ONE OF THE TWELVE
A NUMBER LIKE THAT OF THE TRIBES IN ISRAEL
ALL OF THEM WERE TOLD TO BE AWARE
OF HIS MESSIANIC SECRET TO BE AWARE

THAT HE WOULD SHOW THE WORLD THAT HE WAS THE MESSIAH
WITH MIRACLE FEEDINGS AND HEALING S BUT TO KEEP IT QUIET
THAT HE WAS TO GO TO JERUSALEM EVENTUALLY
TO SUFFER AND DIE ON THE CROSS TO SAVE ALL MEN

THEOLOGIANS HAVE MADE JUDAS GUILTY OF TREACHERY
BUT WOULD JESUS PUT HIM IN CHARGE OF THE APOSTLE'S TREASURY
OR EVEN HAVE SELECTED HIM AS A DISCIPLE AT ALL
JUDAS AS DEPICTED WOULD HAVE NEVER RECEIVED THE "CALL"

IF JESUS IS GOD AND KNOWS EVERYTHING
WOULD HE SELECT THE TWELVE INCLUDING A THIEF?
THEN PUT HIM IN CHARGE OF THE TREASURY
MAYBE HE COULD IMBIBE OF THE FUNDS BE GUILTY

THE PEOPLE THAT GO AROUND CARRYING PLAQUES
THAT ALL MEN ARE EQUAL JUST LOOK AT THE FACTS
ARE THE VERY ONES WHO EAT HAM ON EASTER,
SO PARTAKING OF PORK WILL HUMILIATE HEBREWS
WHY DO WE ALWAYS LOOK DOWN ON THE HEBREWS IN HISTORY
AS THE ONES WHO KILLED JESUS WHEN THEY FULFILLED HIS DESTINY

WHOM THEY SAY ARE RESPONSIBLE FOR HIS DEATH
WHEN ASKED BY PILATE WHO SHOULD BE RELEASED
THEY ALL CRIED OUT TO RELEASE BARABBAS
SO TWO THIEVES WERE THE FIRST SAVED BY JESUS

THE GOSPEL OF JUDAS WAS DISCOVERED IN NAG HAMMADI
IN AN EARTHEN JAR DUG UP BY A SHEPHERD IN NORTH AFRICA
INCLUDED AS ONE OF THE GNOSTIC GOSPELS THIS WRITING
WAS TRANSLATED BY ELAINE PAGELS AND KAREN L. KING

DISPROVING EVERYTHING THAT WE'VE ALWAYS BEEN TOLD
FOR IT SAYS THAT JUDAS IS <u>THE DISCIPLE JESUS LOVED MOST</u>
THE HEBREWS ARE STILL AWAITING THEIR MESSIAH
AT PENTATEUCH HE WAS BAPTIZING WITH THE HOLY SPIRIT AND FIRE

SO WITH THAT KIND OF REASONING IT COULD BE DIAGNOSED
THAT JUDAS COULD BE THE DISCIPLE JESUS LOVED MOST
IF AS THEY SAY THE BIBLE IS TRUE
WHICH OF THESE VERSIONS DO YOU THINK IS TRUE?

JESUS ASKS THEM TO PRAY WITH HIM
THESE ARE HIS LAST HOURS HE'S AWARE OF THIS
BUT THEY ARE TOO FULL OF PASSOVER WINE
AND LIE FAST ASLEEP THOUGH THE HOUR IS NIGH

AFTER SETTING HIMSELF UP TO BE THE SAVIOR OF YOU AND ME
HE CRIES OUT FOR GOD TO "TAKE THIS CUP FROM ME"
FOR HIS EXISTENCE HAS NOW COME TO THIS POINT IN HIS LIFE
IN COMING BACK TO JERUSALEM WHERE HE WAS CIRCUMCISED

HE HAS FULFILLED ALL OF THE PROPHECIES
BY GOD TELLING MOSES HE WOULD RAISE UP "ONE LIKE ME"
SO THE PEOPLE HAVE BEEN WAITING FOR CENTURIES
AND HE'S COME TO TAKE THEM OUT OF THEIR MISERIES

ALL THEY MUST DO IS COPE WITH THE EARLY MISERIES
OF SICKNESS TRIBULATIONS BUT WITH THEIR BELIEVING
THEY WILL BE RAISED TO JOIN HIM ON DEATH'S DOOR
SO HOW CAN THEY HELP IT BUT TO LOVE AND ADORE

THERE IS ONE FACET WHERE THE GOSPELS AGREE
THERE WERE 30 PIECES OF SILVER WHICH JUDAS RECEIVED
THE SAME AMOUNT THAT THE BROTHERS OF JOSEPH
RECEIVED AS BOUNTY FROM THE MIDIANITE SLAVERS

THESE DAYS IN OUR LIVES OF RELATIVE PROGRESS
IS THE POLITICAL SITUATION IN SUCH A MESS?
WILL THERE EVER BE A DAY IN OUR IMMEDIATE FUTURE
WHERE ALLIANCES CAN BE MADE AND HEALED AND SUTURED

EXPLAIN IT TO ME FOR I AM SO DUMB
WHY THE PEACEMAKER WOULD ORDER
HIS DISCIPLES TO EXCHANGE THEIR CLOAKS FOR A SWORD
THEN ONE THE THEM CHOPPED OFF THE EAR OF A SOLDIER

IF WE BELIEVE ALL THE BIBLE IS TRUE
WHICH OF THESE VERSIONS IS BEST FOR YOU
THAT JUDAS WAS THE TRAITOR WHO HIM DISCLOSED
OR WAS HE THE DISCIPLE JESUS LOVED MOST

SO ALL THESE DEPICTIONS ARE A DECEPTIVE MYSTERY
A COMPLETE DISTORTION OF HISTORY-
THE TRUE STORY MAY EVEN NEVER BE KNOWN
WITH THESE FACTS WE HAVE TO FIGURE IT OUT ALL ON OUR OWN

RB WELSH, 4 1 21

CRUCIFIXION

AM I ON GOOD FRIDAY ONCE A YEAR, FORGIVEN
AT THREE O'CLOCK, ABSOLVED OF ALL SIN
WHEN THE LORD EXPIRED DYING FOR ME
THAT'S THE WAY IT HAS BEEN FOR CENTURIES

IT SEEMS LIKE I SHOULD PAY MYSELF
FOR ALL THE SINS THAT I HAVE REPRESSED
FORGIVE AND FORGET, THEY ALWAYS SAY
SOMEHOW MY SIN IS REPEATED EVERY DAY

THERE'S BEEN A HARDENING OF MY HEART
LIKE AS IF I DON'T THINK I NEED A NEW START
LIKE AS IF I DON'T APPRECIATE ALL THAT HE DID
I HAVE ALL THESE EXCUSES FOR MY BEING BAD

I'M NOT ASKING THAT THE FEROCIOUS LION
LIE DOWN WITH THE LAMB OR ANYTHING LIKE THAT
I'M JUST ASKING FOR SIMPLE JUSTICE
FOR THE WORLD OF NATIONS TO TRUST US

I HAD THE FEELING LAST YEAR THAT GOD'S PATIENCE HAD ENDED
INSTEAD OF A FLOOD, COVID-19 WAS TO BE OUR CRUCIFIXION
THAT YOU'D HAD ENOUGH OF PERVERSION OF COMMANDMENTS
THAT WE WERE TO BE CRUCIFIED SINCE YOU COULDN'T STAND IT

PERHAPS MAN WOULD HAVE BEEN EXTERMINATED BY THE COVID-19
EXCEPT FOR THE CRASH PROGRAM IN DEVELOPING A VACCINE
THE LABS ARE STILL WORKING ON A SWINE-FLU VACCINATION
BUT THEY ARE STYMIED BY TOO MANY REGULATIONS

FORGIVE ME, LORD AND et al. FOR STILL BEING SARCASTIC
I MUST NOT HAVE BEEN ABLE TO BECOME DEMOCRATIC
WHAT WE ALL NEED IS A SEVEN-FOLD VACCINATION
AGAINST HATE, JEALOUSY, EMBITTERMENT, AND SARCASM

THAT'S THE REASON I STILL HAVEN'T YET HEARD OF ANY CONFESSIONS
OR YET SEEN ANY JUSTICE DONE FOR SINFUL COMMISSIONS.
THEY MUST HAVE BEEN VACCINATED FOR TRIALS AND CRUCIFIXIONS;
FOR PAST SINS, LET ALONE THE INJUSTICE THAT WAS COMMITTED.

BUT THE CRUCIFIXION OF JESUS SATISFIED ALL SIMPLE SIN
REMOVED ALL GUILT AND THE TROUBLE MAN SHOULD HAVE BEEN IN
WITH THIS NEW BEGINNING, THERE SHOULD BE A NEW START
WITH THE REMOVAL OF ALL SIN MAN WILL GET A NEW HEART

I WISH JESUS' DEATH WOULD HAVE KILLED ALL DISEASE
CREATED MORE THAN THE WORD LOVE BUT MAKE IT REAL
TAKEN AWAY ALL HUNGER AND PAIN
MADE THIS A NEW HEAVEN FOR ALL TO GET IN

BUT THANKS ANYWAY FOR GIVING IT A TRY
TO SETTLE MEN DOWN TO BE SATISFIED
FOR THEIR EXISTENCE ON THIS GREAT EARTH
PLEASE GIVE EVERYONE THE PHENOMENON OF REBIRTH

SO THEY CAN ALL AT ONCE BECOME NEW BEINGS
RECEIVE THE SPIRIT OF CHRIST WITH HIS FEELINGS
OF SENSITIVITY TO THEIR NEEDS AND FULFILLING THEM
SO WITH THESE NEW HEARTS, ALL MEN WILL BE FRIENDS

RB WELSH, 4 2 21

HAPPY EASTER

GOD CREATED THE EARTH AND MAN WHO LIVES ON IT
SO IT WAS NOT MUCH OF A TRICK TO CREATE LIFE INCARNATE
EVEN MIRACULOUSLY, FROM THE WOMB OF A VIRGIN
AS PROPHESIED BY ISAIAH, THE SUFFERING SERVANT

FROM BEGINNING TO END, A MIRACULOUS LIFE
WAS LED BY JESUS BUT NOT WITHOUT STRIFE
BORN IN A MANGER UNDER THE STAR OF JACOB
SEARCHED FOR AS THE MESSIAH BY ISRAEL'S KING HEROD

ESCAPING TO EGYPT GROWING IN WORD AND DEED
HE WAS RAISED AS A CARPENTER WHILE LEARNING GOD'S CREED
FINALLY REACHING MANHOOD, HE WAS BAPTIZED BY JOHN
HAVING A SECOND BIRTH BY THE HOLY SPIRIT'S DOVE

GOING OFF TO THE WILDERNESS TO BE TEMPTED BY SATAN
AS ALL MEN DO IF THEY'RE TO BECOME NEW CREATIONS
PROCLAIMING A REVISED VERSION OF THE WORD OF GOD
PERFORMED MIRACLES OF HEALINGS PREACHED A GOSPEL OF LOVE

TO BE KNOWN AS THE PEACEMAKER IT WAS THE OPPOSITE OF THAT
FROM PEACEFUL HILLTOP GATHERINGS OF BELIEVERS TO RIOTS
FOR ON JOURNEYING TO JERUSALEM HE WAS ARRESTED AND TRIED
FOUND TO BE GUILTY OF TREASON BY THE ROMANS, THEN CRUCIFIED

HE DESCENDED INTO HELL TO RAISE PEOPLE LIKE ME
WHO WERE ONCE DEAD BUT RAISED TO BE WITH HIM FOR ETERNITY
THIS IS THE CULMINATION OF HIS LEADING A VIRTUOUS LIFE
SO WE CELEBRATE EASTER AGAIN THIS YEAR WITH THE DIVINE

WE LOOK FORWARD TO A SECOND COMING TO EARTH
TO CELEBRATE THE PENTECOST WHEN HE RETURNS
TO RE-BAPTIZE MEN WITH THE HOLY SPIRIT AND FIRE
THEN LIKE ISAIAH WITH BURNING COALS, WE'LL BE STERILIZED

RB WELSH, 4 4 21

EZRA

EZRA WAS KNOWN AS A PRIEST AND A SCRIBE
INSTRUMENTAL IN THE RETURN OF THE JUDEAN TRIBE
WHO HAD BEEN DEPOSED TO BABYLON
AS PUNISHMENT FOR THE WORSHIP; OF OTHER GODS

GOD HAD TO SEND JUDAH OFF INTO CAPTIVITY
AS THEY HAD BEEN THREATENED IN DEUTERONOMY (DT 11:26)
THAT DEFILING THE COMMANDMENTS AND WORD OF GOD
WOULD SEND YOU OFF IN CAPTIVITY FOR YOU ARE CUT OFF

SO WHILE BEING CAPTIVE IN THE LAND OF BABYLONIA
PRIESTS AND SCRIBES COMPILED THE HISTORY OF
GOD AND THE STORY OF THE MAN HE CREATED
HIS COMMANDMENTS AND LAWS AND HOW THEY WERE RELATED

OF ALL THE BOOKS SCRIBES COMPILED IN THE TALMUD
EZRA WAS RESPONSIBLE FOR THE BOOK OF CHRONICLES
WHERE IT TELLS THE REASON WHERE IT WAS ALLOWED
FOR SOLOMON, NOT DAVID, TO BUILD THE TEMPLE OF GOD

AFTER CYRUS THE GREAT HAD CONQUERED BABYLONIA
IT WAS THEN THAT HE LED THEM BACK INTO PERSIA
WITH QUEEN ESTER THEN ALLOWING THEM TO LIVE
EZRA AND NEHEMIAH RETURNED THEM TO JERUSALEM

EZRA COULD NOT BELIEVE IT WHEN THEY ARRIVED
THAT THE REMAINING HEBREWS HAD FOREIGN WIVES
ONE OF THE VERY REASONS THEY WERE TAKEN CAPTIVE AT FIRST
HE COULDN'T BELIEVE IT RENT HIS GARMENTS KICKED THE DIRT

I, TOO, AM MARRIED TO A FOREIGN WIFE
BUT SHE IS MORE CHRISTIAN THAN I
AND IT SEEMS THAT COUPLES ARE MORE INTERRACIAL
BUT THE HEBREWS, IF SO, WOULD BE EXCOMMUNICATED

GOD, SAD, I HAVE TRIED EVERY ANGLE I CAN THINK OF
TO GET YOUR RESPECT, DEVOTION, AND LOVE
I AM THE ONE WHO CREATED YOU
NOT BAAL OR ASHERA, WHOM YOU'RE DEVOTED TO

SO NOW YOU'VE GONE TOO FAR, AND I'M MAD A SHELL
I'LL MATERIALIZE MYSELF AS JESUS OF NAZARETH
SO YOU CAN SEE AND TOUCH BE CURED AND BE FED
EVEN REALIZE IT'S NOT OVER EVEN IF YOU ARE DEAD

IT SEEMS TO ME THAT YOU ARE TERRIFIED OF ME
SO I WILL CREATE MYSELF AS A GOD. YOU CAN SEE
ONE YOU CAN LOVE AND WORSHIP SO PEACEABLY
THAT YOU CAN BELIEVE AND BE WITH ETERNALLY

THEN PAUL CAME ALONG TO INTEGRATE ME WITH THE CHRIST'S
THAT MY COMMANDMENTS AND LAWS WERE TOO STRINGENT, NOT NICE
THAT IT WOULD BE BETTER TO WORSHIP THE SPIRIT OF CHRIST
JUST FORGET MY COMMANDMENTS AND TAKE HIS ADVICE

I DON'T KNOW HOW I GOT INTO THIS QUANDARY
WHEN A MAN, NOT ANY GOD, CREATED THE TRINITY
I WAS NO LONGER WORSHIPED AS THE GOD OF ONE
SO AS A ONE GOD I'LL DEPORT MYSELF OFF TO ISLAM

I WILL THEN BE WORSHIPED AS THE GOD ALLAH
PLUS, FULFILLING MY PROMISE TO ISHMAEL
WHERE MEN CAN BOW DOWN ON THEIR KNEES
WORSHIPING THEIR ONLY ONE GOD, WHICH IS ME

RB WELSH, 4 8 21

LAMENTING

LAMENTATIONS IS NOT A SUBJECT FOR ME
EXCEPT THAT MARLIS DIED A YEAR AGO SATURDAY
I CAN SEE WHY THE HEBREWS CATERED TO BAAL
BUT BEING TAKEN TO BABYLONIA, IT WAS THE SAME AS HELL

THERE'S A LOT IN THIS STORY THAT'S NOT BEING TOLD
GOD WAS NO LONGER IN HIS ARK IN THE HOLY OF HOLIES
FOR IT DISAPPEARED DURING THE REIGN OF SOLOMON
SO IT'S NO WONDER THE PEOPLE WORSHIPED HIM NO LONGER

WE'VE ALL HEARD THAT IT'S A LONG WAY TO TIPPERARY
BUT IT WAS LONGER IN THOSE DAYS TO THE TEMPLE T O PRAY
BAAL HAD BROUGHT CANAANITES IN THE PROMISED LAND
TO ONE OF CATTLE AND VINEYARDS AND GRAIN OUT OF SAND

THE HEBREWS HAD BEEN SHEPHERDS ALL OF THEIR LIVES
THEN TURNED INTO SOLDIERS JUST TO CAPITALIZE
THEY HAD NO TRANSPORTATION TO GO TO JERUSALEM TO PRAY
SO NO WONDER THEY WORSHIPED AT THE ALTARS OF BAAL EVERY DAY

IT WASN'T TILL AFTER THE MACCABEES RECONSTITUTED THE TEMPLE
AFTER DEFEATING THE SELEUCIDS UNDER ANTIOCHUS THE GREECIAN
THAT SYNAGOGUES APPEARED IN THE DIASPORA ABOUT 70 BCE
ALL THIS IS FOUND IN THE APOCRYPHA ABOUT ISRAEL'S HISTORY

THAT'S WHEN ELEAZAR WAS CRUSHED WHEN HE KILLED THE KINGS ELEPHANT
AND MOTHERS AND SONS HEROICALLY JUMPED INTO BOILING OIL
RATHER THAN EAT PORK AND REMOVE CIRCUMCISIONS
THOSE WHO GAVE THEIR LIVES WOULD BE CANDIDATES FOR THE PROMISED ONE

SO TODAY, WE WORSHIP JESUS THE CHRIST
WHO IS NOW IN THE TEMPLE OF MAN'S HEART
SINCE IT'S BEEN CIRCUMCISED AND ORDAINED (JER 31:31)
WITH GOD'S LAW NOW WRITTEN UPON THEIR BRAINS (2 COR 3:3)

RB WELSH, 4 23 21

ORIGINS OF JESUS

THERE ARE SEVERAL THEORIES
ABOUT THE ORIGIN OF JESUS
THE GOSPEL OF MARK WAS WRITTEN FIRST
THIS IS THE ONE THAT SKIPS JESUS BIRTH

HERE IT IS OBVIOUS TO ME THAT IT IS GOD HIMSELF
APPEARING AS A HUMAN AGAIN ANYTIME IT IS FELT
IN HIS PROTEAN WAY, NOW HE'S BAPTIZED BY JOHN
APPEARING OUT OF NOWHERE, HE IS FULL Y GROWN

MATTHEW THEN THOUGHT JESUS HAD TO BE BORN
SO TWENTY YEARS LATER WROTE THE BIRTH STORY
THE PERSIAN GOD-CHILD MITHRA WAS BORN ON DECEMBER 25TH
WITH KINGS VISITING THE CHILD WITH MYRRH AND GIFTS

PICKING UP ON THE PROPHECY OF ISAIAH CENTURIES BEFORE
DR. LUKE EXPLAINED IT WAS THE HOLY SPIRIT WITH THE SPORE
TO MARY, A VIRGIN BETROTHED TO JOSEPH OF NAZARETH
TO BEAR THE CHILD JESUS SON OF GOD TO BE ALWAYS HERE WITH US

SO IN A.D. NINETY, JOHN DEVISED JESUS AS THE WORD
HAVING JESUS WITH GOD AT THE CREATION OF THE WORLD
WHICH MAY BE ONE REASON FOR DEVISING A TRINITY
THROUGHOUT THE WORLD, THERE WERE MANY

BEFORE THESE GOSPELS, THERE FIRST WERE THE LETTERS OF PAUL
WITH SOME OF HIS THEORIES INCLUDED IN ALL
FOLLOWED BY "SAYINGS" AND THE GERMAN "Q"
AND THE GOSPEL OF THOMAS AS BIBLICAL TOO

WE ARE ALL ADULTS NOW AND SHOULD TAKE IT IN STRIDE
THERE ARE STORIES OF VIRGIN BIRTHS BOTH FAR AND WIDE
FROM THE FAR EAST TO ROME, GREECE, AND EGYPT
SIMILAR BIRTHS ARE RECORDED AS BEING LEGITIMATE

SO SINCE BEING IMPOSSIBLE TO USE BELIEVING IN JUST ONE
WE COMBINE OUR BELIEFS WITH ALL FOUR TO CHOOSE FROM
REMEMBERING THEY WERE SELECTED BY A COMMITTEE OF MEN
THE CHURCH FATHERS DEVISED OUR BELIEFS WHERE AND WHEN

REMEMBERING WE ARE ALL GROWN UP NOW AND NOT SO NAIVE
AS TO HAVE FIRST CENTURY CATHOLICS TELLING US WHAT TO BELIEVE
THERE'S A LOT OF EMPHASIS ON DESCENDING INTO HELL
FRIGHTENING EVERYONE TO WATCH IT OR THEY'LL GO THERE AS WELL

WE KNOW JESUS WAS FIRST IN THE GARDEN WITH MARY
THEN BLESSING THE FOOD ON THE ROAD TO EMMAEUS
LATER BACK IN THE UPPER ROOM WITH HIS DISCIPLES
SO DID HE SPEND THREE DAYS IN THE EARTH'S BOWELS (MT 12:40)

THERE'S ONLY ONE BIBLICAL REFERENCE MADE OF THIS
BUT A MOUNTAIN OF LITERATURE TAKES AWAY ALL BLISS
DESCRIBING THE TORTURE OF THE FIRES OF HELL
IF WE'RE NOT GOOD, WE'LL GO THERE AS WELL

IF SO, THERE WON'T BE ANYBODY IN HEAVEN
SO FORGET THAT YOU'RE SAVED; THERE'S NO INTERCESSION
NOW YOU KNOW WHY FUNERALS ARE IN ALWAYS THREE DAYS
SO MY BODY CAN BURN IN HELL; THAT'S WHY THE DELAY

IF SO I'M JUST AN ICON, A FIGURE OF SPEECH
IF I GET UP THERE TO HAVE WINE WITH JESUS
I'LL JUST TELL SAINT PETER I'M AN ILLEGAL ALIEN
SO I CAN GET THROUGH THE GATE ON THE WALLS AROUND HEAVEN

RB WELSH, 4 19 21

MICAIAH

HERE'S ANOTHER PROPHET OF IGNOMINY
DURING THE REIGN OF THE WORST KING IN HISTORY
WHO HAD IN ADDITION TO CONTINUING CALF WORSHIP IN ISRAEL
MARRIED JEZEBEL OF TYRE BRINGING HER PRIESTS OF BAAL

AS ONE OF THE STUDENTS OF THE PROPHET ELIJAH
MICAIAH LIVED DURING THE REIGN OF AHAB, WHO DECRIED GOD
SINCE AHAB AND HIS QUEEN JEZEBEL WORSHIPPED BAAL
GOD'S NEMESIS WHOM GOD SHOULD HAVE BURIED IN HELL
HE HAD HUNDREDS OF PROPHETS WHO AGREED WITH HIS DEEDS
EXCEPT FOR MICAIAH, WHO MOCKED EVERY BELIEF

WE ARE FAMILIAR WITH AHAB'S MURDER OF NABOTH
JUST TO GET HIS VINEYARD BY BEARING FALSE WITNESS
STRANGELY, AHAB WOULD INVADE RAMOTH-GILEAD
A LAND EAST OF THE JORDAN, NOT EVEN IN ISRAEL
BUT DRUNKEN WITH POWER AND WITH JUDAH IN ALLIANCE
AHAB CALLED IN 400 BAAL PROPHETS TO PREDICT HIS SUCCESS

THEN HESITATINGLY CALLED IN MICAIAH, GOD'S PROPHET
WHO NEVER TOLD THE TRUTH BUT REPEATEDLY MOCKED HIM
THIS TIME AHAB INSISTED ON TRUTH, SO MICAIAH GAVE HIM GOD'S WORD
THAT HE WOULD DIE IN BATTLE AND DOGS WOULD LICK UP HIS BLOOD
SO THOUGH AHAB HAD DISGUISED HIMSELF AS NOT BEING THE KING
HE WAS SHOT WITH AN ARROW AND DIED AS MICAIAH WAS PREDICTING

SO WE ALL HAVE OUR PROPHET BRINGING MESSAGES FROM GOD
BUT DO WE ALWAYS HEED THIS ADVICE AND GO OUT ON OUR OWN
ONLY TO LEARN WITH DISMAY THAT OUR DECISION WAS WRONG
WE SHOULD HAVE HEEDED JESUS'S PREDICTION, THAT WE KNEW ALL ALONG

RB WELSH, 4 22 21

HIS COMING – 2ND OR 1ST

JUST DON'T CONFUSE ME WITH THE FACTS
FOR I LOVE JESUS AND THE WAY HE ACTS
HE LOVES ALL LITTLE BOYS AND GIRLS
AND HE'LL GIVE ME ALL MY JUST DESERTS
FOR SOME, HE WILL ALWAYS BE A BABY CHILD
BORN IN A MANGER, WHO COULD CRY OR SMILE
WHILE THE SHEPHERDS KNELT FOR HIM, THEY COULD ADORE
SINCE THE STAR TOLD THEM THE CHRIST CHILD WAS BORN
THE CATTLE WERE LOWING WHILE KINGS AND WISE MEN
TRAVELED FROM AFAR TO PAY THEIR RESPECTS

SOME SAY THEY DON'T THINK HE WAS EVER BORN
THAT HE CAME TO EARTH ON A CLOUD TO GIVE MAN THE WORD
AS PROPHESIED BY DANIEL SOME ONE THOUSAND YEARS
AGO WHILE IN BABYLON, THE SON OF MAN APPEARED
HE PROMISED TO COME AGAIN LIKE A THIEF IN THE NIGHT
BUT WILL VISIT MAN INDIVIDUALLY AS A BEAM OF LIGHT
THEN HE'LL BAPTIZE MEN WITH THE HOLY SPIRIT AND FIRE
THEY'LL BECOME NEW BEINGS FOR ALL THEIR SINS HE ACQUIRED

RB WELSH, 4 22 21

JESUS ORDERS JUDAS TO DISCLOSE HIM

THE POINT OF ALL THIS THAT THE APOSTLE'S DISAGREE
THAT SATAN ENTER INTO HIM TO GO TO THE AUTHORITIES
BUT JUDAS WAS ORDERED BY JESUS TO DISCLOSE HIS IDENTITY
"WHAT YOU ARE ABOUT TO DO GO DO IT QUICKLY" (JN 13:27)

SO THE MESSIANIC SECRET THAT JESUS SAID HE MUST DIE
IS CULMINATED IN A FINAL ORDER TO JUDAS TO DO IT QUICKLY
IT TOOK JOHN FIFTY YEARS TO REALIZE ALL THIS
THAT EARLIER GOSPEL WRITINGS WERE SIMPLY AMISS

RB WELSH, 4 1 21

BABYLON IS HELL

AS ADAM SINNED AND WAS EJECTED FROM THE GARDEN
ISRAEL SERVED BAAL AND NEVER RECEIVED PARDON
NEITHER EVER RETURNED TO THEIR HOME AS WELL
BUT THE JUDEANS WILL BE SAVED AND RAISED OUT OF HELL

THE KINGDOM OF JUDAH WAS KNOWN AS THE HOLY LAND
IT WAS LIKE THE GARDEN OF EDEN BUT IT GOT OUT OF HAND
AS ADAM THEY SINNED AND WERE KICKED OUT TO BABYLONIA
HOWEVER, GOD REPENTED THIS TIME AND GAVE THEM SALVATION

NOW HIS PEOPLE HAVE RETURNED PAROLED FOR THEIR CRIMES
TO A BOMBED OUT AND BURNED OUT GARDEN IN ITS WORSE DECLINE
DO YOU NOW THINK THE PEOPLE WILL EVER LEARN,
AND DO YOU BELIEVE WHAT HAPPENED TO THEM SHOULD GIVE US CONCERN?

ARE WE SO CONCEITED WE THINK WE'RE NOT GUILTY
BOWING DOWN TO BAAL THEN BEGGING YOU TO BE FORGIVING
WITH OUR EVIL MINDS AND UNLIMITED POWER
WE ARE THE ONES WHO SHOULD BE EXILED RIGHT NOW

RB WELSH, 4 24 21

THE HOLY GRAIL

THEY'VE BEEN LOOKING FOR CENTURIES FOR THE HOLY GRAIL
ALL TO THEIR PROPHECIES AND SEARCHING TO NO AVAIL.
THE REASON, OF COURSE, THAT THEY SHOULD CEASE,
IT IS BECAUSE IT SIMPLY NEVER DID AND DIDN'T EXIST.

JESUS TOLD HIS DISCIPLES AT THE FEAST OF THE PASSOVER
THAT HE WOULD NOT DRINK OF THE VINE TILL THEY PASSED OVER.
THE IDEA WAS PICKED UP FROM ST. PAUL BY GOSPEL WRITERS,
WHO SUBSTITUTED COMMUNION WITH THE FEAST OF DIONYSUS.

RB WELSH, 4 14 22

ENOCH

ENOCH WAS THE GREAT GRANDFATHER OF NOAH
WRITING A BOOK CONSIDERED SCRIPTURE AND MUCH MORE
BUT HIS BOOK WAS REJECTED BY THE JEWS DESPITE
OR MAYBE FOR HIS PROPHECIES ABOUT JESUS CHRIST

THEIR CHURCH FATHERS, IN THEIR INFINITE WISDOM
HE DECIDED HIS BOOKS WERE TOO OUTLANDISH FOR ONE IN THE KINGDOM
SO THEY CLAIMED ENOCH WAS GUILTY OF PLAGIARISM
IN HIS RENDITIONS OR PREDICTIONS, ESPECIALLY ABOUT SIN

ENOCH AGREES WITH THE GOSPEL OF JOHN
THE LOGOS WOULD BE CREATED ALONG WITH THE FIRST MAN
JESUS WAS WAITING IN THE CURTAINS TO BE UNVEILED
AT THE PROPER TIME, WHEN ALL ELSE HAD FAILED

ENOCH'S ANTI-NICENE OUTLOOK WAS THOROUGHLY REJECTED
THOUGH GOD IS ONE, THERE'S NOTHING THAT CAN NOT BE EFFECTED
WE SHOULD BE PRAYING, "GOD THE FATHER, THE SON THE HOLY SPIRIT AND ALLAH
FOR WE HAVE DEFECTED SO NOW, IT'S NOT NORMAL

THE MAIN OBJECTION IS THAT HE WAS RAISED TO HEAVEN ALIVE
HE DIDN'T DESCEND INTO HELL OR SAVE SINNERS TO SURVIVE
NOR DID ENOCH APPEAR WITH ELIJAH AND MOSES
ALONG WITH JESUS ON TRANSFIGURATION MOUNTAIN

SO WHEN GOD THINKS HE'S HAD ENOUGH OF MANKIND
HE'LL RAPTURE US ALL LIKE ENOCH AND ELIJAH
SO THERE'S REALLY NOTHING TO OBJECT TO AS FAR AS I CAN SEE
THERE ARE MORE OFFENSIVE BOOKS IN OUR BIBLE TO READ

RB WELSH, 4 24 21

NEHEMIAH'S RETURN

ONE OF THE SECULAR HEROES IN THE REBUILDING OF JUDAH
NEHEMIAH WAS NOT A PRIEST NOR A PROPHET LIKE EZRA
HE WAS THE CUPBEARER FOR ARTAXERXES 100 YEARS LATER
SO WAS SENT WITH AN ESCORT TO SUPERVISE WALL RAISING

ACCOUNTS NEVER MENTION THE ROUTE THEY TOOK
DID THEY WALK OR RIDE ON CAMELS OR ELEPHANTS?
WE KNOW THAT MANY STAYED IN BABYLON AND PERSIA
FOR THOSE RETURN, ING WERE OF THE NEXT GENERATION

THE TEMPLE WAS FINISHED THE GOLD ARTIFACTS RESTORED
BUT THE WALLS OF THE CITY STILL WERE DESTROYED
THOUGH IT WAS NOT AS PERFECT AS SOLOMON'S TEMPLE
IT WAS THE BEST THEY COULD DO WITH THESE MATERIALS

WHEN IT COMES TO REBUILDING, THEY SHOULD HAVE HAD
JIM FOGARTIE OUR MINISTER WHO WAS AN EXPERT AT
REBUILDING A CHURCH LIKE MYERS PARK PRESBYTERIAN
LOCATED ON OXFORD PLACE, THE CHURCH WE WORSHIP IN

THEY NOW HAD ROOM FOR A NEW LIBRARY BY ELEANOR BELK
WITH THE EXPERIENCE OF CATALOGING BY MARLIS WELSH
WHO HAD ACQUIRED HER EXPERIENCE AND KNOWLEDGE
IN THE AMERICAN ARMED FORCES LIBRARIAN COLLEGE

RB WELSH, 4 28 21

ANTINOMIANISM

THIS ANTIOMIANISM REALLY OPENS A CAN OF WORMS,
CHANGING ONE'S PERCEPTION OF BIBLICAL TERMS.
THIS VIEW IMPLIES THAT THE SPIRIT OF CHRIST,
SUPERSEDES GOD'S LAWS THAT WERE HARD TO ABIDE BY.

SAINT PAUL HAS JUST TAKEN IT ON HIMSELF,
TO MAINTAIN THAT, YOU CAN PUT GOD'S LAW ON A SHELF.
NOW YOU MUST LIVE BY THE SPIRIT OF CHRIST AND BE SAVED
IT'S CALLED JUSTIFICATION BY HIS GRACE THROUGH FAITH.

RB WELSH, 4 30 22

NEHEMIAH

ALL THROUGHOUT THE HISTORY OF ISRAEL
IT READS JUST LIKE A NOVEL SERIAL
IT'S ONE RETURN AFTER ANOTHER
AFTER ALWAYS HAVING TO SUFFER

HAVING TO LEAVE THE PROMISED LAND
BECAUSE OF THE USUAL ANNUAL FAMINE
FIRST TO EGYPT TO BECOME ENSLAVED
RETURN TO CANAAN NOW OF VINEYARDS AND GRAIN

LIKE GOD AS JESUS, WHO IS NOT DEAD THOUGH CRUCIFIED
PROMISED TO RETURN TO AGAIN ON A CLOUD ALIVE
UNLESS HE RETURNS EACH YEAR TO THE PENTECOST
TO BAPTIZE WITH THE HOLY SPIRIT AND FIRE THE LOST

AFTER BEING ENSLAVED IN EGYPT, IT WAS NOW BABYLON
SOME RETURNED TO JERUSALEM WITH EZRA, THE PROPHET
TO WORK WITH NEHEMIAH TO REBUILD GOD'S TEMPLE
INSTEAD OF HAVING NATIONWIDE SYNAGOGUES AS BEING SIMPLE

THEY HAD BEEN RESCUED BY PERSIA'S CYRUS THE GREAT
WHO HAD ENTERED BABYLON USING THE CISTERN'S GRATE
A REPEAT OF TACTICS USED BY DAVID CONQUERING JERUSALEM
DANIEL HAD THE SON OF MAN PERFORMING MIRACLES

WITH REPENTANT PRISONERS NOW RETURNING HOME
THEY FELT LIKE NEW BEINGS AFTER BEING REBORN
WHILE IN EXILE, THE TORAH WAS FINALLY WRITTEN
THE ISRAELITES WERE NOW INFORMED OF WHAT GOD HAD BIDDEN

SOME BABY JEWS WHO REMAINED NOW HAD FOREIGN WIVES
CAUSING NEHEMIAH AND EZRA TO BE HORRIFIED
THESE WERE NOW EXPELLED, WHICH SEEMED DISASTROUS
BUT IT SPREAD THE WORD OF THE LORD BECOMING THE DIASPORA

JUDAH'S KING ZEDEKIAH APPROVED OF EVERYTHING
WITH ZERRUBABEL RECEIVING GOD'S SIGNET RING (Hag 2:23)
MEANING AS BEING ROYALTY AS GOVERNOR OF JERUSALEM
IN DAVID'S LINE TO THE MESSIAH, IS HE THE CHOSEN ONE

NOW THE QUESTION IS HAS GOD MADE MISTAKES
FROM GIVING THEM A KING IN THE FIRST PLACE
DID ALL THE PUNISHMENTS LIKE SPLITTING THE KINGDOM
BRING HIS PEOPLE CLOSER TO HIM TILL THE MESSIAH COMES

RB WELSH, 4 15 21

SON OF MAN

THOUGH WE KNOW THAT JESUS IS THE SON OF GOD
THIS IS SOMETHING THAT SEEMS VERY ODD
FOR HE ALWAYS REFERS TO HIMSELF AS THE SON OF MAN
BORN OF A VIRGIN AND GOD, WE CAN'T UNDERSTAND

IT SEEMS TO ME THAT HE'D BE EITHER ONE OR THE OTHER
AS A HYBRID, IT'S LIKE THE GREEK GODS IN THAT CULTURE
I GUESS I'M ONE WHO LIKES REALITY
LIKE FLYING SAUCERS BING MY SPECIALTY

JESUS, IN REFERRING TO HIMSELF, ALWAYS SAID
THE SON OF MAN HAS NOWHERE TO LAY DOWN HIS HEAD
SO NOW THERE'S NOT ONLY GOD BUT ALSO HIS SON
NOW ADD THE HOLY SPIRIT AND SAY THEY'RE JUST ONE

DANIEL REFERRED TO HIS COMING ON THE CLOUDS
AS THE SON OF MAN TO SAVE THE WORLD
FROM THEMSELVES AND THE RULERS WHOM THEY SERVE NOW
HE WILL BE THE SAVIOR WEARING THE CROWN

A SON OF MAN WOULD BE LIKE YOU AND ME
NOT FROM GOD AND A VIRGIN NAMED MARY
A SON OF MAN WOULD BE MARY'S AND JOSEPH'S
GROWN-UP FROM A BABE, SOMEBODY LIKE MOSES

JESUS NEVER SEEMS EVER TO REST
THOUGH FOXES HAVE HOLES, THE BIRDS HAVE NESTS
HE PRAYS WHILE HIS DISCIPLES SLEEP
MARY IS FOREVER ANOINTING HIS FEET

LIKE A MAGNET, HE ALWAYS DREW BIG CROWDS
WHO LISTENED TO PARABLES OF THEIR SINS TO DISAVOW
WHO HEARD THE MEANING OF THE WORD
WITH MANY BEING MIRACULOUSLY FED AND CURED

IF ANYONE TODAY EVER CLAIMED TO BE THE SON OF GOD
WE WOULD CALL HIM INSANE, AND HE'D BE CRUCIFIED
JESUS WAS CONVICTED FOR BEING KING OF THE JEWS
LED A REVOLT AGAINST THE ROMANS SO PUT IN THE TOMBS

ALL MEN HAVE EXPERIENCED THE FEELING OF PEACE AND LOVE
IT SHOULD BE EXTENDED TO ALL MEN AS COMING FROM ABOVE
THOUGH KNOWN AS THE LAMB, HE CALLS HIS FOLLOWERS SHEEP
THIS SON OF MAN IS THE SYMBOL OF WHAT WE CAN ALL ACHIEVE

I JUST DON'T THINK THAT GOD UNDERSTANDS
WE NEED HEAVEN ON EARTH, NOT IN NEVER-NEVER LAND
EVEN THOUGH WE BELIEVE SO, WE'LL ALL BE SAVED
FOR HEAVEN, BUT WHAT ABOUT NOW AND NOT BE DELAYED

WE NEED FOR A JESUS TO CURE EVERYONE'S ILLS
WE ARE VERY TIRED OF JUST LIVING ON PILLS
SEND JESUS BACK AGAIN TO FINISH THE JOB THIS YEAR
BRING PEACE TO THIS EARTH WHILE WE ARE STILL HERE

THEN WE'LL KNOW HE'S THE SON OF A MAN
ONE WHO'S NOT ONLY GOD BUT IS A HUMAN
NOT ONLY CURING FEEDING AND TEACHING TO JUST A FEW
BUT BRINGING HAPPINESS TO ALL THEN WOULD BE NEW

JESUS HAS SPENT ENOUGH TIME HERE ON THIS EARTH
TO REPORT BACK TO GOD THAT IT NEEDS A REBIRTH
NOT WITH PLAGUES OR COVIDS, FLOODS OR BOMBINGS
IF ALL MEN WERE SONS OF GOD, IT WOULD BE PROMISING

RB WELSH, 4 17 21

GOD'S STRUGGLES

OH GOD, WE WONDER JUST WHO ARE YOU
CREATOR OF THIS EARTH AND HEAVEN TOO
IT WAS WHEN YOU CREATED MAN
THAT YOUR TROUBLES FIRST BEGAN

YOU SET THE RULES FOR ETERNAL LIFE
IN A GARDEN WITH ADAM AND EVE, HIS WIFE
BUT WHEN THIS MAN ONE TIME DISOBEYED
HE SUFFERED CONSEQUENCES THAT WERE NOT DELAYED

THEY WERE THRUST OUT OF THE GARDEN
HAVING NOT RECEIVED A PARDON
IT WOULD TAKE 6000 YEARS OF SINNING
TILL CHRIST WOULD COME FOR ONE TO BE FORGIVEN

GOD HAD, FOR SOME REASON, PROHIBITED KNOWLEDGE
POSING AS A SNAKE TI EVE IN THE FOLIAGE
HE TEMPTED EVE TO EAT THE FRUIT
BRINGING ON MAN'S EVIL PURSUIT

WHY WOULD GOD PROHIBIT MAN FROM OBTAINING KNOWLEDGE?
NOW WE HAVE TO GO TO A LIBERAL COLLEGE
MAN SHOULD NEVER THINK HE'S AS SMART
AS GOD, SO THAT'S WHY WE ARE NOW JUST RETARDS

IT WASN'T LONG TILL NEPHILIM GIANTS
CAME IN FROM OUTER SPACE IN THEIR FLYING SAUCERS
STEALING THE FAIR MAIDENS OF THE EARTH
GIVING GOD EXTREME CONCERN

WITH THAT, GOD BEGAN AGAIN WITH MAN
FLOODING THE EARTH TO START-ALL OVER AGAIN
MAKING COVENANTS OF A RAINBOW AND BLOOD (GEN 9:4)
WITH PAIRS OF ANIMALS AND NOAH'S BROOD

GOD NOW SELECTED THE HEBREWS AS HIS CHOSEN RACE
FROM ALL THOSE COMING HERE FROM OUTER SPACE
HE CALLED ON ABRAM AND SARAI, HIS SISTER/WIFE AND
GIVING HIM AND HIS DESCENDANTS THE PROMISED LAND

BINDING THIS COVENANT WITH THE SYMBOL OF CIRCUMCISION
WITH THE PROMISE AND BLESSING OF LEADING A NATION
AND DESCENDANTS AS MANY AS STARS IN THE SKY
CHANGING THEIR NAMES, MAKING THEM HOLY

THEN GOD REALIZED A MISTAKE WAS MADE
SO THE PRODIGY WAS FOR YEARS DELAYED
FOR A MAN AND WIFE IN HAVING THE SAME FATHER
DESCENDANTS ARE DEFORMED AND THE PROMISE SHATTERED

SO SARAH SINNED LIKE EVE IN THE GARDEN
SAYING HERE, ABRAHAM TAKE THIS CONCUBINE
HAGAR, A HANDMAIDEN FROM ANOTHER RACE
BIRTHING ISHMAEL NOW THE FATHER OF THE ISLAMIC MISTAKE

SO THEN GOD BECAME SO DESPERATE THAT
HE VISITED SARAH AT MAMRE IN HER TENT
PRODUCING ISAAC, THE REAL PROMISED CHILD
WHOM HE READILY WANTED ABRAHAM TO SACRIFICE

BUT HE STRUGGLED WITH HIS PEOPLE FOREVER AND A DAY
TO SACRIFICE JESUS AS A SYMBOL FOR SINS TO ALLAY
AFTER THE FLOOD, IT SEEMS THAT THE PROMISED LAND
IT HAD A DEAD SEA AND WAS MOSTLY OF SAND

SO THE PEOPLE SEVERAL TIMES WERE ALIENS IN EGYPT
WHERE THEY PICKED UP THEIR GODS BUT BECAME CIVILIZED
BECOMING SO POPULOUS, THEY WERE ENSLAVED
HERE IS WHERE MOSES COMES IN SO THEY COULD BE SAVED

THE EGYPTIANS WORSHIPED A CALF BUT WERE A TRINITY
WITH HORUS, ISIS, AND OSIRIS A MODEL FOR CHRISTIANITY
GOD SAID I AM THE GOD OF THIS PLANET, AND I'M JEALOUS
DON'T BRING IN YOUR GODS AND THOSE LITTLE IDOLS

GOD WONDERS WHY HE EVER MADE MAN
TO WORSHIP HIM, BE COMFORTED, AND UNDERSTAND
IT SHOULD BE ONE OF EQUAL PARTICIPATION
OF PROGRESS, INVENTION, AND COOPERATION

GOD HAD BEEN ABSENT FOR FOUR HUNDRED YEARS
IS NOW ENRAGED AT PHARAOH FOR ENSLAVING HIS PEERS
SO MUCH SO HE BRINGS PLAGUES AND KILLS THE FIRSTBORNS WITH A PASSOVER
THE CHILDREN STEAL JEWELRY AND DROWN CHARIOTEERS IN THE EXODUS OVER

THE RED SEA TO WANDER IN THE WILDERNESS FOR FORTY YEARS
RECEIVING COMMANDMENTS TO LOVE HIM BUT NOT TO STEAL OR KILL
BUT ON RETURNING TO ABRAHAM'S PROMISED LAND
WHERE THEY WOULD KILL FOR HOMES WITH VINEYARDS AND CATTLE

SOMEHOW THE CANAANITES, WITH THEIR GOD BAAL
HAD PRODUCED THIS BOUNTY WHERE THE ISRAELITES HAD FAILED
A LAND OF MILK AND HONEY WITH LOCAL ALTARS TO PRAY
TEMPLES WITH PROSTITUTES, ITS NO WONDER ISRAEL STRAYED

NOW THE PEOPLE ARE CLAMORING
THEY SAY OTHER TRIBES ALL HAVE KINGS
GOD SAYS I HAVE TRIED MY BEST TO PROVE I AM THEIR KING
BUT I FINALLY GIVE IN TO GIVE THEM EVERYTHING

I TELL THE PROPHET SAMUEL TO GET THE TALLEST AND BEST
WHOM HE ANOINTS AS KING OF THE ISRAELITES
TO CONDUCT MY POLICIES AND MY WARS
AND ALWAYS IT'S ME WHOM THEY SHOULD ADORE

THERE WERE SOME NEPHILIM LEFT AFTER THE FLOOD
THE PHILISTINES HAVE ONE WHOSE NAME IS GOLIATH
HE IS THE TERROR OF THE ISRAELITE ARMY
CHALLENGING ANYONE WHO DARES TO FIGHT ME

THE SHEPARD BOY DAVID WITH A ROCK IN HIS SLING
HAVING KILLED MANY LIONS SAVED THE ISRAELIS
CREATED SOME JEALOUSY WITH THE NEW KING SAUL
WHO HAD BEEN ADMONISHED BY THE WAY HE CONDUCTED WAR

HE HAD SAVED THE PRIZE HERDS TO GIVE TO THE PRIESTS
AND SOME OF MOSES' RELATIVES HE HAD RELEASED
LIKE MOSES FOR NOT FOLLOWING ORDERS WAS REMOVED
GOD SENT AN EVIL SPIRIT TO HIM, SO HE WAS DOOMED

SO THE ISRAELITES WENT FROM JUDGES THEN TRIED KINGS
THENCE TO PROPHETS WHO RELATED GOD'S THINKING
THE KINGS WERE ALL FAILURES FOR NOT FOLLOWING GOD'S EXAMPLE
DAVID WAS GOD'S PET BUT WAS NOT ALLOWED TO BUILD THE TEMPLE

TO CHASTISE THE NATION, GOD SPLIT IT IN TWO AS INCORRIGIBLE
BUT THEY CONTINUED TO SIN, ESPECIALLY AHAB AND JEZEBEL
NOW WAS THE TIME TO INSTITUTE SYNAGOGUES FOR PURIFICATION
BUT HE ALLOWED ASSYRIA TO CARRY OFF ISRAEL TO THEIR EXTINCTION

DID THIS SET AN EXAMPLE TO JUDAH AT ALL
JOSIAH WAS KILLED FOR READING THE TORAH
JEREMIAH WAS JAILED FOR PROPHESYING JUDAH'S DOOM
THEN JUDAH WAS TAKEN IN CAPTIVITY TO BABYLON

SO THE REAL QUESTION IS, WILL MAN EVER LEARN
CHRISTIANS OPENLY SIN, CHALLENGING GOD AT EVERY TURN
CLAIMING THAT JESUS WILL SAVE THEM NO MATTER WHAT
ALL THEY HAVE TO DO IS BELIEVE AND STILL BE CORRUPT

RB WELSH, 4 20 21

THE PROPHET ISAIAH

ISAIAH WAS ONE OF THE FOUR MAJOR PROPHETS
WITH JEREMIAH, EZEKIEL, AND DANIEL FORETELLING THE FUTURE
GOD HAD BASICALLY FAILED IN TRANSCRIBING HIS THOUGHTS
THROUGH JUDGES AND KINGS, SO THINGS WERE AT A SORE SPOT

IN ADDITION, I WOULD CERTAINLY HAVE SELECTED ELIJAH
FOR NOT ONLY RAISING THE DEAD BUT WAS RAISED TO THE ETERNAL
HAVING A MANTLE TO CROSS OVER THE JORDAN
HE PROMISED MANY WEEKS OF FOOD FOR THE WIDOW

ISAIAH HAS TRANSCRIBED THE EVILS OF EPHRAIM
FROM THE WORDS OF THE LORD, AND HE IS NOW SERIOUS
FOR IT SEEMS THEY HAVE SINNED BEYOND THE PALE
THERE'LL BE NO FORGIVENESS THEY'LL GO TO THE ASSYRIAN HELL

WOE IS ME TOO, FOR I AM A MAN OF UNCLEAN LIPS, HE SAYS
TO BE IN THE PRESENCE OF GOD WITH THESE MANY REGRETS
I HAD SEXUAL RELATIONS WITH A PROPHETESS PERHAPS IT WAS HULDA (IS 8:3)
THE NIECE OF JEREMIAH WHILE HE WAS OFF IN ASSYRIA

THERE BEING NO COMMANDMENTS, A MAN JUST TOOK A WIFE
MARRIAGE VOWS WERE STILL IN THE FUTURE OF LIFE
THERE WAS THE CUSTOM OF BETROTHAL BETWEEN MARY AND JOSEPH
BUT GOD TOOK HER TO BEAR THEIR SON JESUS

I WAS COMMANDED TO TAKE UP A STYLUS AND ADDRESS
THE NAME OF MY SON MAHER-SHALA-HASH-BAZ
FOR BEFORE HE CAN CRY OUT "FATHER" OR "MOTHER"
ISRAEL WILL BE CARRIED OFF TO ASSYRIA BY SHALAMANZER

ISAIAH THEN DENOUNCED EVERY KNOWN COUNTRY
SURROUNDING ISRAEL FOR THEIR EFFRONTERY
AS BEING UNFAITHFUL AND BLIND TO HIS CAUSE
THEY WILL ALL BE DESTROYED JUST LIKE KING AHAB

BUT WHEN SENNACHERIB THREATENED KING HEZEKIAH
AS REPETITIVE LIKE THE KING OF NINEVEH AND JONAH
HE PUT ON SACKCLOTH AND REPENTED BEFORE THE LORD
SO THE ANGEL SLEW 185,00 ASSYRIANS BY THE SWORD

THIS WAS A TIME BEFORE THE EXILE OF A GREAT FEELING FROM GOD
THIS WAS A TIME OF PLENTY FOR JACOB AND HIS TRIBE
IT WAS LIKE THE MESSIAH HAD COME FOR THE BEST TO THE LEAST
THERE WAS LIGHT TO THE BLIND WITH A PLENTEOUS FEAST

BUT IN SPITE OF THIS GLORIOUS SHORT TIME AGAIN
ISRAEL BURDENED GOD WITH THEIR SINS AND SHAME
IT WAS LIKE DYING BEFORE BEING ALLOWED
BY MOSES AND AARON TO GO IN TO THE PROMISED LAND

HOW CAN WE CLAIM EVIL IS CAUSED BY THE DEVIL
WHEN GOD CLAIMS HE'S THE SOURCE OF GOOD OR EVIL (IS 45:7)
WE KNOW THAT HE PUT AN EVIL SPIRIT
INTO THE HEART OF KING SAUL TO KILL DAVID 1SAM (16:14)

IT'S LIKE IF ONE PRAYS AND PLOTS TO BE EVIL, THAT'S WHAT HE'LL GET
THE RUIN AND DESOLATION OF COUNTRIES THEIR PEOPLES REGRET
SUCCUMBING TO IDIOCY, BEING BLIND TO THE END
SLAVES TO UNTRUTHS, BELIEVERS IN SIN

SOMETIME IN THE FUTURE, GOD WILL BRING HIS LIGHT
THE PRINCE OF PEACE SO MEN WILL DO WHAT IS RIGHT, (ISA 9:6)
THOUGH HE WAS BORN OF A VIRGIN AS ISAIAH PREDICTED
THE PEOPLE WERE JOYFUL AT FIRST, BUT THEN THEY REBELLED

FOR THEY STILL LUSTED AFTER SIN LIKE THE DEPRAVED
WITH NO IDEA OF WANTING TO BE SAVED
THEIR WORSHIPING WORDS WERE JUST MEMORIZED
OUT OF THE SIDE OF THEIR MOUTHS LIKE DEMONS, THEY LIED

GOD'S AMBITIOUS PLAN
IN MAKING MAN
WAS IN ITS INCEPTION NOW BOUND TO FAIL
ESPECIALLY WHEN GOD'S PROMISE RAN INTO BAAL

THE ONLY REASON FOR SETTING UP THE COMMANDMENTS
HE KNEW THEY WERE PREDESTINED JUST TO BE BROKEN AND
THAT'S THE REASON WHY PAUL SAID THE SPIRIT OF CHRIST (GAL 3:13)
WOULD BE INSTITUTED TO SUPERSEDE FOR GOD'S LAW IS TOO PRECISE

IF THE HOLY SPIRIT COULDN'T CONTROL ALL THE GODS
THEY WOULD CONSTANTLY BE WARRING WITH EACH OTHER AT ODDS
SO EACH ENDS UP WITH A CASE OF JEALOUSY
IN COMPETITION FOR FOLLOWERS TO PRAISE AND BELIEVE

GOD HAD LOST ALL CONTROL OF HIS PRECIOUS MAN
THERE WAS JUST NO WAY THAT HE COULD UNDERSTAND
SO INSTEAD OF A FLOOD TO RID HIM OF MAN
HE INVOKED THE ASSYRIANS AND BABYLONIANS TO REMOVE MAN AGAIN

JUST A REMNANT RETURNED TO JUDAH THIS TIME
FINDING NOTHING BUT DESOLATION AND SOME FOREIGN WIVES
JUDAH WAS REBORN BUT NOT WITHOUT SLAVERY
IT WAS TIME FOR SOMEONE LIKE DANIEL TO COME AND SAVE THEM

GOD WILL SEND A MEDIATOR TO RESOLVE MEN TO HIM
FOR ALL AXIAL NATIONS HAVE A KRISHNA OR BUDDHA
WITH A HUMAN MINDSET THAT UNDERSTANDS STRIFE
AND A PERPETUAL REBIRTH OR AN AFTERLIFE

THE HEBREW NATION IS STILL WAITING FOR THEIRS
WILL IT BE OF A VIRGIN BIRTH OR COME OUT OF THIN AIR
THE WORSHIP OF CHRIST IS EXPECTED OF ALL MEN
BUT GOD MADE NO EFFORT TO CONVERT THE EGYPTIANS

HE WOULDN'T HAVE ALL HIS PROBLEMS LIKE THIS WITH BAAL
NOW WE HAVE CHURCHES AND LOCAL TEMPLES AS WELL
HOWEVER, FOR BELIEVERS IN THE HOLY SPIRIT FOR WORSHIPING
THERE'S ONLY ONE CHURCH, AND THAT'S IN HEIDELBERG GERMANY

FOR HIS MANY GREAT PROPHECIES AND HIS SPIRITUAL LIFE
HE SHOULD HAVE BEEN RAISED TO HEAVEN LIKE ENOCH AND ELIJAH
BUT MANASSEH, THE WORST KING OF JUDAH, ASSAILED THIS PROPHET OF GOD-
AND KILLED HIM HIDING IN A HOLLOW TREE AND TWO WAS HE SAWED (HEB 11:37)

SO WHAT IS THE FINAL RESULT OF ALL THIS
SOMETHING IN GOD'S PLAN HAS GONE AMISS
FROM THE GARDEN OF EDEN TO THE DESTRUCTION OF ISRAEL
ORDERS AND LAWS WITHOUT BLESSINGS RESULT IN TURMOIL

SO FAR, THERE'S NO SIGN OF LOVE IN GOD'S MIND
DEMANDING LOVE AND WORSHIP WITHOUT ALTARS OR SHRINES
THIS LAND BECAME A DESERT, SO THEY BECAME ALIENS
NOW IT IS PROSPEROUS UNDER THE CANAANITES BAAL (JOS 24:13)

SOMEHOW WE EXPECTED OF GOD A FAIRY TALE LAND
ESPECIALLY AFTER TRUDGING A THOUSAND MILES THROUGH SAND
WITH MAGIC WANDS AND STARS, WE EXPECTED A CIRCUS WITH CLOWNS
ESPECIALLY WHEN OUR TRUMPETS CAUSED THE WALLS TO FALL DOWN

GOD COULD MAKE EARTH HIS HEAVEN IF HE SO DESIRED
BUT MAN HAS TO DIE FIRST AFTER EXHIBITING A GOOD LIFE
I WONDER IF THIS LIFE IS THE HELL JESUS DESCENDED INTO
BEFORE HE WAS RAISED LIKE ELIJAH AND ENOCH

RB WELSH, 5 6 21

THE SUFFERING SERVANT

WHERE ELSE WAS IT PREDICTED THAT ONE COULD TAKE ON YOUR SINS
BY HIS SUFFERING, AT HIS DEATH, FOR THE TROUBLE I CAUSED HIM?
IF HE HADN'T DIED FOR MY LOWNESS OF LIFE,
I WOULD BE TAKING THE WHIP AND BE CRUCIFIED.

IT WAS JOHN THE BAPTIZER WHO SPOKE OF HIM WHO WAS HIGHER
FOR HE WAS COMING TO BAPTIZE US WITH THE HOLY SPIRIT AND FIRE. (MK 1:7)
AT THE PENTECOST EACH YEAR, WE KNOW THIS IS TRUE,
HE RETURNS WITH THE BREATH OF THE HOLY SPIRIT AND GOD TOO.

HE BAPTIZES MEN SO THEY CAN SPEAK OTHER LANGUAGES
THERE FOLLOWS GREAT LOVE AND INTERNATIONAL UNDERSTANDING
GOD HAD FINALLY DECIDED THAT WAR AND TRIBULATION
WOULD HAVE TO BE SUPPLANTED WITH LOVE AND LIBATIONS

GOD SAYS: IT SEEMS THAT I HAVE TRIED EVERY WAY
TO GET YOU TO LOVE ME AND OBEY
SO NOW I WILL SEND YOU ANOTHER SON
AS THE SYMBOL OF MY GREAT LOVE

HE WILL BE THE ONE WHO WILL STAND TRIAL
FOR ALL YOUR SINS AND ETERNAL SURVIVAL
HE WILL BE THE ONE YOU PRAY TO AND SAY
PLEASE HELP ME, LORD, WITH THIS TASK TODAY

SO ISAIAH SAYS: SO LOOK OUT FOR A CHILD BORN OF A VIRGIN
FOR HE WILL BE THE ONE TO HELP CARRY YOUR BURDENS
THEN WHEN IT COMES TIME FOR YOU TO PAY UP
FOR YOUR MANY SINS, HE WILL DRINK THE CUP

RB WELSH, 5 7 21

ISAAC, SON OF GOD

KNOWN AS THE SON OF ABRAHAM
ISAAC WAS THE SON OF A MAN
TO BEAR A CHILD AT AGE NINETY-NINE
IS LIKE A BEGINNING VIRGINAL, NOT KNOWING A MAN.

RB WELSH, 1 17 22

JEREMIAH

THE THING THAT MAKES A PROPHET EITHER MAJOR OR MINOR
IS WHETHER HE CAN DELIVER MORE THAN A ONE-LINER
YOU WOULD THINK IT'S THE CONTENT AND NOT THE LENGTH
LIKE HOW MANY CHAPTERS ARE IN HIS BOOK, NOT THE CONTENT IN STRENGTH

WHAT DISTINGUISHES A MAJOR PROPHET FROM THAT OF A MINOR
IS THE LENGTH OF OF HIS BOOK AND NOT OF HIS BEING A DIVINER
THE TWELVE BOOKS OF THE MINORS DEAL WITH ISRAEL'S INIQUITY
FOLLOWED BY THOSE OF RESOLUTION TO WORSHIP OF THE DIVINITY

JUST WHO WAS THE GREATEST PROPHET IN EITHER NATION
IT WAS CERTAINLY ELIJAH, THOUGH CONSIDERED TO BE MINOR
HE RAISED THE DEAD, FED THE POOR HAD THE BAAL PROPHETS KILLED
THEN CARRIED UP TO HEAVEN IN A WHIRLWIND

SO YOU KNOW WHY WE WORSHIP BAAL
HE'S AVAILABLE RIGHT OUT MY DOOR IN THE TOWN SQUARE
I KNOW THAT MANY TIMES HAVE I SINNED
BUT NEVER HAVE I EVER KNOWN THAT I'VE BEEN FORGIVEN

GOD JUST WANTS A SIMPLE SACRIFICE
BUT I DON'T SEE HOW A BIRD CAN MAKE IT ALL RIGHT
MAYBE THAT MAKES GOD FEELS ALL THE BETTER
BUT WHATEVER IS MY GUILT, IT JUST FOLLOWS ME FOREVER

WHEN AN ALTAR TO BAAL IS RIGHT OUT THE DOOR
I FEEL FORGIVEN AND READY TO SIN ONCE MORE
TODAY WE WORSHIP ILLICIT SEX AND DRUGS
IT'S STILL THE SAME BAAL TO WHOM MAN SUCCUMBS

WASN'T THERE A WAY GOD COULD PUNISH EACH ONE
FOR THEIR INDIVIDUAL SINS INSTEAD OF EVERYONE
SENDING THE WHOLE NATION OFF TO SIBERIA
INSTEAD OF EACH ONE AS IF IT WERE TERRORISM

WERE THEY INTOXICATED WHEN THEY SINNED
WERE THEY ALWAYS FORGIVEN AGAIN AND AGAIN
TILL GOD WAS SICK AND TIRED THEN GETTING MAD
ALLOWING THE ASSYRIANS TO DRAG OFF ISRAELIAN DAMNED

DO YOU THINK THIS INCIDENT WAS A HINT TO JUDEANS
THAT IF THEY DIDN'T SHAPE UP, THEY'D BE OFF TO THE CHALDEANS
DO YOU THINK GOD GAVE THEM ANY ALTERNATIVE WAYS
TO WORSHIP HIM INSTEAD OF BAAL WITH SIMPLE PRAYERS

HAVING LOCAL SHRINES INSTEAD OF ONE TEMPLE
SERVICING EACH CITY ALL OVER, MAKING WORSHIP SIMPLE
THE PEOPLE HATED JEREMIAH FOR HIS PERSISTENT WARNINGS
THROWING HIM INTO THE DUNGEON AND KEPT ON IGNORING

SOMEONE EVEN BOUGHT JEREMIAH'S PROPERTY
NO ONE PAID ATTENTION TO HIS PROPHECIES
SADLY ENOUGH, JEREMIAH WAS ALSO TAKEN
ALONG WITH THE KING AND THE OTHERS IN CAPTIVATION

ISAIAH HAD TAKEN THE PROPHETESS HULDA IN MARRIAGE,
THE NIECE OF JEREMIAH. IT WAS WITHOUT CEREMONY IN THOSE DAYS
IF HE DIED, HIS BROTHER TOOK OVER, SO HE MAY HAVE HAD MANY WIVES
JUST THINK HOW MANY CEREMONIES KINGS WOULD HAVE HAD AND SURVIVED

IT WAS LIKE AS IF GOD HAD JUST TAKEN OVER MARY AS A WIFE
WITH THE HOLY SPIRIT GIVING JESUS HIS LIFE
AS PORTRAYED BY LUKE IN HIS VERSION AS THE CUSTOM
THIS MEANS THAT MARY HAD GOD AND JOSEPH AS HUSBANDS

JESUS HIMSELF WAS A TRINITY LIKE IN OUR RELIGION
INSUFFLATED BY THE SPIRIT AND BORN OF A VIRGIN
THEN CALLING HIMSELF THE SON OF MAN
THAT'S ALL THREE, SO FIGURE THAT OUT IF YOU CAN

SUDDENLY NEBUCHADNEZZAR BECOMES GOD'S "SERVANT"
FULFILLING GOD'S ORDERS TO REMOVE THEM FOR INTERNMENT
THE KING WAS DRAGGED OFF WITH A RING IN HIS NOSE AS A HALTER
THEY WERE JUST LIKE SOME CATTLE HERDED OFF FOR THE SLAUGHTER

CATHOLICS JUST CONFESS, SO IT RIDS THEM OF SIN
THAT WAY, IT'S EASY TO SIN AGAIN AND AGAIN
JUST PAY INDULGENCES EACH TIME TO BE ABSOLVED
THEIR SIN AGAINST GOD WILL THEN BE RESOLVED

AT THE TIME OF DEATH, ONE WILL JUST STEP OVER PURGATORY
IS THAT TRUE, OR IS IT JUST A BEDTIME STORY
THE BISHOP'S EARS MUST REALLY BE RED
FOR LISTENING TO THOSE WALLOPING STORIES IN DEPTH

AT FIRST, JEREMIAH SOMEHOW GOT TO RETURN
TO JERUSALEM AND HELP THOSE IN A CITY DESTROYED AND BURNED
SEEING THE IMPOSSIBILITY, HE TOOK SOME REFUGEES TO EGYPT
NEVER SOLVING THE PROBLEMS OF JUDAH'S REGENT

FUNERALS ARE ALWAYS HELD THREE DAYS AFTER ONE DIES
THEY MUST THINK THE DECEASED HAS TO REALIZE
HOW LUCKY IT IS FOR HIM TO BE RAISED
FOR AN ATONEMENT WITH GOD ASTONISHED TO BEING SAVED

NOW WAS THE TIME FOR THE SIMPLICITY OF A CHRIST
FOR ONE'S SINS TO BE CARRIED OFF INTO PARADISE
BY ADMITTING TO HIM THAT YOU WERE JUST A BUMMER
BUT THAT WAS A TUNE FOR A DISTANT DRUMMER

RB WELSH, 5 10 21

HUNCH

WHEN I GET A HUNCH IT'S THE SPIRIT OF GOD
NUDGING ME TO DO SOMETHING I DIDN'T THINK OF AT ALL.
I USED TO IGNORE THIS FOR I DIDN'T KNOW WHAT
IT WAS, TILL AFTER A WHILE HE KICKED ME IN THE BUTT.

NOW WHEN I GET TO A CROSSROAD AND DON'T KNOW,
IS IT LEFT OR RIGHT? HE'LL TELL ME WHICH WAY TO GO.
THE HOLY SPIRIT IS IN CHARGE OF ALL THE BIG STUFF,
LIKE WHOM YOU WILL MARRY, SO YOU WON'T MUFF.

IF YOU THINK IT'S JESUS WHO MAKES UP YOUR MIND.
THAT'S OKAY FOR GOD AND JESUS ARE OF ONE KIND.
GOD IS JESUS SO THE SPIRIT THEY POSSESS
IS GOD'S NO MATTER WHOM YOU ADDRESS.

THIS IS THE SPIRIT THAT FOLLOWS ME AROUND,
TELLING ME NOT TO WAIT, BUT TO DO IT NOW.
DON'T PUT IT OFF OR THERE'LL BE A LAPSE,
THE MOMENT OF OPPORTUNITY WILL SOON PASS.

SOMETIMES IT'S SUDDEN, LIKE AN ALARM,
BUT MAINLY IT'S JUST A NUDGE, AN IDEA HAS FORMED.
SO I PAY ATTENTION TO SEE WHERE THIS GOES,
IF IT'S GREAT I PATENT IT BEFORE LOSING CONTROL.

RB WELSH, 5 30 23

GOD SAYS TO JEREMIAH

GOD: SOMETIMES I REALLY SIT AND WONDER,
WHY MAKING MAN WAS SUCH A BLUNDER.
OF COURSE, I NEEDED SOPHIA'S BLOOD
I MUST HAVE USED TOO MUCH MUD
SIMPLY, I MADE HIM FREE,
JUST TO LOVE AND OBEY ME.

I WARN HIM, BUT IT'S ALL IN VAIN,
HE JUST REPEATS HIS SAME OLD SINS
HE'S TOO SMART TO ACT SO DUMB,
HE SHOULD STAY BENEATH MY THUMB.
I KEEP ON GIVING HIM EXTRA CHANCES, BUT
HE KEEPS GIVING ME THE SAME OLD ANSWERS.

WORSHIPING THOSE IDOL GODS,
NO WONDER I GAVE HIM THE ROD
WHEN THEY CLAMORED FOR A KING
I GAVE HIM THAT AND EVERYTHING
I HAVE LOST ALL CONTROL,
OF HIS HEART AND HIS SOUL.
SO OFF THEY'LL GO TO BABYLON,
PERHAPS THEY'LL SING A DIFFERENT SONG.

RB WELSH, 5 15 21

SYNAGOGUE

THE CAPTIVES OF THE NORTHERN KINGDOM NEVER RETURNED
AFTER ASSYRIAN FORCES CAPTURED THEM, NOTHING WAS LEARNED
JUDAH KEPT ON WITH THEIR SINS, AND THE WORSHIP
OF BAAL AND ASHERAH TILL JERUSALEM BURNED.

SOME OF THE PRIESTS WHO ESCAPED
THEY WENT TO TUNISIA, WHERE THEY THEN BUILT
THE FIRST SYNAGOGUE IN BC 586
WHEN SOLOMON'S TEMPLE WAS DESTROYED IN THE CONFLICT

SOLOMON HAD TO BUILD THE ORIGINAL AT GOD'S COMMAND
FOR DAVID HAD TOO MUCH BLOOD ON HIS HANDS
NOW HERE IT WAS TO LIE IN RUINS
THIS SHOULD BE AN EXAMPLE TO US, BUT IT'S FUTILE

WITH GOD MAKING NEBECHADRESSER HIS SERVANT,
TELLING THE PEOPLE TO PEACEABLY SURRENDER IS JUST APPEASEMENT;
SO ONLY THAT GOD CAN SAVE THE CITY WALLS AND HIS TEMPLE
IS SO RIDICULOUS IN THE BIG PICTURE. THIS IS JUST AN EXAMPLE.

FOR THE WHOLE SCENARIO OF GOD'S ONLY HUMANS LEFT TO RETURN,
SINCE AFTER JUDGES PROPHETS AND KINGS, NOTHING WAS LEARNED,
WAS TO START THE TRIBE OF THE ISRAELITES WORSHIPING GOD
BEGINNING ALL OVER AGAIN IN NEIGHBORHOOD SYNAGOGUES.

THEN THEY WOULDN'T BE SO ATTRACTED TO BAAL
OR TRAVEL MANY MILES TO JERUSALEM, THAT FAILED
BUT THEY WENT BACK TO THE SAME OLD SCENARIO
REBUILDING THE TEMPLE RESTARTING THE FIASCO

RB WELSH, 5 18 21

ONE OF THREE

IF YOU HAD THE CHOICE OF CHOOSING JUST ONE OF ALL THREE
WHICH ONE WOULD YOU TAKE IN THIS TRINITY
YOU HAVE GOD THE FATHER AND HIS SON
RELYING ON THE ADVOCATE TO GET THINGS DONE

THOUGH JESUS WAS NOT YET BORN
THE SPIRIT WAS NEVER HEARD OF BEFORE
IN ALL THE YEARS OF THE TALMUD
WERE WE EVER INTRODUCED

SO GOD WENT THROUGH ALL CREATION
FROM ADAM TO MARY'S INSUFFLATION
WHEN THE HOLY SPIRIT FIRST SHOWED UP
IN HISTORY, IT WAS SUDDENLY ABRUPT

THE SPIRIT HASN'T DISAPPEARED SINCE IT FINALLY SHOWED UP
LIKE GOD LEFT WHEN THE ISRAELITES WERE SLAVES IN EGYPT
THAT THEY ARE SPIRITS NOW THEY DO HAVE THIS IN COMMON
EXCEPTING FOR JESUS'S HUMANITY AS BEING THE SON OF MAN

GOD MAY HAVE HAD A RELATIONSHIP WITH THE HOLY SPIRIT
HE SAID, "LET US MAKE MAN," BUT THAT HAD TO BE SOPHIA
JOHN SAYS AS THE LOGOS WAS THE JESUS TO BE
SO TWO OUT OF THREE JUST DOESN'T MAKE A TRINITY

SCRIPTURE SAYS I CAN TAKE THE LORD'S NAME IN VAIN
AND STILL, BE FORGIVEN
BUT NOT THAT OF THE HOLY SPIRIT
OR I'LL NEVER GO TO HEAVEN (MT 12:31)

DOES THAT GIVE ONE A CLUE
AS TO WHETHER THIS IS PROOF
THAT THE HOLY SPIRIT IS THE HIGHEST
OF THESE GODS, SO IS THE MIGHTIEST

THIS IS SO OBVIOUS I CAN'T BELIEVE
THAT MEN STILL THINK THERE'S A TRINITY
ESPECIALLY SINCE WE THINK THAT GOD'S NOT GONE
FOR LIKE IN EGYPT HE'S DISAPPEARED TO BE ALLAH AS *ONE* (NOT THREE)

PEOPLE SHOULD RE-ORIENT THEIR BRAINS
THEY KEEP REPEATING THE SAME OLD REFRAIN
THE WORD TRINITY IS NOT IN THE BIBLE
FOR CONSTANTINE IS THE ONE WHO'S LIABLE

DO YOU WANT TO KNOW WHAT THE HOLY SPIRIT IS
IT'S NOT A MAN SO SHOULD BE ADDRESSED AS "IT"
JESUS AND GOD MAY BE KNOWN AS A "HE"
BUT THE SPIRIT HAS BEEN AROUND UNIVERSALLY

THAT IT GAVE EACH GOD LIKE BAAL BUDDHA AND YAHWEH
THEIR OWN SOLAR SYSTEMS AND PLANETS TO OPERATE
BUT WHEN TIME CAME FOR DESTRUCTION BY A SUPER-NOVAS
THE GOD WITH IT'S RACE FLEW TO EARTH TO START OVER

SOME PEOPLE WILL SAY GOD CREATED YOU
BE IN FOR A SHOCK HE ONLY MADE THE HEBREW
HOW MANY RACES CAME TO THIS EARTH NOT A FEW
BLACK, WHITE AND YELLOW I'M SURPRISED THERE ARE NO BLUES

EACH ONE BRINGING THEIR OWN GODS
DO YOU THINK THE CRUSADERS KNEW THEY WERE FIGHTING AGAINST GOD
AS THEY CAME ALL THE WAY FROM EUROPE TO SAVE ISRAEL FROM ALLAH
NOT REMEMBERING THAT GOD'S ANGEL GABRIEL
WAS SENT TO MUHAMMAD TO WRITE THE KORAN

DO YOU THINK YOU'D BE REMINDED BOTH DAY AND NIGHT
AN ILLOGICAL LIE HAVING NO REASONING THEN IT WAS RIGHT
BUT PSYCHOLOGICALLY YOU KEEP ON BELIEVING
EVEN THOUGH IT HAS ALWAYS BEEN DECEIVING

YES, WE BELIEVE IN THE APOSTLES' CREED
WHERE NOTHING IS SAID ABOUT EQUALITY OF ALL THREE
IT MUST HAVE BEEN AT ITS INCEPTION TO BE SUSPECT
FOR GOD TO NOT ONLY BE HIS OWN BABY AS THE MESSIAH
BUT TO ALSO BE A NEW SPIRIT NEVER HEARD OF OR PROPHESIED OF

TO BELIEVE IN A TRINITY IS LIKE BELIEVING IN SANTA
TO BE TAUGHT AS A CHILD, IT'S BELIEVABLE LIKE PROPAGANDA
SO GET DOWN TO BASICS IS MY ADVICE
A TRINITY IS UNFEASIBLE, IMPRACTICAL, AND JUST DEVISED

IF I EVER AGREED TO JOIN IN THIS BELIEF
I'D HAVE TO INCLUDE MARY WITH THE OTHER THREE
FOR WITHOUT HER, THERE WOULD ONLY BE TWO
JUST GOD AND THE SPIRIT IS CALLED THE DUO

ISRAEL HAS ALWAYS BEEN THE VULVA OF HISTORY
RAPED EVEN BY GOD AND ALWAYS IN MISERY
BORN AND REBORN HEBREWS EVENTUALLY SUCCEED
FOR THEY WORSHIP THE ONE GOD AND ALWAYS EXCEED

RB WELSH, 5 18 21

EZEKIEL

HAS ANY OTHER PROPHET HAD A MORE INTERESTING AGENDA,
THEN THE DESCENDANT OF THE PROSTITUTE RAHAB AND JOSHUA,
THE SON OF JEREMIAH, ALSO PROPHESIED IN JUDAH
ANOTHER MAJOR PROPHET WHOSE TREATISE IS LUDICROUS.

FOR WHOEVER HAS WITNESSED GOD IN HIS GOLDEN CHARIOT,
A CRAFT THAT MAY HAVE RAISED JESUS AND ELIJAH,
A FLYING SAUCER WITH ITS WHIRLING EYES,
FLITTING ABOUT IN STORM-LADEN SKIES?

GOD HAS COME CLOSE SO HE CAN WITNESS THESE UNREPENTANT
OF MAJESTIC PEOPLE'S DETERMINATION TO BE INDEPENDENT
ALL THIS MUST HAVE BEEN SIMPLY A FORECAST
OF JEWS IN THE 20TH CENTURY OF THE HOLOCAUST

NOW HERE HE WAS IN A VALLEY OF DRY BONES
GOD SAID SPEAK TO THEM, AND THEY ALL AROSE
THE SKELETONS GREW SINEWS BREATH CAME TO THEIR LUNGS
THEY WERE RESURRECTED; THEY WERE SPEAKING IN TONGUES.

THIS IS ALL A PROPHECY OF JESUS'S MESSIANIC SECRET
TO GO TO JERUSALEM TO DIE AND DESCEND INTO HELL
TO THE VALLEY OF DRY BONES RAISE THEM FROM THE DEAD
RAISE THEM TO HEAVEN FOR ETERNAL LIFE INSTEAD

RB WELSH, 5 20 21

IS THERE A TRINITY

I'LL HAVE TO ADMIT THAT TODAY IT WAS PROVED
AFTER READING THE GOSPEL THAT GOD IS JESUS TOO
I HAD TO ADMIT THAT THE CLASS HAD A POINT TO SELL
BUT A TRINITY INCLUDES THE HOLY SPIRIT AS WELL

SO AS JESUS SAID I'M IN HIM; HE'S IN ME
THAT MAKES JESUS GOD, AND GOD IS HE
THE HOLY SPIRIT IS SUPERIOR IN THIS UNIVERSE
GOD IS THE ONLY MAKER OF THIS HEAVEN AND EARTH

THE OTHER CONSTELLATIONS HAD BAAL AND OTHER GODS
WHO CAME TO THIS PLANET WHEN THEIR SUPERNOVAS
THE LANDING PAD IN LEBANON IS CALLED BAALBAK
FOR THEIR FLYING SAUCERS, SO LOOK IT UP ON THE INTERNET

GOD JUST BECAME JESUS, SO WE'D HAVE HIM TO SEE
TO EXPLAIN HIS COMMANDMENTS WITH SIMPLICITY
THAT LIFE IS NOT PERFECT LIKE HEAVEN WILL BE
THE CHALLENGES WE MUST SOLVE PROGRESSIVELY

DID GOD OR JESUS EVER SAY THEY WERE ALSO THE SPIRIT
EVEN THOUGH THEY'RE NOW LIKE A GHOST SINCE WE CAN'T SEE IT
TO OUR HUMAN VISION, THEY ARE LIKE AN X-RAY
BEYOND VISUAL RANGE LIKE ULTRAVIOLET OR INFRARED

THESE SCRIPTURES SHOWED THAT JESUS AND GOD ARE ONE
HE SAID THAT HE IS IN THE FATHER, SO THE FATHER IS THE SON
THAT'S FINE AS FAR AS IT GOES CAUSE IT'S ONLY TWO, NOT THREE
THEY DIDN'T INCLUDE THE HOLY SPIRIT TO MAKE IT A TRINITY

SO I'VE FIGURED IT OUT THAT THERE'S NO TRINITY
THE WORD IS NOT BIBLICAL AS FAR AS I CAN SEE
THE CONCEPTION INVENTED BY CONSTANTINE
FOR THE RELIGIONS IN HIS EMPIRE NEEDED UNITY

SO IN CONVENING A COUNCIL AT NICEA
CONSTANTINE HAD THEM VOTE YES ON HIS IDEA
SO GOD JUST WENT OFF TO MU HAMMED AS ALLAH
WHERE HE WOULD STILL BE ONE LIKE BAGTIVAGITA

GOD MAY BE JESUS; THAT'S EASY TO SEE
FOR GOD BECOMES MAN WHENEVER IT'S NECESSARY
FOR GOD TO UNDERSTAND MAN
IT WAS NECESSARY TO BECOME HIS OWN MESSIAH

THE GOSPEL OF MARK IN 40 AD WAS WRITTEN FIRST
THEN MATHEW AND LUKE HAD THE VIRGIN BIRTH
WITH THE GOSPEL OF JOHN, SIXTY YEARS LATER
WHERE JESUS WAS THE LOGOS WITH THE CREATOR

TAKING THE PROPHECY OF ISAIAH OF A VIRGIN BIRTH
THE HOLY SPIRIT INSUFFLATING MARY'S WOMB OCCURRED
SAYING HE WAS TO BE CALLED THE SON OF GOD
THIS SEEMS TO BE THE ONLY INCIDENT OF ALL FOUR BEING INVOLVED

JOSEPH THE BETROTHED WAS LEFT OUT OF THIS TRYST
BUT ENDED UP BEING CALLED JESUS'S FATHER ON THIS LIST
IT'S STRANGE THAT JESUS CALLED HIMSELF "SON OF MAN"
ONLY DANIEL WOULD BE SOMEONE WHO COULD UNDERSTAND

SO WITH ALL THIS CONFUSION WHY SHOULD I BELIEVE
WITHOUT BEING IN THE BIBLE, THE WORD "TRINITY"
THE HOLY SPIRIT SAID IF ONE TOOK ITS NAME IN VAIN
HE WOULD NOT BE FORGIVEN AS THAT'S TOO PROFANE (MT 12:32)

THEN THERE WAS THE TIME WHEN PETER AND JOHN
WENT TO SAMARIA TO REBAPTIZE THEM ALL
FOR THEY HAD ONLY BEEN BAPTIZED IN JESUS' NAME (ACTS 8:16)
THAT PROVES TO ME THE SPIRIT HAS MORE FAME

SO HOW CAN JESUS BE THE HOLY SPIRIT
WHEN THE SPERM MARY'S WOMB WAS INFUSED BY IT?
WAS IT JESUS'S VOICE WE HEARD TO SAY, "THIS IS MY BELOVED SON"
WHILE HE WAS BEING BAPTIZED BY THE SPIRIT'S DOVE?

SO I JUST GAVE UP WITH A FALSEHOOD ABOUT THESE THREE
TRYING TO HYPNOTIZE MYSELF AGAINST REALITY
WHEN I MUST DECLARE WITH ALL THIS EVIDENCE AGAINST
THAT THE TRINITY IS A HOAX AND HAS LED TO DISASTERS SINCE

RB WELSH, 5 13 21

MORE EZEKIEL

GOD ALSO HAD CONDEMNATION FOR THE JUDEANS TO HEAR
TAKE THIS SCROLL AND EAT IT; MY WORDS WILL BRING FEAR
DIGEST THESE CONTENTS WRITTEN ON BOTH SIDES
SO WHEN IT TASTED SWEET AS HONEY, I WAS SURPRISED

BUT IN MY STOMACH, IT WAS BITTER WITH CONTEMPT
MEANING THEY WILL BE RETURNED IF ONLY THEY REPENT
THEY WILL HAVE NEW BEGINNINGS IN JERUSALEM
A RECONSTRUCTED LIFE AND TEMPLE FOR RESTITUTION

A REPETITION OF THE TIME OF MOSES WHEN ONLY THE NEXT GENERATION
WAS ALLOWED TO ENTER ISRAEL FOR THEIR SALVATION
THE REBELLIOUS ISRAELITES WITH MOSES FAILED
TO TRUST GOD SO IN THE WILDERNESS, THEY REMAINED

RB WELSH, 5 20 21

PENTECOST SUNDAY

JOHN THE BAPTIST SAID AS HE PROPHESIED
THAT ONE WAS COMING WHOSE LACES HE COULDN'T TIE
FOR AS I BAPTIZE YOU ONLY WITH WATER OF NEW LIFE
HE WILL BAPTIZE YOU WITH THE HOLY SPIRIT AND FIRE

SO ON THIS DAY OF THE PENTECOST
ALL THREE APPEAR TO BAPTIZE THE LOST
WITH JESUS BAPTIZING THEIR TONGUES WITH FIRE
BY THE BREATH OF THE HOLY SPIRIT RAISING YOU HIGHER

RB WELSH, 5 23 21

FORGIVENESS

YES, I HAVE SINNED BUT HAVE I BEEN FORGIVEN
FOR THE MEMORY OF THEM HAUNTS ME FOREVER
I HAVE ALL THESE EXCUSES, THAT I STILL GO OVER
TIME AND AGAIN, THINKING I WAS SO CLEVER

I LIKE TO THINK I WAS FORCED INTO THIS
IT WAS A MATTER OF LOVE AND OF BLISS
THERE IS SOMETHING GOOD, AND THE ONLY THING
ABOUT ALL THIS AND IT WON'T HAPPEN AGAIN

FOR I HAVE BEEN TEMPTED AGAIN SEVERAL TIMES
BUT HAVE EASILY RESISTED ANYTHING OF THIS KIND
I BRAG TOO LATE ABOUT BEING SO PURE
THE MAIN THING IS THAT IT WAS SO STUPID

WE HAVE GOD AND JESUS TO GIVE US FORGIVENESS
SINCE IT STILL HAUNTS US SO WE'LL ASK THE HOLY SPIRIT
FOR I KNOW MAN IS PSYCHIC, AND THOUGHTS TRAVEL FAST
TO GET THE RESPONSES NOT REALLY POSSIBLE AGAIN

GOD SAYS IF I VIOLATED MY OWN COMMANDMENTS
COMMUTING THOSE SINS OF KILLING CANAANITES
STEALING THEIR HOMES THEIR VINEYARDS AND CATTLE
I GUESS I CAN FORGIVE YOU FOR SINS I CAN'T FATHOM

I HAVE NAMED YOU AS MY CHOSEN RACE
WHAT I HAVE DONE IS JUST A DISGRACE
MURDERS OF NEPHILIM EGYPTIAN FIRSTBORN
DESTRUCTION OF ISRAEL FOR WHOM I WILL MOURN

SO I WILL MAKE REPARATIONS FOR WHAT I BLAMED ON YOU
I WILL SACRIFICE MYSELF AS THE TRINITY AND THEN WHO
WILL BE LEFT FOR YOU TO BOW DOWN TO SO OFTEN
BUT ALL THOSE OTHER GODS YOU WORSHIP FOR FUN

RB WELSH, 5 24 21

JONAH

JONAH AND THE WHALE IS A GREAT STORY
WE LAUGH AT THE EFFORT EXPENDED IN JONAH'S ORGY
IN HIS EFFORTS TO ESCAPE FROM GOD
WHO GAVE HIM THE ORDER TO WARN NINEVEH

FOR THEIR LICENTIOUSNESS THEY WILL BE DOOMED
UNLESS THEY REPENT THEIR DESTRUCTION IS SOON
DOES JONAH HEED THE ORDERS OF GOD AND OBEY
NO HE SETS OFF SAILING FOR SPAIN TO HIDE AWAY

GOD COUNTERS THIS MOVE WITH A GIANT STORM
THE SAILORS REALIZE SOMEONE OFFENDS GOD AND BRINGS HARM
ONLY BE THROWING HIM OFF WILL THE STORM ABIDE
WHERE GOD AS A WHALE SWALLOWS JONAH NOW READY TO COMPLY

THREE DAYS AND THREE NIGHTS JONAH'S DISGORGED AT LAST
ON THE BEACH IN ASSYRIA WHERE HE MUST MAKE NINEVEH REPENT
AFTER WARNING THE KING WHO PUTS ON SACKCLOTH AND ASHES
ORDERING THE CITIZENS TO DO LIKEWISE OR PERISH

RETREATING TO THE BEACH TO SIT PATIENTLY UNDER A TREE
EXPECTING THE FIRESTORM TO MAKE NINEVEH SO MUCH HISTORY
BUT THE KING AND THE CITIZENS AND EVEN THE CATTLE
HAD REPENTED SUFFICIENTLY FOR GOD TO RESCIND HIS ORDER

DO YOU THINK THAT JONAH WAS SATISFIED ABOUT ALL THIS
AFTER ALL THIS ROUNDABOUT EFFORT HE WANTED JUSTICE
NINEVEH WAS A CESSPOOL OF SINNERS ALIENATED FROM GOD
JUST PUTTING ON SACKCLOTH DIDN'T SATISFY HIM AT ALL

SO IN SEEING THE FRUITS OF HIS ACTIONS COMING NIL
IN GOING THROUGH THE STORM AND IN THE BELLY OF THE WHALE
HE REQUESTED THAT GOD JUST GO AHEAD TAKE HIS LIFE
EXISTENCE IS STUPID GOING THROUGH ALL OF THIS STRIFE

FOR THIS WAS THE NATION WHICH HAD DESTROYED ISRAEL
THE PEOPLE HAD BEEN CARRIED OFF INTO SLAVERY IN NINEVEH
SO WHY DIDN'T HE SAVE HIS OWN CREATION INSTEAD
GOD FOUND THAT THE GENTILES OBEYED WHAT HE SAID

RB WELSH, 5 25 21

PETER'S FAITH

LIKE THROWING YOURSELF FROM A PINNACLE WHICH WOULD BE ABSURD
WE WOULD BE DEFYING THE LAWS OF NATURE AS IF WE COULD FLY LIKE A BIRD
SO PETER HAVING FAITH TRIED WALKING ON WATER, BUT SANK
AND WAS CRITICIZED UNJUSTLY FOR HAVING A LACK OF FAITH

WHAT EXACTLY WOULD BE FAITH BEYOND REASON OR DOUBT
IT WOULD HAVE TO BE SOMETHING GIVING A PRACTICAL RESULT
BUT WHEN I AM SICK, I CALL UPON THE MASTER
TO DEFY NATURE SO I CAN GET WELL FASTER

THAT'S WHAT CHRISTIAN SCIENTISTS DO TO GET WELL
THEY DON'T EVEN MEDICATE THEMSELVES; IT'S AU' NATUR EL
THEY CALL UPON JESUS AND THEIR FAITH TO GET THEMSELVES THRU
SO PETER MAY HAVE BEEN A CHRISTIAN SCIENTIST TOO

JESUS JUST WASN'T THERE WHEN THE LEVIATHAN CHALLENGED JOB
JOB LEFT ALL HIS FAITH IN THE POWER OF GOD
TO MAKE HIM OR BREAK HIM IN THE TURMOIL OF LIFE
FOR EVERYTHING CAME FROM GOD IN HIS TIME OF STRIFE

RB WELSH, 5 27 21

DANIEL

WHY IS NOT THE MAJOR PROPHET DANIEL INCLUDED IN THIS COURSE
OUT OF THE THOUSANDS TAKEN TO BABYLON, DANIEL'S IN THE KING'S COURT
LIKE JOSEPH IN EGYPT, DANIEL INTERPRETED THE KING'S DREAM
BECAME GOVERNOR OF BABYLONIA AND HELD IN THE HIGHEST ESTEEM

IS DANIEL A PROPHET OR MORE LIKE THE PROMISED MESSIAH
BY MIRACLE, HE WAS SAVED FROM THE LION'S DEN AND THE FURNACE OF FIRE
\IT MAKES YOU WONDER IF RE-INCARNATION IS TRUE
IF DANIEL IS JOSEPH REBORN, IT DEPENDS ON ONE'S POINT OF VIEW

IT IS CERTAIN THAT DANIEL AND ALL THAT TRANSPIRED
WITH ALL THE ACTIONS THAT WERE DIVINELY-INSPIRED
ONLY JESUS WAS KNOWN AS THE LAMB OF GOD
IT COULDN'T BE DANIEL, FOR THAT WOULD SEEM ODD

THE LION SHALL LIE DOWN WITH THE LAMB SAID ISAIAH (IS 11:6)
NOT THREE BUT FOUR WALKED AROUND IN THE FLAMES
THE PROMISED MESSIAH MUST SURELY HAVE COME
TO SAVE MANKIND, SO WAS DANIEL, THE PROMISED ONE

IT MADE NEBUCHADNEZZAR LOSE HIS MIND
HE WAS EATING GRASS AS IF ALL THIS WERE DIVINED
IT'S GOD'S CHILDREN WHO ARE ALWAYS ACTING LIKE BRATS
ALWAYS GETTING THEIR WAY TILL THEY FINALLY GET THE AXE

HE WAS COMING ON THE CLOUDS AS THE GOD OF HEAVEN. (DAN 7:13)
ALL THIS HAD BEEN PREDICTED AS A CERTAIN REVELATION
IT'S NO WONDER THAT THE POWERS WHO RE-WRITE THE BIBLE
RE-INTERPRET IT OR REMOVE LINES SO OUR SOULS WON'T BE LIABLE

THEY WANT THE BOOK OF DANIEL REMOVED LIKE THE APOCRYPHA
OUR TENDER EARS SHOULDN'T BE EXPOSED TO ANOTHER MORIAH
OUR MINDS ARE BEING SUPERVISED AS IF WE WERE CHILDREN
IN THE SERIES ON PROPHETS, AT LEAST WE LEARNED ABOUT HULDAH

LIKE A MESSIAH WHO PERFORMED MIRACLES WITH THE POOR WAS CONCERNED
DANIEL HAD ONLY SAVED THE TRIBE OF JUDAH, THAT WAS RETURNED.
THE TROUBLE IS HE DIDN'T GO TO THE CROSS,
HE DIDN'T SAVE SINNERS AND THOSE WHO WERE LOST.

RB WELSH, 5 27 21

THE MACCABEES

ALEXANDER THE GREAT TOOK OVER THE KNOWN WORLD
INTRODUCING TO JUDEA GREEK THEOLOGY AND RULES
GIVING OVER THE TERRITORY TO ANTIOCHUS, THE SELEUCID KING
HEBREWS WERE COMPELLED TO EAT PORK AND STOP CIRCUMCISING

THE GROUP OF MACCABEES WOULD HAVE NONE OF THIS
THEY THREW DOWN THE STATUES RETOOK THE TEMPLE
WORSHIPING GOD AND PUTTING ON SACKCLOTH AND ASHES
ELIJAH'S CHARIOTS OF GOD APPEARED, ROUTING THEM IN BATTLE

THIS WAS A GROUP OF PEOPLE WHO GAVE UP THEIR LIVES
IN THE NAME OF GOD, THEY SELF-SACRIFICED
THIS WAS THE PERIOD IN ISRAEL'S HISTORY AFTER RETURNING FROM BABYLON
TILL THE BIRTH OF JESUS THAT THEOLOGIANS USED MIND CONTROL

CLAIMING THE HEROES DID NOT HAVE A SAVING GRACE
IN THEIR WARS ON THE ENEMIES OF GOD DID NOT SAVE FACE
THESE HEROES WHO VOLUNTARILY GAVE UP THEIR LIVES
COULD HAVE EASILY ADAPTED TO GREEK LAW AND SURVIVED.

IT IS WE CHRISTIANS WHO ARE AT FAULT FOR THIS TRAVESTY
WE ARE THE ONES WHO HAVE BEEN BRAINWASHED
WITH TRINITIES BREAD AND BLOOD AND THE SACRIFICE,
TO STILL SIN AND AT THE SAME TIME BE HOLY WILL SUFFICE.

CHURCH FATHERS JUST DUMPED THREE HUNDRED YEARS
OF EXCITING FEATS OF BRAVERY AND CHIVALRY
TO SAVE WHAT'S LEFT OF THE SHAMBLES LEFT BY JUDEANS
THE WARS AND THE VALOR OF THE MEN AND WOMEN

LIKE JUDITH, WHO WENT FOR A WEEK INTO THE SYRIAN CAMP
DISGUISED AS A LOVER OF HOLIFERIUS AND ENCHANT
HIM TO COME TO HER, SO SHE CUT OFF HIS HEAD
PLACING IT ON THE ISRAELI WALL, THE SYRIANS SAW IT AND FLED

THEY JUST DON'T WANT YOU TO KNOW ABOUT HEROIC SACRIFICES
WHERE PEOPLE WENT TO THEIR DEATHS TO SAVE OTHER LIVES
THE TROUBLE WAS THEY DIDN'T CLAIM TO BE KING
THEY WERE JUST LOYAL TO GOD AND STILL SAVED EVERYTHING

THERE WAS ELEAZAR MACCABEES WHO SPIED ON THE KING'S ELEPHANT
HE RAN THROUGH A GAUNTLET AND STABBED IT, BUT IT FELL ON HIM
THOUGH HE NEVER SAID THIS HEROISM WOULD SAVE THE WORLD
HE DIED TO SAVE HIS COUNTRY FROM SLAVERY BY THE SELEUCIDS

THE ONLY MIRACLE WAS THAT OF A FLAME
THAT KEPT ON BURNING AGAIN AND AGAIN
BUT IT SHOWED THAT A PERSON COULD BE SAVED BY WORKS
THEY WORSHIPED GOD, NOT A LOT OF FICTIONAL JERKS

THE REASON THE APOCRYPHA WAS REMOVED FROM BEING BIBLICAL
THOUGH THE LADY AND SONS THREW THEMSELVES IN BOILING OIL
IS THAT THOUGH THEY ARE HISTORY, THEY ARE NOT DIVINELY INSPIRED
THIS WAS GIVING UP OF LIFE WAS ONLY BY WORKS AND NOT FAITH AS REQUIRED

THIS SOUNDS LIKE SAINT PAUL ARGUING WITH JAMES
THE BROTHER OF JESUS AND JERUSALEM COURT WAS HIS FAME
WHO CONTINUALLY ARGUED ABOUT HAVING FAITH OR WORKS
WHERE JESUS SAYS, MARY'S FAITH IS GREATER THAN MARTHA WHO COOKS

THE FAITH OF THE MACCABEES SURPASSED THEM ALL
THEY WOULD HAVE THOUGHT OF BAAL AS BANAL
ONLY THEIR GOD WAS MAJESTIC FOR THEM
THEY WERE NOT AWAITING ANY SAVIOR BUT HIM

GOD WAS THEIR SAVIOR AND WAS TO BE THE MESSIAH
IN HIS PROTEAN WAY, HE BECAME JESUS TO SAVE US
THERE IS ONLY ONE GOD, AND THAT'S ALL THAT'S REQUIRED
WE DON'T NEED A TRINITY THAT'S HUMANLY INSPIRED

ESPECIALLY ONE CONJURED UP BY AN UNCHRISTIAN EMPEROR
IT MAY HAVE UNIFIED HIS EMPIRE, BUT IT CREATED THE ALLAH
AND HIS HOARDS OF ISHMAELITES WITH WARS WE'RE STILL FIGHTING
I'M SURE GOD WILL FORGIVE US AS THE HOLY SPIRIT IS LIKE LIGHTNING
COMING AND GOING AT WILL OR OUR BECKON CALL
FOR IT IS WHAT FORMED THE UNIVERSE AND THE GODS ALL

WE CAN TAKE BOOKS OUT OF THE BIBLE, BUT IT DOESN'T CHANGE HISTORY
WE CAN RE-WRITE THE BOOKS TO RE-INTERPRET TO SUIT RELIGION'S MYSTERY
BUT IT DOESN'T ALTER REALITY IN ANY WAY, SHAPE, OR FORM
THE APOCRYPHA IS STILL HISTORY; THERE'S NO REASON TO TRANSFORM

RB WELSH, 5 28 21

JONAH PREDICTION

WHY WOULD GOD CARE IF THE ASSYRIANS REPENTED
THEY HAD NEVER WORSHIPED GOD, WHOM PERHAPS THEY RESENTED
THEY HAD CARRIED OFF GOD'S PEOPLE, THE ISRAELITES
GOD SHOULD HAVE RESCUED THEM FROM THE INVITES

JONAH MUST HAVE SENSED THIS AS A PREDICAMENT
HE WANTED NOTHING TO DO WITH SAVING NINEVEH
BEING A PROPHET, HE COULD FORESEE EVENTS OF THE FUTURE
GOD'S REPUTATION HAD PRECEDED HIM, AND CONJECTURE

THOSE EVENTS WOULD END UP LIKE GOD'S SHADE TREE,
THAT GETTING NINEVEH TO REPENT WOULD BE A DISASTER.
IF ANYTHING, GOD SHOULD FORGIVE THE ISRAELITES,
WHO WERE NOW ENSLAVED BY THE NINEVITES.

RETURN THEM BACK TO ISRAEL WHERE THEY COULD REPENT
JUDAH HAS BEEN SAVED BY CYRUS, HEAVEN SENT TO
RECOMBINE THE TWO NATIONS INTO A SOLID COUNTRY
HAVING ALTARS TO GOD WHERE THEY COULD WORSHIP REGULARLY.

JONAH COULD THEN COOL DOWN FROM HIS RANTING AND RAILING
FOR THINGS WOULD RETURN TO NORMAL WITH GOD AS THEIR KING.

RB WELSH, 5 29 21

TRINITY VIEW

ON THE WAY TO DAMASCUS, PAUL SAW THE LIGHT
AND HEARD THE VOICE OF JESUS THE CHRIST
SAYING, PAUL, WHY DO YOU PERSECUTE ME
FOR I AM A PART OF THE TRINITY

FIRST, THERE WAS GOD, OR WAS IT THE SPIRIT
THAT CREATED THE UNIVERSE AND ALL OF THE PLANETS
LETTING GOD OUR FATHER CREATE THIS HEAVEN AND EARTH
THEN TOLD A VIRGIN THAT SHE WOULD GIVE BIRTH

TO A HOLY BABY TO BE CALLED THE SON OF GOD
THUS THE EXPECTED MESSIAH FINALLY ARRIVED
AS HUMAN AS FEMALE AS GOD AND SPIRIT IN UNITY
SO THAT'S WHY JESUS IS CALLED PART OF THE TRINITY

I KNOW YOU LOVE GOD AND FOLLOW HIS COMMANDMENTS
EXCEPT FOR ONE TIME WHEN YOU FELL FOR ENCHANTMENTS
BUT WE HAVE BEEN FORGIVEN FOR ALL THIS
FOR THEY WILL LISTEN AND CANCEL A REMISS

WHEN DIAGRAMMED, THEY APPEAR AS A TRIANGLE
WHEN IT REALLY SHOULD BE AS A MANDALA
FOR THE HOLY SPIRIT IS ALWAYS THE APEX
GOD AND JESUS BELOW, WHICH DOESN'T MAKE SENSE

IF THEY WERE DEPICTED AS ONENESS IN A MANDALA
IT WOULD BE EQUAL CONFIGURATIONS IN A CIRCLE
WAS IT JESUS WHO PROMISED ABRAHAM
THE GARDEN OF ISRAEL AS THE PROMISED LAND

WAS IT THE HOLY SPIRIT THAT SENT THE CHILDREN TO EGYPT
TO ESCAPE THE HOLOCAUST OF FAMINES, THAT WERE FREQUENT
FINALLY, TO BE ENSLAVED WHILE GOD WAS AWAY
THE ONLY WAY TO ESCAPE WAS GOD SENDING TEN PLAGUES

WAS IT THE SPIRIT OR JESUS WHO CALLED FROM THE BUSH
ORDERING MOSES TO TAKE OFF HIS SANDALS, IT'S GOD, OF COURSE
THEN YOU PRAY FOR SOMEBODY WHO IS NOW SICK
WHO GETS THEM WELL? IS IT GOD OR JESUS OR THE HOLY SPIRIT
NO, I COVERED ALL BASES AND PRAYED TO THE TRINITY

WORSHIPING BAAL IS LIKE WORSHIPING SATAN
FOR JUDAH ALSO HAD THE BAAL INFATUATION
WHEN GOD SENT THEM OFF TO THEIR EXTERMINATION
NO ONE WAS LEFT OF GOD'S CREATION

RB WELSH, 5 22 21

NATURE

HOW DOES JESUS SERMON PERTAIN TO ME?
HE ONLY SPEAKS OF A STORMS HE HALTED ON THE SEA
BUT WE COULD IF WE ONLY HAD FAITH
EVEN WALK ON WATER OR BLAST OFF IN SPACE

JESUS NEVER SAW IT SNOW IN ISRAEL
IT WAS ALWAYS SUMMER OR SPRING, WITH THE AIR BEING STILL
STORMS ON THE SEA WERE NEVER HURRICANES OR TORNADOES
THERE WERE NO SUCH THINGS AS EARTHQUAKES OR VOLCANOES

A RICH MAN WENT TO HELL FOR BUILDING MORE BARNS
TO GET RICHER FROM STORING UP WHEAT ON HIS FARM (LK 12:16)
BUT PHARAOH PRAISED JOSEPH DURING THE SEVEN YEAR FAMINE (GEN 41:54)
BY MAKING HIM RULER FOR PROPHESYING, THIS WOULD SOON HAPPEN

JESUS JUST EXPERIENCED THE LILIES OF THE FIELD
OF DEEP SNOWS IN WINTER, HE NEVER DREAMED
HE HASN'T HAD HIS HOUSE JUST BLOWN AWAY,
BY A HURRICANE OR TORNADO, IN A SECOND ON ONE DAY

WERE THERE NEVER ANY FLOODS IN ISRAEL
HE WOULD JUST SNAP HIS FINGERS, AND THE WATERS WOULD STILL
SO DO WE TAKE THIS SERMON ON THE MOUNT WITH A GRAIN OF SALT
HOW DOES JUST FEEDING THE POOR GIVE THE PROPER RESULT

THERE SHOULD BE NO HANDICAPPED OR POOR AS FAR AS I CAN SEE
MAN SHOULD BE BORN MENTALLY AND PHYSICALLY ABLE AS GUARANTEED
NO, IT IS NOW NECESSARY TO INVENT A VACCINE
INOCULATE EVERYONE FOR COVID-NINETEEN

IF WE CONTRACT COVID NINETEEN OR SOME OTHER DISEASE
A WAVE OF THE HAND SHOULD CURE OR HEAL IT WITH EASE
WE FED THE HOMELESS PUT THEM UP IN HOTELS
NOW IS IT POSSIBLE THEY'LL BECOME RELIABLE SELVES

WHAT DO WE DO WITH PROBLEMS LIKE THESE?
FOR THE COVID CRASH, DEVELOP A SUCCESSFUL VACCINE
THEN WE'LL KNOW ALL THIS HAS BEEN MIRACULOUS
EVEN SO, DENY HIM THREE TIMES, TAKING AWAY ALL THIS TRUST

EVERY NOW AND THEN, WE HEAR
OF SOME UNHEARD OF MIRACULOUS CURE
OF SOMEONE BEING CURED OF A DREADED DISEASE
WITH NO HOPE NOW, HE'S WELL BUT WITH NO GUARANTEE

LAZARUS WAS ONLY HUMAN AND WOULD EVENTUALLY DIE
HE WASN'T A GOD-LIKE JESUS WHO IS ALWAYS ALIVE
WHO FEEDS AND CURES HERE AND THERE, THOUGH ALL BELIEVE
IT'S LIKE THROWING THE DICE OR SPINNING THE ROULETTE WHEEL

AS TO WHICH ONE OF US WILL MAKE IT THROUGH LIFE'S WAR
BLESSED WITHOUT BIRTH BLEMISHES HUNGER, OR MORE
IS IMPOSSIBLE NOW, FOR THAT'S RESERVED FOR ETERNITY
TO FLIT ABOUT AS AN ICON WITHOUT NEGATIVITY

IF JESUS DIED ON THE CROSS SHEDDING HIS BLOOD FOR US
HOW IS IT POSSIBLE TO EAT HIS FLESH AND DRINK MORE BLOOD?
FOR WHEN THE ROMAN SOLDIER PIERCED JESUS'S SIDE
BLOOD AND WATER ISSUED FORTH, PROVING HE WAS NO LONGER ALIVE

JUST THINK HOW MIRACULOUS IT IS TO EAT BREAD AND DRINK WINE
IT IS JESUS, NOT GEORGE WASHINGTON, WHO WAS DEAD AND NOW ALIVE
WHERE ARE GOD AND THE HOLY SPIRIT IN ALL THIS CEREMONY?
THEY HAVE BEEN IGNORED FOR THE MOMENT, THOUGH THEY'RE IN MAN'S TRINITY.

IT SEEMS THAT DEATH SEEMS MORE IMPORTANT THAN LIFE ITSELF
WHETHER NATURALLY OR BY VIOLENT DRUG DOSES OR ELSE
OUR SPIRITS WILL BE RAISED FROM HERE TO SOME ETERNAL SOUL
WHETHER TO HEAVEN OR STRETCHED OUT FOREVER IN A BLACK HOLE

IT SEEMS THERE'S NEVER ANY PROGRESS WITHOUT A BIG WAR
THEIR TROOPS SHEDDING BLOOD AND DYING WITH HONOR AND VALOR
THEIR LEADERSHIP PROVES THEIR TRUSTWORTHINESS TO LEAD
SO INSTALL THEM AS PRESIDENT; IT'S PREDESTINATED CONCEIVED

JESUS REMINDS US NEVER TO WORRY
BUT IT'S THE RICH WHO GIVE TO CHARITY
SO WE POOR PRAY TO GOD TO GIVE US THE WEALTHY
SO THEY CAN PROVIDE FUNDS TO KEEP US HEALTHY

IT'S LIKE WE ARE ONLY THE BABY BIRD
WHO DEPENDS ON ITS MOTHER TO GIVE IT THE WORM
SO WHEN I PRAY, IT'S FOR MORE AND MORE THAT I DESIRE
FOR IF I HAVE FAITH, HEALTH AND PLENTY WILL BE ACQUIRED

RB WELSH, 6 1 21

TRUTH

YE SHALL KNOW THE TRUTH, AND IT WILL MAKE YOU FREE
THE BIBLE IS THE SYMBOL OF TRUTH IN EVERYTHING YOU READ
GOD CAN GIVE ORDERS TO MOSES FROM A BURNING BUSH
CHALLENGE JOSHUA AT THE GATES OF JERICHO IN LIVING FLESH

GOD APPEARED TO ABRAHAM FOR A PICNIC IN THE PARK
WITH THE MOTIVE OF IMPREGNATING SARAH FOR ISAAC
AS A DIVINE INTERVENTION, THE PROMISE KEPT
GENERATIONS OF HEBREWS EMANCIPATED FROM HER TENT

GOD COULD HAVE, AS IN THE GOSPEL OF MARK
APPEARED FULLY GROWN AS THE EXPECTED MESSIAH
OR SOMEHOW JUST BEING BORN OF A VIRGIN
WITH GOD AS THE FATHER IN LUKE'S VERSION

GOD, AS IT WAS ARGUED LAST WEEK, BECOME A WHALE
SAVING JONAH, WHO LIVED IN ITS BELLY THREE DAYS
THAT' MUST HAVE BEEN LIKE DESCENDING INTO HELL
BUT UNLIKE JESUS, WHO SAVED SINNERS, JONAH REBELLED

THIS IS THE PROOF OF GOD-LOVING ONE'S ENEMIES
FOR IT WAS GENTILES WHO TOOK JESUS IN THE GARDEN OF GETHSEMANE
HE WANTS TO SAVE EVERYONE, EVEN NINEVEH
JESUS SAID, JUST REPENT. YOU WILL ALWAYS BE FORGIVEN.

RB WELSH, 6 4 21

JOSEPH'S VERSION

MY NAME IS JOSEPH HAVING A HOME IN NAZARETH
I HAVE BEEN IN A SITUATION THAT YOU JUST CAN'T IMAGINE
I AM RESPONSIBLE AS A STONE MASON OR CARPENTER
BETROTHED TO A GIRL AND TRIED TO KEEP CHARMING HER

TAKING OUR VOWS AT QUMRAN AS CUSTOM REQUIRES
WE'VE HAD TO SUPPRESS OUR NATURAL DESIRES
WHILE LIVING TOGETHER ALL OF THESE MONTHS
WE'VE HAD TO SEE IF WE ARE COMPATIBLE AND IF WE MUST

THEN OUT OF ALL THE HOMES IN NAZARETH OR EVEN IN THE WORLD
AN ANGEL STEPS IN, SAYING MARY IS TO BEAR THE CHILD OF THE LORD
GOD IS TO TAKE OVER AS THE BABY'S FATHER, AS PROPHESIED BY ISAIAH
TO TEACH HIM OF HIS WAYS AND BECOME THE MESSIAH

I CAN SEE RIGHT NOW THAT TONGUES WILL BE WAGGING
SHE'S ONLY SIXTEEN YEARS OLD, AND HE'S TAKEN ADVANTAGE
BUT WHEN I WAS GOING TO THREATEN TO PUT HER AWAY
AN ANGEL STEPPED IN, PERSUADING ME TO STAY

SO IF BY NOW YOU BELIEVE ALL OF THIS
JUST STICK AROUND; THIS ONLY BEGINS
YOU COULDN'T MAKE THIS UP IN A THOUSAND YEARS
A TRINITY OF GODS, THE HOLY SPIRIT GOD, AND MARY

RUMORS ABOUNDED OF A COMING MESSIAH
TO RID US OF THE ROMANS WITH THEIR TAXES AND REQUIREMENTS
I KNEW IN A MOMENT THAT THIS WAS TO BE HE
THE CHILD OF MY WIFE, THE VIRGIN MARY

NOW THIS STORY BECOMES MORE BIZARRE
THE ROMANS HAVE CALLED FOR A CENSUS OF ALL
SO WE TRAVELED ON DONKEYS IN HER CONDITION
BACK TO BETHLEHEM, WHERE THERE'S NO PLACE TO STAY IN

THEY SAID A STAR WAS FOLLOWING JUST OVERHEAD
PROPHESIED BY THE FALSE PROPHET BALAAM WHO SAID
THE STAR OF JACOB WILL ANNOUNCE OVERHEAD
THE BIRTH OF THE MESSIAH WHO WILL RULE THE WORLD

AS SOON AS THE BABY WAS BORN, IT WAS TELEGRAPHED
ALL OVER THE WORLD, AS KINGS AND MAGI BRING GIFTS
BUT HEROD IS WORRIED ABOUT ANY KING
WHO IS BORN TO RULE, SO THIS IS STARTLING

WHEN HE ORDERS THE KILLING OF ALL BABIES
AN ANGEL TELLS ME TO TAKE MARY AND FLEE
DOWN TO EGYPT TILL THE KING HEROD IS DEAD
WE GO BACK TO QUMRAN, TWENTY MILES AWAY INSTEAD

SO, IN ADDITION TO JESUS GETTING A RELIGIOUS EDUCATION
MARY AND I GET MARRIED COUNTING ON JESUS FOR OUR SALVATION
IF THIS VERSION HAPPENS TO BE TOO COMPLICATED AND SERIOUS
THERE'S ALWAYS THAT OF MARK, WHERE GOD APPEARS AS THE JESUS

RB WELSH, 6 16 21

CURE

I SUSPECT JUST WHAT'S THE REASON
GOD BECAME THE CHRIST TO INCLUDE ALL RACES
GOD IS STILL GOD OF THE HEBREWS
WHICH NOW INCLUDES THE CHINESE TOO.

I DON'T GET IT THOUGH, WHAT'S THE POINT
OF JESUS CURING WITH JUST A TOUCH?
WHEN IT SEEMS LIKE HE COULD HEAL
ALL MEN AT ONCE FROM THEIR ORDEALS.

THEN THAT WOULD INCLUDE
AND CURE ALL KIDS AT ST. JUDE
IT SEEMS TO ME THAT HE CURED TEN MEN OF LEPROSY,
BUT ONLY A SAMARITAN RETURNED TO THANK HIM. (LK 17:11)

PAUL IS FANATICAL IN WHATEVER HE DOES,
HE HAS TO BE BLINDED AND KNOCKED OFF HIS HORSE.
WHILE ON THE WAY, WHICH IS OUT OF HIS JURISDICTION,
TO FIND FOLLOWERS OF CHRIST THAT NEED PERSECUTION.

BUT PAUL WAS CONVERTED AND HEALED THE SICK,
HE WENT OVERBOARD FOR HE WAS A FANATIC.
I GUESS THE ONLY WAY TO KEEP POPULATION DOWN,
IS TO HAVE WAR AND COVID-19 TO CONTROL THE CROWD.

RB WELSH, 5 26 23

JOSEPH'S VERSION

MY NAME IS JOSEPH HAVING A HOME IN NAZARETH
I HAVE BEEN IN A SITUATION THAT YOU JUST CAN'T IMAGINE
I AM RESPONSIBLE AS A STONE MASON OR CARPENTER
BETROTHED TO A GIRL AND TRIED TO KEEP CHARMING HER

TAKING OUR VOWS AT QUMRAN AS CUSTOM REQUIRES
WE'VE HAD TO SUPPRESS OUR NATURAL DESIRES
WHILE LIVING TOGETHER ALL OF THESE MONTHS
WE'VE HAD TO SEE IF WE ARE COMPATIBLE AND IF WE MUST

THEN OUT OF ALL THE HOMES IN NAZARETH OR EVEN IN THE WORLD
AN ANGEL STEPS IN, SAYING MARY IS TO BEAR THE CHILD OF THE LORD
GOD IS TO TAKE OVER AS THE BABY'S FATHER, AS PROPHESIED BY ISAIAH
TO TEACH HIM OF HIS WAYS AND BECOME THE MESSIAH

I CAN SEE RIGHT NOW THAT TONGUES WILL BE WAGGING
SHE'S ONLY SIXTEEN YEARS OLD, AND HE'S TAKEN ADVANTAGE
BUT WHEN I WAS GOING TO THREATEN TO PUT HER AWAY
AN ANGEL STEPPED IN, PERSUADING ME TO STAY

SO IF BY NOW YOU BELIEVE ALL OF THIS
JUST STICK AROUND; THIS ONLY BEGINS
YOU COULDN'T MAKE THIS UP IN A THOUSAND YEARS
A TRINITY OF GODS, THE HOLY SPIRIT GOD, AND MARY

RUMORS ABOUNDED OF A COMING MESSIAH
TO RID US OF THE ROMANS WITH THEIR TAXES AND REQUIREMENTS
I KNEW IN A MOMENT THAT THIS WAS TO BE HE
THE CHILD OF MY WIFE, THE VIRGIN MARY

NOW THIS STORY BECOMES MORE BIZARRE
THE ROMANS HAVE CALLED FOR A CENSUS OF ALL
SO WE TRAVELED ON DONKEYS IN HER CONDITION
BACK TO BETHLEHEM, WHERE THERE'S NO PLACE TO STAY IN

THEY SAID A STAR WAS FOLLOWING JUST OVERHEAD
PROPHESIED BY THE FALSE PROPHET BALAAM WHO SAID
THE STAR OF JACOB WILL ANNOUNCE OVERHEAD
THE BIRTH OF THE MESSIAH WHO WILL RULE THE WORLD

AS SOON AS THE BABY WAS BORN, IT WAS TELEGRAPHED
ALL OVER THE WORLD, AS KINGS AND MAGI BRING GIFTS
BUT HEROD IS WORRIED ABOUT ANY KING
WHO IS BORN TO RULE, SO THIS IS STARTLING

WHEN HE ORDERS THE KILLING OF ALL BABIES
AN ANGEL TELLS ME TO TAKE MARY AND FLEE
DOWN TO EGYPT TILL THE KING HEROD IS DEAD
WE GO BACK TO QUMRAN, TWENTY MILES AWAY INSTEAD

SO, IN ADDITION TO JESUS GETTING A RELIGIOUS EDUCATION
MARY AND I GET MARRIED COUNTING ON JESUS FOR OUR SALVATION
IF THIS VERSION HAPPENS TO BE TOO COMPLICATED AND SERIOUS
THERE'S ALWAYS THAT OF MARK, WHERE GOD APPEARS AS THE JESUS

RB WELSH, 6 16 21

THAT'S HIS JOB

IT'S LIKE BRINGING A LITTLE BIT OF HEAVEN TO EARTH
WHEN JESUS PERFORMS WHAT WE CALL MIRACLES, WE DON'T DESERVE
IF WE MUST WALK UPON WATER
TO KEEP FROM DROWNING THAT'S ANOTHER MATTER

BUT TO DO IT JUST FOR A LARK, IT SEEMS TO ME
TO BE PUSHING MY LUCK JUST TO LOOK HEAVENLY
THOUGH MOST OF THE TIME, I NEED JESUS'S HELP
TO LIVE ONE DAY MORE AND KEEP IN STEP.

THAT'S THE MAIN POINT. I FINALLY GOT IT
THAT'S WHY I PRAY TO THE LORD CONSTANTLY TO LET HIM
HELP ME TO DO WHAT ALWAYS SEEMS IMPOSSIBLE
AS YOU KNOW, I AM MOSTLY IRRESPONSIBLE

I WILL PRACTICE THIS WALKING WHERE IT IS SHALLOW
LIKE LOOKING FOR PENNIES IN A ROMAN FOUNTAIN
EVEN IF MOTHER NATURE IS STILL CREATING THE EARTH
WITH HURRICANES, VOLCANOES, AND FLOODS FOR THE WORLD'S REBIRTH

LIKE ME, THE EARTH NEEDS A NEW BEGINNING
MAN HAS RUINED ITS ATMOSPHERE WITH HIS SINNING
THE CO_2 ATMOSPHERE IS SAID TO BE THE CAUSE
OF ANOTHER ICE AGE AND MELTING WITH MAN'S DEMISE

IF THEY ARE ALL GOING TO HEAVEN ANYWAY
JUST BLOW IT UP AND LET THEM HAVE IT THEIR WAY
THEY CAN LOOK DOWN AND CONTINUE WITH THEIR CURSE
SEE, I TOLD YOU SO, BUT YOU GOT WHAT YOU DESERVE

IT'S ALL THIS ANIMOSITY THAT GETS ON MY NERVES
WE'LL ONLY BE FREE, BUT THE TRUTH'S IN REVERSE
EVEN IF I ADMIT AND CONFESS MY GUILT ALL THE TIME
WHAT HAPPENED STILL NAGS AND PESTERS MY MIND

NO WONDER SOME HERMITS TAKE REFUGE
INTO NATURE TO LIVE ALONE WITHOUT BOTHERSOME NEWS
OF WHAT ONE PERSON OR COUNTRY DID TO ANOTHER
THAT CAUSES ENMITY LEADING TO TARIFFS OR WAR

YES, PETER WAS RIGHT IN HIS ATTEMPT TO WALK ON WATER
HIS FAITH GAVE OUT ON HIS THIRD STEP, AND HE FALTERED
THAT IS WHY SOME ARE BELIEVERS AND OTHERS UNSURE
IT'S BECAUSE THERE ARE QUESTIONABLE FACTS TOO OBSCURE

RB WELSH, 6 28 21

TO BE OR NOT TO BE

TO BE OR NOT TO BE THAT IS THE QUESTION
LETS JUST CALL THEM JSG JUST FOR PERFECTION
INSTEAD OF CELEBRATING ONLY THE BIRTH OF CHRIST
ON DECEMBER TWENTY-FIFTH, JSG WOULD BE RIGHT

WHEN THE ANGEL VISITED MARY AT HIS INCEPTION
SHE WOULD BECOME PREGNANT BY INSUFFLATION
NO WONDER HE WAS CALLED THE SON AND SPIRIT OF GOD
FOR JESUS AS A MIRACLE WAS CONCEIVED BY THEMSELVES

IN THAT CASE, IT IS TRUE THERE IS A TRINITY
FOR JESUS CALLED HIMSELF THE SON OF MAN, NOT THREE
AND THAT WOULD BE JOSEPH, WHO IS MAINLY IGNORED
FOR HE AND MARY LIVED TOGETHER AS BETROTHED

MARY, THE MOTHER, IS COMPLETELY IGNORED
FOR SHE IS BUT THE CARRIER AND BROUGHT HIM UP AS A BOY
IF THERE IS SUCH A THING AS A TRINITY
IT WOULD INCLUDE THE SPIRIT THE CHRIST AND THE MOTHER MARY

BUT JESUS ALWAYS CALLED GOD HIS FATHER
A SEPARATE ENTITY WITH WHOM HE WAS ALWAYS IN PRAYER
THERE IS ONE THING THAT MAKES THEM A TRINITY
THEY ALL HAD THE SAME PERSONALITY

SOMETIMES JESUS SAID HE WOULD HELP THEM BY CALLING ON THE SPIRIT
AS WHEN HE VISITED THE DISCIPLES IN THE UPPER ROOM WHEN HE VISITED
WE SHOULD INCLUDE THE GARDENER FOR MARY THOUGHT JESUS TO BE DEAD
OR THE MAN ON THE WAY TO EMMAUS WHO BROKE BREAD

WE'VE HEARD ABOUT SHAPE-SHIFTERS WHO CAN CHANGE THEMSELVES
FROM ONE FORM TO ANOTHER AT WILL
SO WITH ALL THESE VARIOUS ALTERNATIVES
JUST HOW DID MAN COME UP WITH SUCH A CONCEPT AS A TRINITY

IT WAS COMMON IN MANY OF THE OTHER RELIGIONS
THE PHILOSOPHY OF PLATO AND CONSTANTINE HAD A REASON
IN THE THIRD CENTURY, AT THE COUNCIL OF NICEA
MEN VOTED IN FAVOR OF GOD HOLY SPIRIT AND JESUS BEING ONE

GOD AS ONENESS HIMSELF DID NOT AUTHORIZE
ANYTHING SO STUPID SO HE WAS DEMORALIZED
MEN HAD ALWAYS ERRED WHEN TAKING OVER THEMSELVES
LIKE SARAH GIVING HAGAR TO ABRAHAM NOW WE'LL HAVE TWO REALMS

GOD WAS NOW GOING TO KEEP HIS PROMISE TO ISHMAEL
CREATING HIMSELF AS ALLAH THREE HUNDRED YEARS LATER
ALL THE PRESENT FIASCO OCCURRED WHEN ISLAM WAS BORN
MO HAMMED AS LEADER HAS BEEN A PERPETUAL THORN

SO YOUR SO-CALLED CONCEPT CALLED THE TRINITY
MAY IN THE FUTURE BE REFERRED TO AS A DUALITY
AS GOD IS NOW ABSENT AS AFTER THE HAGAR INCIDENT
HAVING TO RETURN AT MAN'S PRAYER FOR THE EXODUS FROM EGYPT

SO IT'S MAN'S EXISTENTIAL BEING OR BEING DEPENDENT UPON GOD
THERE HAVE BEEN PLAGUES AND COVIDS TO GET RID OF US ALL
YES, GOD IS JESUS IN A PROTEAN WAY SINCE HE CAN APPEAR TO EVE AS A SNAKE
SO I WILL HAVE TO AGREE THAT IF THIS IS SO, THERE IS A TRINITY

RB WELSH, 6 4 21

STORM AT SEA

THIS IS A STORY ABOUT HAVING FAITH
AND IT'S A BAD EXAMPLE IN THE FIRST PLACE
THESE WERE ALL EXPERIENCED SAILORS
WHO HAD BEEN IN SUCH STORMS WITH NO FAILURES

IN THE FIRST PLACE, NO ONE IN A STORM IS EVER ASLEEP
WITH THE BOAT PITCHING AND YAWING, HEARING THE WIND SHRIEK
THIS STORY IS SO OBVIOUSLY CONTRIVED
BY SOME LANDLUBBER NEVER ON A BOAT RIDE

ABRAHAM WAS OBEDIENT WHEN TOLD TO SACRIFICE ISAAC
HE KNEW ISHMAEL WAS THE FIRSTBORN, SO THEY WOULD BE BACK
CONSEQUENTLY, THERE WAS NO PROBLEM WITH HIS HAVING FAITH
THEOLOGIANS ARE ALWAYS STRETCHING THE TRUTH TO MAKE THEIR CASE

THE SADDEST STORY IN HISTORY
AND STILL IS TO ALL A BIG MYSTERY
IS ABOUT THE SINKING IN ICEBERGS OF THE TITANIC
FOR THE FAITH OF ITS CAPTAIN IN SAILING THE ATLANTIC

RB WELSH, 6 11 21

QUANDARY

WITH THE CHILDREN OF ISRAEL IN THE PROMISED LAND
GOD EXPRESSED HIS ONENESS FOR THEIR BELIEF IN HIM
FOR THEY WERE TO WORSHIP HIM, NOT AN IDOL OR KING
BUT THERE WAS ALSO THE PROMISE OF A MESSIAH FORTHCOMING

THEY HADN'T WORSHIPED ATON OR THE BULL AS SLAVES IN EGYPT
WHERE THE TRINITARIAN GOD ISIS, OSIRIS, AND HORUS WAS WORSHIPED
BUT IN CANAAN, THERE WAS THE CONVENIENCE OF BAAL
WITH HIS ALTARS AND TEMPLES WERE AVAILABLE EVERYWHERE

I'M OW ASKING MYSELF, HAVE I NOT BEEN BRAIN-WASHED
WITH JESUS, THE ONENESS OF OF GOD HAS NOW BEEN HALVED
THE TRINITY WON'T BECOME THE BELIEF TILL NICEA IN 300 CE
SO FOR THREE HUNDRED YEARS, THE DUALITY'S THE BELIEF

WE NEVER HEARD A BIBLICAL REPORT ABOUT THE MARRIAGE
OF ISAIAH'S PROPHESIED COUPLE, JOSEPH AND MARY
BUT WE CAN READ OF THESE CEREMONIES AT THE ESSENES
WHERE THERE WERE BOTH BETROTHAL AND MARRIAGE SCENES

THE CATHOLICS HAVE NOW IMMORTALIZED MARY
IT'S NOW A FOURSOME WITH ROSARY BEADS TO CARRY
SO WE WONDER ABOUT JOSEPH'S PART IN THIS BIRTHING SCENE
MAYBE IT WOULD BE BETTER TO NAME GOD THE INFINITY

RB WELSH, 7 11 21

CONVERSION OF SAUL

WHAT IS IT THAT WE KNOW ABOUT THE JEW NAMED SAUL
THE TENTMAKER OF TARSUS PROFICIENT IN GOD'S LAW
WHO STUDIED THE TORAH UNDER GAMALIEL
PERSECUTING BELIEVERS IN JESUS WITH PHARISAIC ZEAL

ROUNDING UP PEOPLE OF THE WAY
HIS TROOP STONED THEM OR PUT THEM IN JAIL
AFTER STEPHEN DIED AFTER BEING STONED
JESUS DECIDED TO MAKE SAUL ATONE

JAILING BELIEVERS WAS ONE THING
BUT KILLING NEW CHRISTIANS WAS SERIOUS INDEED
JESUS LAMENTED THIS SERIOUS LOSS
ENDING UP GIVING SAUL A SERIOUS RIGHT CROSS

JESUS WAS TIRED OF TURNING HIS OTHER CHEEK
THIS WAS A NEW RELIGION WITH ITS MYSTIQUE
THE CAMEL'S BACK WAS BROKEN WHEN STEPHEN DIED
JESUS HAD HAD ENOUGH THAT HIS PATIENCE WAS TRIED

SAUL WAS BLINDED AND KNOCKED OFF HIS HORSE
HE HAD TO BE HALTED FROM HIS INSOLENT COURSE
JESUS HAD CONVERTED SAUL INSTANTLY
ASKING WHY DO YOU PERSIST IN PERSECUTING ME

SAUL BECAME FANATICAL IN HIS JESUS' BELIEF
THE COMMANDMENTS OF GOD WERE IN JEOPARDY
HEBREWS HAD ONCE TURNED TO BAAL AND BEING EXILED
HERE AGAIN, HIS GOD SHOULD HAVE BEEN RILED

WHEN PEOPLE FINALLY SEE THE LIGHT
IT IS THEIR CALL TO BELIEVE IN THE RISEN CHRIST
BUT THIS TIME, JESUS KNOCKED SAUL OFF OF HIS HORSE
BLINDING HIM AS WELL, IT ALTERED HIS COURSE

PAUL WAS CONVERTED IN A TWINKLING OF AN EYE
BECOMING SO FANATICAL IT WAS AS IF GOD HAD DIED
THE SPIRIT OF CHRIST SUPERSEDED GOD'S LAW
PAUL WAS SPREADING THE WORD CLAIMING TO BE AN APOSTLE

BECOMING NOW MORE FANATICAL THAN EVER BEFORE
IN SPREADING THE WORD GOING OUT TO THE WORLD
IMAGINING GREEKS COULD READ HEBREW IS A MYSTERY
NEVERTHELESS, SAUL BECAME PAUL TO CHANGE HISTORY

THERE IS NO RECORD OF HIS BEGGING FORGIVENESS
FOR THE MURDER OF STEPHEN AND OTHER CHRISTIANS

AFTER BEING ARRESTED FOR CONSTANT AGITATIONS
RESULTING IN IMPRISONMENT FOR ROMAN VIOLATIONS
ENCOURAGING LETTERS WERE SENT TO VISITED CITIES
URGING THEM TO REMAIN FAITHFUL AND SPIRITUAL CHRISTIANS

RB WELSH, 7 18 21

JESUS SAID

I AM THE BREAD OF LIFE
THAT WHICH SUSTAINS YOU, SO YOU SURVIVE

I AM THE LIGHT
OF PEACE AND LOVE ETERNAL AND BRIGHT

I AM THE DOOR
TO HEAVEN WITH GOD AND ALL YOURS

I AM THE GOOD SHEPHERD
WHO GUIDES AND PROTECTS WITH THE WORD

I AM THE RESURRECTION AND THE LIFE
IN THIS CREATION AS YOUR PERFECT GUIDE

I AM THE WAY THE TRUTH AND THE LIFE
FOLLOW ME SPEAK THE TRUTH TO AVOID STRIFE

I AM THE VINE
THE AFFINITY MAKES YOUR BRANCHES DIVINE

RB WELSH, 7 21 21

BIZARRE

GOD HAS FORGOTTEN HIS WIFE SOPHIA
IN FAVOR OF MARY OF JUDEA
TAKING HER TO HAVE A CHILD
FOR BEING A VIRGIN, SHE IS SURPRISED

GOD'S MOTIVE IS TO BECOME A MAN
HAVING A MIND LIKE JESUS TO UNDERSTAND
THEN EXPLAIN TO THEM IN THEIR TERMS
HIS LAW FED THE POOR AND HEALED THE INFIRM

SOME JESUS STORIES ARE BIZARRE
SHE'S ALREADY PREGNANT BUT ALARMED
THEY LIVE IN NAZARETH, BUT HE'S BORN IN BETHLEHEM
AFTER REGISTERING FOR THE CENSUS IN JERUSALEM

THIS TIME THE FAMILY GOES TO CELEBRATE PASSOVER
JESUS REMAINS BOUND, STUDYING TORAH AT THE TEMPLE
SHE KNOWS WHO JESUS IS
BUT IS SURPRISED HE'S MISSING

THIS IS TYPICAL OF MARY NOT MAKING SURE JESUS IS WITH THE PARTY
RETURNING TO NAZARETH AFTER CELEBRATING FOR A WEEK IN JERUSALEM.

IT IS LIKE LUKE'S VERSION OF JESUS' BIRTH WHERE SHE IS BETROTHED TO
JOSEPH, WHICH IS A CEREMONY ALMOST LIKE A WEDDING TO SEE IF THE
COUPLE IS COMPATIBLE AND THEY LIVE TOGETHER. SHE CLAIMS SHE HAS NOT
KNOWN A MAN, BUT SOME SEMEN MUST HAVE SLIPPED THROUGH THE CRACKS.
FOR AS LUKE SAYS, SHE IS IN HER SIXTH MONTH.

THEN AT CANA OF GALILEE, THEY ARE AT A WEDDING, AND MARY ASKS JESUS
TO PRODUCE MORE WINE...AND HE HAS NEVER BEFORE PERFORMED ANY
MIRACLE UNLESS AS A KID IT IS REPORTED HE MADE MUD-PIE SPARROWS-, BUT
THE POINT IS

HE WANTS TO SAVE HIS MIRACLES TO FEED THE POOR AND CURE THE LAME
BEFORE ACHIEVING FAME BY GETTING PEOPLE DRUNKER.

SO THIS IS TYPICAL MARY TO GO OFF TO NAZARETH WITHOUT MAKING SURE
JESUS IS WITH THE PARTY.

RB WELSH, 7 12 20

JUSTIFICATION

IT SEEMS THAT I HAVE A LOT OF FAITH
GIVEN TO ME BY GOD'S GOOD GRACE
IT'S NOT THAT IT'S JUSTIFIED, I WILL ADMIT
BUT IT'S FREE TO THOSE WHO WILLINGLY SUBMIT

JUST WHERE DO THESE BIG WORDS COME FROM
NOT FROM GOD, WHO'S A SIMPLE BEING WITH US
HE KNOWS OF ALL OF OUR LIMITATIONS
AND INTELLIGENCE IS THE LEAST OF HIS EXPECTATIONS

WE DON'T SEEK GOD; HE IS LOOKING FOR US
TO CAPTURE EVERY SOUL IN HIS BOOK OF LOVE
MOST PEOPLE ALWAYS TRY TO RUN AWAY
HIDING THEIR SIN FROM HIM EVERY DAY

BUT FOOLING ONLY THEMSELVES, OF COURSE
FOR HE HAS HIS FINGER ON EVERY PULSE
BUT AFTER A WHILE, WE ALL SUBMIT
SURRENDERING TO HIS GRACE THOUGH WE'RE UNFIT

WE TIRE OF PLODDING THE WAY THROUGH LIFE
OUR INSPIRATIONS SEEM TO LEAD TO STRIFE
HAPPY IS THE MAN WHO SITS IN GOD'S LAP
WITH LOVING ARMS AROUND HIM CONTINUALLY WRAPPED

GIVING HIM THANKS FOR EVERY BENEVOLENCE
ALSO BLAMING HIM TOO FOR ALL CONDOLENCES
FOR HE IS THE SOURCE OF EVERYTHING
THE GOOD, THE BAD, AND THE UGLY

SO GOD GIVETH AND HE TAKETH AWAY
HE IS THE MESSIAH, SO THROUGH HIM, WE CAN PRAY
SO WE GET DOWN ON OUR KNEES AND BEG
FOR JUSTIFICATION OF GRACE THROUGH FAITH

RB WELSH, 7 22 21

THE PATRIARCHS

THE PATRIARCHS ARE ABRAHAM ISAAC, JACOB, AND JOSEPH
THE STORY IS LITERAL, NOT EMBELLISHED WITH WHITEWASHES
THE HISTORY OF ISRAEL, ITS DOOMS, AND THE FAILURES OF THE NATION
THE FATHERS OF GOD'S CHOSEN RACE IN EXAMINATION

THIS IS GOING TO BE MY INTERPRETATION
OF WHAT THERE IS IN BIBLICAL SAYINGS
THEOLOGIANS GIVE THEIR SLANTS
SINCE THEY ARE HOLIER THAN THOU AND YOU WON'T OR CAN'T

IN THE BEGINNING, WAS THE WORD
THE STARS IN THE HEAVENS AND THE EARTH
A GARDEN WITH ONLY ONE FORBIDDEN TREE
ATTRACTIVE AS KNOWLEDGE BY ADAM AND EVE

EACH STAR MUST HAVE HAD ITS RACE OF MEN
WHO FOUND EARTH'S WOMEN ATTRACTIVE TO THEM?
FOR THEY INFILTRATED WI TH THESE OTHER RACES
THE ORIENTAL THE INDIAN NORDICS FROM OUTER SPACE

THIS INCENSED GOD, WHO BROUGHT ON THE FLOOD
RAISING ENOCH TO HEAVEN NOAH AND ANIMALS IN A BOAT
MAKING COVENANTS WITH HIM OF A RAINBOW
AND ANOTHER TO NOT TO EAT OF LIFE'S BLOOD Gen 9:4

IT SEEMS THAT SOMEHOW OUR SAINT PAUL FORGOT
WHEN HE TOLD THE CORINTHIANS TO EAT JESUS'S BLOOD
TO GET INTERCESSION ABOUT WORRY AND TRIAL
DO WHATEVER WORKS, EVEN JUST FOR A WHILE

THEN GOD DECIDED ON HEBREWS TO BE HIS CHOSEN RACE
TO MAKE A COVENANT WITH ABRAM GIVING HIM A PROPER PLACE
SIGNIFIED BY CIRCUMCISION OF MEN'S FORESKINS
NOT OF THEIR HEARTS OR BRAINS WRITING HIS LAW ON THEM

IT 'S A FUNNY THING ABOUT OUR PATRIARCHS
YOU'D THINK ALL WAS PERFECTION RIGHT FROM THE START
BUT WITH THE SHORTAGE OF PEOPLE IN HARAN
ABRAM AND SARAI HAD THE SAME FATHER

GOD SEEMED TO HAVE TAKEN NO NOTICE OF THIS
WHEN HE MADE A COVENANT FOR HIS CHOSEN RACE
IN THESE DAYS OF SCIENCE, WE NOW KNOW
BROTHERS AND SISTERS HAVE CHILDREN DEFORMED

SO IF YOU THINK EVE'S EATING AN APPLE IS BAD
WHAT ABOUT ORDERING YOUR HUSBAND TO COMMIT ADULTERY
THINKING THIS WOULD FINALLY GET GOD'S LEGACY
TO CARRY ON THE RACE WITH THE PROMISED BLESSING

AFTER GOD SUDDENLY REALIZED THAT THE RACE WOULD BE DEFILED
HE PUT A HALT TO SARAI HAVING THE PROMISED CHILD
PERFORMING THE FEAT HIMSELF, VISITING HER IN HER TENT
AFTER THE PICNIC AT MAMRE, AS HE WAS A HUMAN PROTEAN

SO THE APOSTLE'S CREED SHOULD AVOID
STATING JESUS IS "HIS ONLY SON, OUR LORD"
FOR ISAAC ALSO WAS TO BE SACRIFICED
INSTEAD OF THE FIRSTBORN, ISHMAEL BORN OF ABRAHAM'S VICE

MUCH IS MADE OF ABRAHAM'S FAITH
IN GOING TO MOUNT MORIAH, WHERE JESUS WAS SLAIN
HIS FAITH MUST HAVE BEEN THAT ISAAC WOULD NOT BE BURNED
TELLING THE DONKEY ATTENDEES THAT *THEY* BOTH WOULD RETURN

DID YOU NOTICE THAT THIS TIME ABRAHAM DIDN'T ARGUE
WITH GOD LIKE HE DID AT SODOM AND GOMORRAH
WHEN HE KEPT ASKING, "WHAT IF THERE ARE MAYBE TEN MEN"
HE JUST PICKED UP ISAAC THE FIREWOOD AND WENT

SINCE A RAM CAUGHT IN A THICKET WAS SUBSTITUTED FOR ISAAC
IT'S SURMISED THAT NOW GOD NOW PREFERS ANIMAL SACRIFICES
EXCEPT FOR THE EGYPTIAN FIRSTBORN SLAIN DURING THE EXODUS
WITH ATONEMENT BEING MADE WITH THE CRUCIFIXION OF JESUS

FOR THE TWO DAYS WHILE THEY WERE GONE
SARAH'S HAIR MUST HAVE TURNED WHITE BEING FRANTIC SO LONG
THEN FOR NO REASON, GOD BECAME ABSENT FOR 400 YEARS
THE PROMISED LAND TURNED TO SAND JORDAN'S SEA LIKE LOT'S WIFE TO SALT

THE ILLEGAL ALIENS FLOODED INTO EGYPT
SARAH WAS HIDDEN IN A CASKET BUT WAS CAUGHT
AND SINCE SHE WAS THE MOST BEAUTIFUL WOMAN SINCE EVE
INSTEAD OF PHARAOH KILLING ABRAHAM, GOD ORDERED HIS REPRIEVE

THOUGH NEVER PERFORMING MIRACLES, ONE
ISAAC AND REBEKAH HAD TWO SONS
ESAU, THE FIRSTBORN, WAS BORN TWICE
THE FIRST REBORN PERSON JESUS COULD HAVE IDENTIFIED

ESAU IN BEING LITERALLY REBORN
ACQUIRED THE FAMILY BIRTHRIGHT, THE CAUSE OF HIS SCORN
FOR HE HAD BEEN DUPED OUT OF THIS BIRTHRIGHT
BY REBEKAH AND JACOB DEVIOUS FAMILY OF ISAAC

CAN YOU BELIEVE
ESAU TRADED HIS BIRTHRIGHT FOR A POT OF LENTILS
JACOB RECEIVES BY DECEPTION THE PROMISED BLESSING
BY LYING TO BLIND ISAAC ABOUT BEING ESAU WITH GOAT HAIRDRESSING

SAYING <u>YOUR LORD</u> HELPED ME IN KILLING THE GAME YOU ARE RELISHING
SO NOW, FATHER, GIVE ME THE BLESSING
AFTER WHICH HIS BROTHER WAS STUPEFIED
THREATENING TO KILL JACOB AS SOON AS HE COULD FIND

BUT REBEKAH, IN HER PRECOGNITIVE WAY
SENT JACOB OFF TO HARAN OUT OF HARM'S WAY
TO GET FOR HIMSELF A WIFE
FROM THE SAME CLAN, AGAIN DECEPTIVE WITH VICE

BUT THE LORD, IN HIS MYSTERIOUS WAYS
HE HAD A REPROBATE LIKE JACOB IN HIS SIGHTS TO PROPAGATE
THE HERITAGE OF ALL HIS CHOSEN RACE TO BELIEVE IN
WITH ANGELS ASCENDING AND DESCENDING ON LADDERS AS A VISION

BUT JACOB CONTINUED ON HIS MISSION TO MARY RACHEL
AS THE FIRST GIRL HE MET AND KISSED IN THE CITY, WELL
THEY HAD TO WAIT TILL HE WORKED TWENTY YEARS FOR HER HAND
HAVING TO MARRY HER SISTER THE FIRSTBORN DAUGHTER OF LABAN

ALL THIS WAS PREORDAINED BY GOD IN HIS INTERCEDING
FOR JACOB TO LEARN \CATTLE INTERBREEDING
TO GAIN WEALTH AND FAMILY TO RETURN HOME
STOPPING ON THE BANKS OF THE JABBOCK, HE REMAINED THERE ALONE

ON LEARNING ESAU HAD COME, IT BROUGHT ON GREAT FRIGHT
HE SENT HIS FAMILY ACROSS WITH GIFTS WHILE HE WRESTLED ALL NIGHT
WITH A MYSTERIOUS STRANGER THAT HAD TO BE GOD
FOR HE THREW OUT HIS HIP, CHANGING HIS NAME TO ISRAEL

ALL THIS HAS BEEN STRANGE SINCE CAIN SLEW ABEL
GOD SELECTED ONE OVER THE OTHER, EVEN THE MOST SHAMEFUL
NO WONDER THERE'S SOMETIMES SEEMINGLY NO JUSTICE AT ALL
WHEN TYRANTS BECOME RULERS WITHOUT HAVING A FALL

FINALLY GETTING UP HIS NERVE JACOB-ISRAEL WENT ON ACROSS
AND ON MEETING WITH ESAU SAID HE HAD THE FACE OF GOD
LIKE WHEN JACOB SAID, "GOD IS IN THIS PLACE," WITH A MEMORIAL
USING HIS STONE PILLOW AS A MONUMENT AT PENUEL

WHY IS IT THAT CHURCH FATHERS SOFT PEDAL THEIR WARES
ALTERING THE FACTS TO SHOW THEIR POINT OF VIEW OF AFFAIRS
LIKE IN OUR LESSON BOOK IT'S AS IF JACOB WAS ALWAYS LOYAL TO GOD
WHEREAS HE HAD TO BE CONVERTED WHETHER HE LIKED IT OR NOT

EVEN SKIP TO THE ONE PERSON PEOPLE DETEST MOST
THAT'S SATAN PERSONIFIED, WHOM JESUS ORDERED TO GO
DIVULGE TO THE ROMANS WITH A KISS TO IDENTIFY
TO ARREST HIM, TRY TO CONVICT AND CRUCIFY

THEN WHY WAS JUDAS THE DISCIPLE'S TREASURER
THE ONE WHO WOULD STAND UP TO GIVE AN ANSWER
EXPLAINING A PARABLE, THE ONE JESUS TRUSTED
THE ANSWER TO WONDERING WHOM JESUS LOVED MOST

ALL WE EVER DO IS SPOUT CLICHE'S OR THE APOSTLE'S CREED
WITHOUT A THOUGHT IN OUR HEADS REPEATING THE SAME OLD THING
WE LEARN THE SAME OLD SAME OLD SINCE WE WERE CHILDREN
AS AN INVESTMENT WITH A GUARANTEE OF MAKING IT TO HEAVEN

WE ARE VICTIMS OF WHAT WE HEAR INCESSANTLY
IN CHURCH AND SCHOOL, THE RADIO AND TV
IT'S REALLY NOT IN ONE EAR AND OUT THE OTHER
IT STICKS BECOMES EMBEDDED IN OUR MEMOIRS

WE HAVE NOT HEARD THE LAST OF THAT STUPID JACOB
HE'S REPENTED HIS WAYS AND MADE UP WITH ESAU
HE IS THE ONE WHO'S TO BE PROCLAIMED
AS PROPHESYING THE STAR BY THE FALSE PROPHET BALAAM

NOW IF THAT'S NOT CONFUSING ENOUGH
JOSEPH AS THE FAVORITE SON OF ISAAC
HAS A COAT OF MANY COLORS AS HE
PROPHESIES THE FUTURE OF THE COUNTRY

PROVOKING HIS BROTHERS SO MUCH THAT THEY
THROW HIM IN A PIT AND SELL HIM AWAY
BLOODYING HIS COAT TO EXPLAIN IN A LIE
THAT JOSEPH WAS KILLED BY A LION AND DIED

WHEREAS HE WAS SOLD TO SOME MIDIANITES FOR THIRTY PIECES
ENTERING POTIPHAR'S HOUSEHOLD AS A SERVANT TO HIS MISSUS
AFTER BEING ACCUSED OF TAKING ADVANCES, HE WAS THRUST INTO PRISON
INTERPRETING DREAMS OF THE BAKER AND CUPBEARER OF PHARAOH

THE BOTTOM LINE IS THAT HE BECOMES THE PHARAOH'S SECOND IN COMMAND
BUILDING BARNS TO STORE GRAIN DURING THE UPCOMING FAMINE
JOSEPH ENDED UP MARRYING POTIPHER'S DAUGHTER;
JACOB AND WITH HIS BROTHERS FINALLY COME TOGETHER

RB WELSH, 7 24 21

HERITAGE

THERE ARE SEVERAL THEORIES ABOUT THE JESUS CLAN.
HE CALLED HIMSELF THE SON OF MAN.
JOHN DECLARED THAT JESUS WAS THE WORD
WHILE MATTHEW SAID HE WAS BORN OF A VIRGIN.

IT'S NO WONDER THAT JESUS SAID TO HATE YOUR PARENTS,
FOR GOD TOOK INDECENT LIBERTIES WITH MARY.
NO MATTER WHAT THE PROPHET ISAIAH SAID,
BUT IT FITS RIGHT IN WITH HIS HERITAGE AS EXPRESSED.

IT WAS EVIDENT THAT GOD IS HIS SON,
FOR THOSE MIRACLES ONLY GOD HIMSELF COULD PERFORM.
UPON ENTERING JERUSALEM, JESUS WOULD HAVE GONE
DIRECTLY TO THE PRISON TO RELEASE THE BAPTIZER, JOHN.

IN ALL THE GOSPELS, JOHN IS COMPLETELY IGNORED,
ONLY GOD WOULD TELL HIS DISCIPLES TO SELL THEIR CLOAKS TO BUY SWORDS.
MARY DIDN'T RECOGNIZE JESUS AT THE TOMB,
NOR DID THOMAS IN THE UPPER ROOM.

SO THE EVIDENCE SHOWS THAT JESUS WAS GOD ALL ALONG
IN HIS PROTEAN WAY, GOD BECOMES ANYBODY HE WANTS.
SO I'M DISCOUNTING THAT HERITAGE AS EXPRESSED
OF TAMAR, JUDAH, RAHAB, OR KING DAVID, NO LESS.

GOD IS JUST ONE, A SPIRIT DIVINE,
THE WORLD OPERATES ON OPPOSITES ALL THE TIME.
SO IF YOU BELIEVE IN A TRINITY,
THEN GOD IS JESUS OF REALITY.

RB WELSH, 9 22 22

THE NEW COVENANT AND CIRCUMCISION

WITH THE COMING OF THE CHRIST
LIFE IS SEEN IN A NEW LIGHT
PAUL SAYS THE COVENANT OF OLD IS PASSE'
GOD BROUGHT ON A BRAND NEW DAY

THE LAW WRITTEN ON TABLETS OF STONE
NOW IT COVERS THE CONSCIOUS OF MAN
THE LIST NOW COVERS ALL INFRACTIONS
FOR ALL THINGS ARE NEW WITHOUT

PAUL IS A SELF APPOINTED AUTHORITY
OF GOD'S LAWS AND NEW DECREES
BRINGING UP OLD PROPHECIES
FULFILLING THEM ON HIS OWN INITIATIVE

NO ONE HAVING GIVEN DIVINE AUTHORITY
HE SUCCORED IT AFTER BEING KNOCKED TO HIS KNEES

IF HE WERE HERE THE BAPTISM OF JESUS FOR THE LOST
WOULD BE WITH SPIRIT AND THE FIRE AT PENTECOST
AS PROPHESIED BY THE BAPTIST
AFTER BEING

GOD SAID HE WOULD BAPTIZE THE HEART
WRITE HIS LAW ON ONE'S BRAIN
NOW PAUL WRITES THE CORINTHIANS
THIS AS A FACT BUT I'M NOT CERTAIN

IT'S LIKE THE BREAD AND THE WINE TO COMMUNE
WHICH FACT JUST CAME TO YOU OUT OF THE BLUE

PAUL HAD A FETISH ABOUT HEAD COVERINGS OR LONG HAIR

IF IT'S IN THE BIBLE THEN IT'S TRUE
IS AN ADAGE WE AL KNEW
BUT FOR THIS ONE WE HAVE OUR TONGUE IN CHEEK
GOD HAS TO FULFILL THIS PROPHESY

TO HAVE ONE'S HEART NOW CIRCUMCISED
MUST BE PROCLAIMED BY GOD I REALIZED
PROPHESIED BY A PROPHET
FOR IT TOO TO BECOME INCARNATE

NOT AS GOSPEL JUST BESTOWED IN A LETTER
LIKE 11:23 TO THE CORINTHIANS SOUNDS DEMENTED
SAYING THIS JUST CAME TO ME RIGHT OUT OF THE BLUE
TO DRINK HIS BLOOD EATING HIS FLESH TOO

THOUGH JEREMIAH PROPHESIED IT
THOUSANDS OF YEARS AGO WE CAN'T DENY THIS
THAT IT MUST BE AUTHORIZED
BY GOD HIMSELF I REALIZED

PAUL JUST PROCLAIMED THIS IN A LETTER
HOPING TO HELP THEM SEE CHRIST BETTER
SUBSTITUTE JESUS FOR DIONYSUS
IN DRINKING WINE IN ORGIES OF BULLS BLOOD

THE GOSPEL WRITERS THEN IMAGINED
THAT THIS ALL REALLY HAPPENED
THAT ON THE NIGHT HE WAS BETRAYED
HE DRANK HIS BLOOD AND ATE THE BREAD

HOW FAR-FETCHED CAN SOMETHING BE
TWENTY YEARS LATER WHEN MARK WROTE HISTORY
TOOK THIS FROM PAUL'S LETTER AS IF THE TRUTH
EVEN PASSING IT ALONG TO MATTHEW AND LUKE

THE LIGHT OF JESUS STOPPED POLICING OF SAUL
THIS DIDN'T MAKE HIM AN APOSTLE
HE USURPED THIS BY HIMSELF
HE COULD EVEN BECOME BOB WELSH

GOING BACK TO CIRCUMCISION CORRECTION
MAKING MAN WITH THIS DEFECTION
IN THE BEGINNING SHOULD BE THE HEART
MALE AND FEMALE RIGHT FROM THE START

NOW IT'S JESUS WHO MUST PERFORM
THIS OPERATION TO GET US NORM
THIS MUST BE DONE UPON OUR SPIRIT
HIS SECOND COMING SHOULD GUARANTEE IT

BUT SINCE CANNABLISM"S SUCH A BUGABOO
GIVES COW MADNESS AND PRIMITIVE TOO
NO WONDER SOME MEN DO REBEL
THE WINE GLASS BACK IN THE SHELF

HIDING BREAD CRUMBS IN THEIR POCKET
SOME MEN JUST GET NAUSEATED
BUT HERE WITH A CIRCUMCISED HEART (JER 31:31)
THIS IS IGNORED IT'S IN THE DARK

IF I WERE A MEMBER OF THE CLERGY
THIS WOULD BE RITUAL THAT'S FOR CERTAIN
FURTHERMORE, THE LAW WOULD BE WRITTEN
ON MEN'S BRAINS THEY'D NE'ER FORGET THEM

WELL NOW WITH THIS DISSERTATION
I'M ALL THROUGH WITH HEART CIRCUMCISION
IT WAS ONLY A LETTER FROM JESUS CHRIST
NOT CIRCUMCISION OF THE HEART OR MIND

SO JUST FORGET I BROUGHT IT UP
NEXT TIME I'LL JUST KEEP MY MOUTH SHUT

RB WELSH, 7 26 21

THE HIERARCHY

I CAN'T FIGURE OUT THE HEIRARCHY
WHICH GOD IS FIRST IN THE TRINITY
THE USUAL ORDER THAT'S HEARD THE MOST
IS GOD THE SON AND THE HOLY GHOST

BUT ONE SUNDAY RICHARD SAID
SO I WONDER THEN IF GOD IS DEAD
THAT "JESUS IS KING OF THE UNIVERSE"
THAT'S LIKE JESUS SAID THE LAST BECAME FIRST

THE HOLY SPIRIT WAS THE ONE COMING TO MARY
TELLING HER THAT JESUS WAS THE ONE SHE WOULD CARRY
WHO WOULD THEN BE CALLED THE SON OF GOD
THAT'S WHAT MAKES THEM ALL THREE INVOLVED

IS THAT HOW COME THERE'S A TRINITY
HOW ONE GOD CAN THEN BECOME ALL THREE
GOD HIMSELF JUST COULDN'T FIGURE THIS OUT
AS TO HIS ONENESS, THERE NOW WAS SOME DOUBT

TO HIS DISCIPLES IN THE UPPER ROOM JESUS SAID
I'LL ASK GOD TO CALL ON HIS ADVOCATE TO HELP
PETER AND JOHN WENT TO SAMARA AND RE-BAPTIZED
BECAUSE THEY HAD ONLY BEEN BY JESUS THE CHRIST

SO AFTER THE NICEAN COUNCIL OF 300 AD
GOD SENT GABRIEL TO MOHAMED TO SEE
EVEN THOUGH HE WAS ONE OF WORST OF THE KNAVES
IF HE COULD WRITE OUT THE KORAN IN A CAVE

THIS WOULD FULFILL HIS PROMISE TO ISHMAEL
A WILD ASS OF A MAN WHO COULD RAISE ALL KINDS OF HELL
SO IN 600 AD GOD BECAME THE ALLAH OF THE MUSLIMS
HAVING HIS SUBJECTS SUBMIT TO BOWING WITH CUSTOMS

IT MAY JUST BE AS NEITZCHE DECLARED
WE KILLED HIM, GOD IS DEAD
THAT LEAVES ONLY TWO, JESUS AND THE SPIRIT,
WHO CREATED THE UNIVERSE AND ALL THAT IS IN IT

THERE ARE TOO MANY OTHER GODS LIKE BAAL AROUND
WITH THEIR OWN RACES WHICH DO ABOUND
AND EXTRATERRESTRIALS WITH THEIR FLYING SAUCERS
LEAVING ME IN A QUANDRY PERPLEXED AS ALWAYS

RB WELSH, 9 3 21

THE ARK OF THE COVENANT

THE NEW COVENANT WITH GOD WAS NOT A RESCISSION
OF THE FIRST ONE TO BE HIS CHOSEN PEOPLE OF CIRCUMCISION
LITERALLY KNOWN AS THAT OF THE LAW OF MOSES
IF ONLY THEY ARE ABIDED BY WITH LOVE AND DEVOTION

SIMPLE IN SCOPE, EASILY UNDERSTOOD
TAKING FORTY DAYS TO WRITE THEM IN STONE
THE FIRST TABLETS WERE BROKEN BEFORE THEY WERE READ
AS MOSES WAS SHOCKED AS A GOLDEN BULL WAS WORSHIPED INSTEAD

AFTER EIGHTY DAYS JUST BEING AROUND GOD
MOSES VEILED HIS FACE SO THE PEOPLE WOULD REMAIN CALM
NOW HEADING TO CANAAN, THEY WERE PUT IN GOD'S ARK
WITH GOD ON THE MERCY SEAT ATTENDED BY CHERUBS, SO THEY EMBARKED

AS THEY CROSSED THE JORDAN INTO THE PROMISED LAND
IT DIDN'T FLOAT THEM OVER LIKE NOAH'S ARK HAD
THE PRIESTS PLACED THE ARK DOWN, SO THE JORDAN WAS DAMMED
HISTORY REPEATS THE RED SEA THEY CROSSED TO THE PROMISED LAND

THEN THE TABERNACLE WAS SET UP IN SHILOH FOR FESTIVALS
WHERE ISRAELITES COULD OBSERVE THE HOLY DAYS WITH LAMBS OR TURTLES
SOMETIMES THE ARK WAS TAKEN TO BATTLE FOR VICTORY
WHEN CAPTURED BY THE PHILISTINES, THEY DIED BEING NEAR TO IT

WHEN FINALLY RETURNED BY DAVID IN A PARADE
LEAPING AND DANCING IN AN ECSTATIC CHARADE
THE CHEERING GIRLS THOUGHT HE WAS QUITE A SPARK
BUT HIS WIFE MICHAL WAS REALLY QUITE SHOCKED

DAVID REQUESTED GOD THAT HE BUILD A PERMANENT TEMPLE
FOR THE GLORY OF HIM IN HIS ARK DURING THE FESTIVALS
BUT IT WAS DENIED SINCE DAVID HAD TOO MUCH BLOOD ON HIS HANDS
THAT ONLY HIS SON WOULD BE ALLOWED TO BUILD ONE EVER SO GRAND

DURING SOLOMON'S REIGN THE ARK DISAPPEARED
IT HASN'T BEEN SEEN FOR THOUSANDS OF YEARS
IT'S LIKE AS IF IT IS RADIO-ACTIVE FOR IT SET UP FEARS
ONLY THE HIGH PRIEST WAS ALLOWED IN THERE ONCE A YEAR

IT WAS A REPEAT OF SINAI, WHERE ONLY THE HIGH PRIEST
LIKE MOSES, BE NEAR TO GOD, AND THEN ONCE A YEAR TO SEE
WAS A VEIL IN THIS TEMPLE THAT SOLOMON BUILT, REPLACING THE TENT
THEN AGAIN, WHEN JESUS DIED, AND THE HOLY OF HOLES VEIL WAS RENT

GOD'S GLOWING LIGHT THAT HAD AFFLICTED MOSES
HAS BEEN MASKING THE GLORY OF HIM WHO CHOSE US
THE SPIRIT OF JESUS HAS REPLACED THE VEIL AND THE ARK
THE VEIL HAS BEEN TORN; LIGHT HAS REPLACED THE DARK

RB WELSH, 9 6 21

PRAISE

TO CATEGORIZE GOD MAKES ME LIKE A FOOL
I CAN ONLY SAY HE'S MYSTERIOUS; THAT IS MY RULE
SIN AND EVIL SEEM TO ME TO OUTWEIGH
THE GOOD, SO HOW CAN I GIVE GOD THAT PRAISE

WE CAN SING AND DANCE AND, AT TIMES, PRAISE HIM
BUT THAT'S JUST TO STAY IN HIS GOOD GRACES
WHY DID JESUS HAVE TO PERFORM ALL THOSE MIRACLES
IF EVERYTHING IS SO GREAT, WHY DO WE HAVE TO TAKE PILLS?

THEN THERE'S THIS THING ABOUT MOTHER NATURE
IT SEEMS SHE'S STILL CREATING THE EARTH AS IF ITS A FAILURE
AND EVERYBODY'S COMPLAINING ABOUT GLOBAL WARMING
IT SEEMS THE MIRACLES OF OUR INVENTIONS HAVE NOW ALARMED MAN

IT SEEMS THAT WHEN I AM SUCCESSFUL, I SAY
"GOD, YOU MUST HAVE HAD A GOOD TIME TODAY"
FOR I COULD NOT HAVE DONE THAT THING
IN A THOUSAND YEARS, SO THAT'S MY PRAYER TO THE KING

RB WELSH, 10 2 21

THE HOLY SPIRIT AND THE LIGHT

THE VEIL IN THE TEMPLE OF THE HOLY OF HOLIES
IS LIKENED TO THE MASK COVERING THE FACE OF MOSES
BOTH SHIELDED MEN'S EYES FROM GOD'S GLOWING LIGHT
OF PEACE AND LOVE SO INTENSE IT KILLS BEFORE ONE'S TIME

THIS VEIL IS THE HOLY SPIRIT OF WIND AND FIRE
THAT PIERCES MAN'S BRAIN KILLING SINS ACQUIRED
THAT MAN CAN ONCE AGAIN BE BORN ANEW
LIKE GOD HIMSELF AS HIS OWN MESSIAH DID FOR YOU

THE HOLY SPIRIT IS THE GOD ABOVE GOD
CREATOR OF THE UNIVERSE AND US ALL
APPEARING IN HISTORY EVERY NOW AND THEN
EACH GOD AND RACE FROM THEIR PLANETS

IT IS THE PSYCHE OF THE SOUL
ALL THAT'S LEFT IN DAYS OF OLD
IT SPINS THE WORLDS EVEN IN SPITE
OF MAN'S EGO, WHICH IS SO TRITE

RB WELSH, 9 7 21

DELIVERANCE

YES, GOD, IT SEEMS LIKE IT'S ALWAYS DELIVERANCE
US FROM THE WOMB AS OUR FIRST EXPERIENCE
FOR CHILDISH PRANKS, WE WERE CONFINED TO OUR ROOMS
SITTING IN THE CORNER FACING A WHIPPING OR DOOM

RULES BY OUR PARENTS WERE LIKE COMMANDMENTS
WE WERE EXPECTED TO OBEY WITHOUT ANY ARGUMENT
DEVIATIONS BROUGHT OUT THE WHIP
THERE WAS A SEVERANCE OF RELATIONSHIP

TO GO OFF ON A WORSHIPING OF SOME OTHER PARENT OR GOD
IS LIKENED TO ADULTERY WHICH IS SOME FRAUD
WE ARE ALSO YOUR SONS, AND YOU ARE OUR FATHER
NOW WE'VE MATURED TO OBEY AND HONOR

THERE IS A THREAD HOLDING US TOGETHER
THE SYMBOL IS LOVE OF THIS BINDING FOREVER

RB WELSH, 10 16 21

KING OF THE UNIVERSE

IT IS INTERESTING TO NOTE THAT THE SUFFERING SERVANT
IS CALLED KING OF THE UNIVERSE BY THE RELIGIOUS FERVENT
GOD SELECTED MARY, A VIRGIN, TO BEAR HIS CHILD
THE HOLY SPIRIT IS WITHIN HIM; HE HAS THE ONENESS REQUIRED

SO I DON'T KNOW WHY THERE IS STILL A TRINITY
JESUS WAS BAPTIZED WHEN HE REACHED MATURITY
CALLED BY A VOICE ECHOING OUT FROM THE HEAVENS
THIS IS MY SON. I'M RETIRING WITH NO APPREHENSIONS

HIS INITIATION WILL BE WITH MEN ON EARTH
BY BEING ONE, HE WILL UNDERSTAND ALL THEIR QUIRKS
I'LL FIX IT SO HE CAN SAVE ALL THEIR SOULS
SIMPLY HAVE HIM CRUCIFIED SO THEIR SINS CAN BE ATONED

THEN I CAN CLOSE THIS HEAVENLY COURT
WHERE THOSE TREMBLING SOULS REPORT
CONFESSING ALL OF THEIR DREADFUL DEEDS
PERFORMED OUT OF DECEPTION AND GREED

THE PERSIANS STILL WORSHIP ME AS THEIR ALLAH
IT'S LIKE OLD TIMES WHEN I WAS CALLED AHURA-MAZDA
I'VE FULFILLED ALL MY PROMISES TO ABRAHAM
DEPARTING A TRINITY FOR ISHMAEL, THE WILD ASS OF A MAN

I AM TIRED OF DEALING WITH THESE INTERRACIAL NATIONS
WHO CAME TO EARTH WITH THEIR GODS MAKING BAD RELATIONS
THE EXTRA-TERRESTRIALS ARE SO FAR ADVANCED
WE WILL NEVER CATCH UP THOUGH I GRADUALLY ENHANCE

MODERN MAN IS SO EGOTISTICAL HE VIOLATES MY TABOOS
WITH SODOMY, GOMORRAH DECORATED THEMSELVES WITH TATTOOS
I THOUGHT MY EDICTS WERE PLAIN AND SIMPLE
EVEN DENOMINATIONS ARGUE NOT LIKE DISCIPLES

SINCE JESUS WAS HUMAN, HE WILL BETTER UNDERSTAND
I PASS ON MY ROD SO HE CAN TAKE OVER MY COMMAND
BUT THE EARTH IS ENOUGH OF A CHALLENGE FOR INTERCESSION
BEING KING OF THE UNIVERSE IS BEYOND COMPREHENSION

RB WELSH, 10 4 21

JUSTICE AND RIGHTEOUSNESS

WE KNOW THAT GOD CREATED THE JEW
AND THAT GOD STARTED MANKIND OVER ANEW
WHEN THE NEPHILIM CAME HERE FROM OUTER SPACE
THESE EXTRA-TERRESTRIALS BROUGHT IN A NEW RACE

SO, WHERE IS THE JUSTICE FOR STARTING A FLOOD
MAKING A COVENANT WITH NOAH NOT TO EAT BLOOD
FOR IT RUINED CREATION AND THE PROMISED LAND
THAT NEVER RECOVERED; IT'S NOTHING BUT SAND

THEN GOD GAVE THEM UP FOR HUNDREDS OF YEARS
THE EXODUS SHOULD HAVE FINALLY CALMED ALL THEIR FEARS
BUT AFTER THE TRAVAIL IN THE DESERT AND BATTLE WITH CANAAN
THEY RETURNED TO ENCOUNTER THE GOD BAAL WITH EXASPERATION

ALL THIS AFTER THE EXECUTION OF EGYPT'S FIRSTBORN
SPLITTING KINGDOM AND EXILE AFTER CONTINUALLY BEING WARNED
SO THE ISRAELITES RECEIVED THE JUSTICE THEY DESERVE
WE ELIMINATED THE MACABEE SELF-SACRIFICES THAT OCCURRED

NOW JESUS IS THE SOURCE OR RIGHTEOUSNESS AND JUSTICE
THAT THERE IS A HEAVEN FOR THOSE WHO ARE RIGHTEOUS
ALL SINS ARE FORGIVEN IF YOU CONFESS AND BELIEVE
FOR HE SUFFERED AND WAS CRUCIFIED IF YOU'RE SO NAIVE

REMEMBER ON THE MOUNT OF TRANSFIGURATION
MOSES, WHO WAS DEAD FOR A THOUSAND GENERATIONS
APPEARED WITH ELIJAH, WHO WAS CARRIED UP
IN GOD'S CHARIOT LIKE ENOCH, SO APPROPRIATE

FIRST, IT IS NECESSARY TO RECEIVE THE LIGHT
BE RIGHTEOUS WITH JUSTICE TO ALL AND BECOME CONTRITE
THIS IS GOD'S CALL TO WORSHIP HIM
AS WE WEND OUR WAY THROUGH THIS WORLD OF SIN

RB WELSH, 10 9 21

EXODUS

ABRAHAM BOUGHT AND PAID FOR A CAVE
AS A BURIAL SITE FOR SARAH'S GRAVE
THOUGH GOD HAD GIVEN THE LAND TO HIS CHOSEN RACE
FAMINES HAD COME AND GONE, SO AN EXODUS TOOK PLACE

IT IS DIFFICULT TO FORECAST WHAT GOD HAS IN MIND
THEY SAY ALL WERE PREDESTINED FOR CENTURIES AHEAD

AFTER CREATING MAN AND SELECTING HIS CHOSEN RACE
GOD GIVES HIM THE PROMISED LAND LEAVING HIM TO HIS OWN FATE
THE ICE AGE IS OVER OCEANS HAD FLOODED THE LAND
THE HEBREWS LEFT ISRAEL FOR GOD WAS ABSENT AGAIN

FLEEING AS ILLEGAL ALIENS TO EGYPT FOR FOOD
AND THOUGH JOSEPH HAD SAVED THEM FROM DOOM
THEY WERE LATER ENSLAVED, AND WE WONDER WHY
WAS IT SO THEY WOULD BECOME MORE CIVILIZED

TO SAVE HIS MANKIND, ISRAEL WAS REBORN
BUT ONLY WITH VIOLENCE AS THE ONLY RECOURSE
EGYPTIANS WERE ROBBED AND CHARIOTEERS WERE DROWNED
FIRSTBORN WERE CRUCIFIED, BUT ISRAEL WAS HOMEWARD BOUND

THE NEXT EXODUS WAS THE ONE FROM BABYLON
EXECUTED BY CYRUS WITH THE HELP OF AHURA MAZDA
THE GOD OF THE PERSIANS WITH THE GLOW OF LIGHT
A RETURN FROM CAPTIVITY TO JERUSALEM WITHOUT A FIGHT

GOD TRIED EVERY ANGLE TO WIN HIS PEOPLE OVER
BUT THEY WERE STUBBORN SO NEVER WERE KOSHER
KINGS PROPHETS SPLITTING THE KINGDOM TO SATISFY
NOT EVEN THE MESSIAH WOULD THEY RATIFY

DURING THE TWENTIETH CENTURY, THEY WERE AGAIN
TAKEN INTO CAPTIVITY BY HITLER'S REGIME
BUT THE REMNANT RETURNED TO ISRAEL ONCE MORE
FIGHTING BATTLES, BEING SURROUNDED BY DRAGONS OF WAR

RB WELSH, 9 2 21

CHRIST THE KING

DID YOU KNOW OR EVER WERE TOLD
THAT JESUS, WHEN RAISED, WAS NOT VERY OLD
HE IS NOW CHRIST THE KING OF THE UNIVERSE
AS ELICITED BY POPE PIUS AFTER 2000 YEARS

ONLY THE APOSTLES CREED CLAIMS HE DESCENDED INTO HELL
TO RAISE THE MURDERERS, RAPISTS, AND EVEN PROSTITUTES AS WELL
SO IF POPE PIUS HAD A GUILTY CONSCIENCE OR GOOD REASON
CHRIST AS KING HAS SAVED HIM FROM SODOMY OR TREASON

SO WHEN THE HEAVEN S AND EARTH WERE CREATED BY GOD
JESUS WAS THE LOGOS AS PRESENTED BY THE GOSPEL OF JOHN
THE HOLY SPIRIT PERVADES EVERYTHING, EVERY BEING
WAS HE GOD ABOVE GOD NOW SUCCEEDED BY THE POPE'S REASONING

BUT WITH CONSTANTINE'S COUNCIL AT NICEA
DECLARING A TRINITY DOESN'T CHANGE A THING
FOR GOD BEING ONE DEPARTED AFTER 300 YEARS TO BECOME
ALLAH FULFILLING HIS PROMISE TO ISHMAEL THE MOHAMMEDAN

SO IF JESUS IS KING OF THE UNIVERSE
IT PROVES THAT THE LAST SHALL BE FIRST

RB WELSH, 11 22 21

THE SONS OF GOD

NOW THAT WE ARE AGE-RELATED
GROWING OLD AND SOPHISTICATED
IT'S TIME WE LEARNED AS WE PAUSE
THAT THERE JUST IS NO SANTA CLAUSE

WHAT I'M SAYING IS JUST THIS
THE EARTH IS ROUND; IT'S NOT A MYTH
OUR GOD HAS OTHER NAMES TO GO BY
ROMAN AND EASTERN AXIAL BABES DIVINE

BORN ON THE SAME DATE, IT APPEARS
DECEMBER TWENTY-FIFTH OF DIFFERENT YEARS
SO ALL THE WORLD CAN NOW CELEBRATE
THAT CHRIST HAS COME ON THE SAME DATE

THERE'S MITHRA DIONYSUS OSIRIS ADONIS
BUDDHA KRISHNA HOROS AND ATTIS
ALL FROM GOD WHO IS AHURA -MAZDA
MOST FROM VIRGINS AS THEIR MOTHER

KINGS AND WISE MEN CAME FROM THE EAST
TO CELEBRATE THIS NEWEST NAMED PRIEST
THE MESSIAH THAT CAN SAVE THE WORLD
TO HEAL AND FEED MAKE PEACE IS THE WORD

RB WELSH, 12 1 21

CHRISTMAS LESSONS

CHRISTMAS IS COMING, THERE'S EXCITEMENT IN THE AIR
BELLS ARE RINGING, LIGHTS ARE STREAMING EVERYWHERE
IT'S TIME FOR THE CELEBRATION OF JESUS' BIRTH AND JOY
COMBINED WITH SANTA AND HIS SLEIGH FULL OF TOYS

THIS IS AGAIN A TIME FULL OF WONDER AND DELIGHT
HOW SANTA CAN GET TO EVERY HOUSE ALL IN ONE NIGHT
AND HOW A VIRGIN CAN BEAR A CHILD WITHOUT HAVING TO CONCEIVE
BOTH FEATS ARE AMAZING, BUT ALL WE HAVE TO DO IS BELIEVE

HAVEN'T YOU EVER HEARD OF MIRACLES BOB
THINGS HAPPEN WITHOUT PROOF, SO DON'T QUESTION AT ALL
MERCHANTS ADS ARE PLAYING CHRISTMAS HYMNS
POLAR BEARS ARE DYING; THEIR ICE FLOES ARE THIN

NOW THAT IT'S TIME FOR THE CHRISTMAS SEASON
OUR LESSON BOOK HAS US STUDY GOD'S LAW AND USE REASON
THIS IS THE TIME FOR JESUS, SO DON'T THEY KNOW
IT'S ALSO ABOUT REINDEER BELLS, FROLIC, AND SNOW

ANYHOW SAINT PAUL HAS TOLD MEN NUMEROUS TIMES
THAT MOSES'S MASK COVERS GOD'S WANING LIGHT
THAT THE SPIRIT OF CHRIST HAS SUPERSEDED GOD'S LAW
THIS IS CHRIST'S BIRTHDAY WITH JINGLE BELLS AND SANTA CLAUS

GAL 2:15 2 COR 3:15-18 GAL 5:1 RO 3:28 ACTS 21:21

RB WELSH, 12 3 21

THE TALMUD

I AM NOT A PRIEST OR ANY CHURCH FATHER-
BUT 500 YEARS OF JEWISH HISTORY IS FODDER
OMITTED BECAUSE OF ITS CONNOTATIONS
ABOUT SELF SACRIFICE BY OUR JEWISH RELATIONS

EACH ONE COULD HAVE BEEN THE ANTICIPATED MESSIAH.
THE HISTORY OF THE PERIOD FROM DANIEL TO CHRIST

WHO WAS ONE OF THESE FIGURES, THE PROMISED MESSIAH,
OR DANIEL IN THE FIERY FURNACE OR DEN OF LIONS-
THE HEBREWS HAD A MIRACLE MENORAH CANDLE
BURNING FOR EIGHT DAYS, NOW KNOWN AS THE HANUKKAH

ENOCH AND ELIJAH WERE REMOVED STRAIGHTWAY INTO HEAVEN
ENOCH AND HISTORIES HAVE BEEN EXTRADITED
PERHAPS JESUS CAME AS IN DANIEL THE FOURTH IN THE FIRE
BUT THEY WERE NOT READY TO HAVE JESUS DECLARED THE MESSIAH

NOW WE HAVE PEOPLE LIKE YOU IN THE MACCABEE STORIES
WHO SACRIFICED THEMSELVES BY BEING HEROIC
IT WASN'T THE ROMANS BUT NOW THE GREEKS
LED BY ANTIOCHUS EPIPHANIES AGAINST THE MACCABEES

DEFYING ORDERS TO EAT PORK AND WORSHIP FALSE IDOLS
MATTHIAS MACABEE KILLED THE KINGS OFFICER IN REPRISAL
TAKING TO THE HILLS WITH HIS REBELLIOUS FORCE TO DEFY THEM
HE FOUGHT FOR GOD AND HIS LAWS WHILE AWAITING THE MESSIAH

THE QUESTION ARISES COULD IT BE ONE OF THEM
WHO DIED HEROICALLY Y WITH SELF SACRIFICE ON A WHIM
LIKE THE WOMAN AND HER SONS JUMPING INTO BURNING OIL, RECOGNIZED
RATHER THAN WORSHIP FALSE GODS AND HAVING HER FAITH DESPISED

SEEING ANTIOCHUS ON AN ELEPHANT WITH A GOLD CANOPY
ELEAZAR RAN OUT WITH HIS KNIFE RIPPED OPEN ITS BELLY
AS IT DIED, IT FELL, KILLING THIS HEROIC MACCABEE TOO
THIS HEROISM AND SELF SACRIFICE IS CHRIST-LIKE ANEW

BUT IN THIS SEASON, LET US GET INTO THE SPIRIT AND CELEBRATE
THE GIFT OF LIFE WE HAVE AND JESUS'S BIRTH TO COMMEMORATE,

RB WELSH, 12 4 21

SON OF MAN

WHATEVER MADE JESUS USE THIS TERM
IN DESCRIBING HIMSELF WHILE HE WAS ON EARTH
DIDN'T HE KNOW HE WAS THE "SON OF GOD"
WE ALL KNEW HE WAS, SO THIS ALWAYS SEEMS ODD

FOXES HAVE HOLES; THE BIRDS HAVE A NEST
THE SON OF MAN KNOWS NOT WHERE TO REST HIS HEAD
SO IS HE A GOD-MAN OR GOD FROM A MOTHER
OR CAN HE BE BOTH OR ONE OR THE OTHER

THE" SON OF MAN" IS AN ANOMALY TO BE SOLVED
THE MEANING'S NOT OBVIOUS, SO IT MUST BE RESOLVED
BY MEN AS PRIESTS THEOLOGIANS OR JUST MEN
FOR JESUS SOMETIMES IS GOD AND AT OTHERS A MAN

TO BE A MAN HE MUST HAVE A HUMAN FATHER
-LIKE JOSEPH THE BETROTHED TO MARY THE MOTHER
A HUMAN BEING THROUGH AND THROUGH
NOT LIKE A SPIRIT BUT LIKE ME AND YOU

WHY DO WE KEEP CALLING HIM THE SON OF GOD?
WHEN HE OUGHT TO KNOW WHO HE IS, SEEMS ODD
HE IS, SOMETIMES, REFERRED TO AS THE SECOND ADAM
WHO WAS, OUT OF SPIT AND MUD, CREATED

SO HERE IS THE DILEMMA TO BE SOLVED IF YOU CAN
CAN HE AT ONE TIME BE GOD AND THEN AT ANOTHER BE MAN
ONE PART OF ME SAYS YES, FOR HE SAYS THAT HE'S "IN" GOD
AND THAT GOD IS "IN "HIM AS WE HOPE TRUE FOR US ALL

MARY SAID THAT SHE WAS BETROTHED,
BUT HAD NOT EVER KNOWN A MAN.
BUT THIS WAS THE WAY OF BETROTHAL BACK THEN
TO SEE IF THEY'RE COMPATIBLE AND WAS NOT A SIN.

SO IF JESUS WAS THEN ONLY A MAN
IN GOD'S PROTEAN WAY, HE DOES, AND HE CAN
MAKE HIMSELF INTO ANYONE HE WANTS
AS AT MAMRE JERICHO OR NOW AS AN INFANT

THEN IT REALLY MUST ALL BE TRUE
AS IT SAYS IN THE BOOKS OF DANIEL AND LUKE
HE'S ONLY TO BE CALLED 'THE SON OF MAN"
SIGNIFYING "ALL OF MANKIND" LIKE YOU AND ALL MEN

IF NOAH COULD BE IN THE BELLY OF A WHALE,
JESUS COULD BE IN THE WOMB OF A GIRL
WITHOUT ANY KIND OF INTERCOURSE
FROM GOD OR JOSEPH AS IT PURPORTS.

THE WHOLE POINT IS THAT GOD REALLY BECAME A MAN
WAS SO THAT HE COULD THEN UNDERSTAND
THE WHATS AND WHEREFORES OF MANKIND
HIS ACTIONS, DECISIONS, AND WHAT'S ON HIS MIND

WITH ALL THIS BIBLICAL EVIDENCE TO ME
IT SHOWS CONVINCINGLY, SO I CAN SEE
THAT GOD CAN EVEN BE A BUSH CALLED "I AM."
CAN REPRESENT HIMSELF AS A WHALE OR A MAN

WOULD GOD FEEL PAIN WHEN CRUCIFIED?
THAT WAS THE IMPRESSION WHEN HE DIED
BUT IN TAKING THE ROBBER THAT DAY TO PARADISE
HE COULDN'T HAVE ALSO BEEN IN HELL AND THEN RISE

IF CRUCIFIED, ONLY A SON OF GOD COULD TAKE THE PAIN
AND ONLY GOD PERFORMS MIRACLES, CURING THE LAME
AFTER HIS DEFENSELESS TRIAL TO DIE
HIS MESSIANIC MISSION WAS A SUICIDE

SO WAS HE GOD OR WAS HE A MAN
FIGURE THIS ONE OUT IF YOU CAN
THERE'S NO REASON HE CAN'T BE BOTH
DEPENDING ON THE SITUATION, OF COURSE

IF HE'S TO RETURN AS SCRIPTURE SAID
ON THE CLOUDS AFTER HIS DEATH
AND AS JOHN THE BAPTIST PROPHESIED
ONE WILL COME AFTER ME TO BAPTIZE WITH THE HOLY SPIRIT AND FIRE,
IT SEEMS LIKE THE PENTECOST FILLS THAT REQUIRE.

ISAIAH'S LIPS WERE PURIFIED
BY THE CHERUBIM WITH A COAL OF FIRE
SO FROM THEN ON, HE SPOKE ONLY THE TRUTH
IF ALL WERE THUS BAPTIZED, GOD WOULD APPROVE

LIKE NOAH IN THE BELLY OF A WHALE
GOD CAN PLACE A BABE INTO THE WOMB OF A MAID
THE HOLY SPIRIT CAN THEN WI TH HOLINESS INSUFFLATE
SO SANTA CLAUS CAN DELIVER ON CHRISTMAS DAY

RB WELSH, 12 8 21

REBIRTH

JESUS SAID 'YE MUST BE BORN AGAIN"
TO ENTER THE KINGDOM OF HEAVEN
THE NATION OF ISRAEL WAS FIRSTBORN
ON THE BANKS OF THE RIVER JABBOCK

THE NATION OF THE CHOSEN PEOPLE OF HAVOC
BECAME ISRAEL ON THE BANKS OF THE RIVER JABBOCK
THAT'S WHEN GOD WRESTLED JACOB ALL NIGHT
AFTER WRENCHING HIS HIP CHANGED HIS BIRTHRIGHT

FOR JACOB AS A BELIEVER WAS NOT ONE OF THEM
A PERPETUAL DECEIVER, A CON MAN AT BEST
INHERITING IT ALL FROM HIS MOTHER REBEL
HE STOLE ESAU'S BIRTHRIGHT AND HAD NO RESPECT

YET GOD SELECTED HIM THOUGH NEFARIOUS INDEED
THE TWELVE TRIBES ARE NAMED AFTER HIS SEED
HIS STAR WILL SHINE OVER THE NATIVITY SCENE
JACOB'S WELL IS WHERE JESUS AND THE SAMARITAN GIRL MEET

DUE TO FAMINE IN THE PROMISED LAND
THE ISRAELITES MIGRATE TO EGYPT AGAIN
THIS TIME THEY BECOME ENSLAVED
BUT THROUGH THE RED SEA, THEY ARE SAVED

A DETOUR TO THE MOUNTAIN OF GOD
RECEIVING COMMANDMENTS TO CARRY ON
THEY PLOD ON TO THEIR GOAL OF GOING HOME
PERPETUALLY HUNGRY, THIRSTY, AND ALONE

NOT REALIZING THEY HAD TO FIGHT
FOR THEY WERE SHEPHERDS, SO THEY GRIPED
IN DECLARING THEMSELVES UNFIT
GOD LET THEM DIE IN THE DESERT

ONLY THE NEXT GENERATION BORN
WERE ALLOWED TO CROSS THE RIVER JORDAN
HEAVEN BEING THE PROMISED LAND
WITH LAWS, THEY HAD TO UNDERSTAND

MAYBE YOU, TOO, GOD MUST BE REBORN
LIKE AS A SAVIOR, MAYBE AS YOUR SON
HE CAN BRING THE HEALINGS AND THE LOVE
NECESSARY FOR THEIR HEARTS TO BE WON

I CAN NOT BE COMPELLED TO LOVE
FROM THE HEART AND SOUL, IT MUST COME
LOVE IS RECEIVING GOD'S LIGHT AND SPIRIT
ONE MUST BE PSYCHIC JUST TO FEEL IT

THIS IS A LOVE THAT YOU CAN'T SEE
THAT WILL LAST AS LONG AS PERPETUITY
LOVE IS GUIDED BY GOD'S PROVIDENCE
IT'S SYNCHRONICITY IN REVERENCE

LOVE IS A MEETING OF THE MINDS
PERPETUALLY READING THE OTHER'S MIND
LOVE, IN ESSENCE, IS A ONENESS
OF MIND, SOUL AND BODY IN HEAVINESS

SO WHENEVER I DO SOMETHING GREAT, I SAY
GOD, YOU MUST HAVE HAD A GOOD TIME TODAY
HIS OTHER COMMANDS JUST FALL INLINE
ONE CAN'T KILL EVEN BY DESIGN

LATER ON IN HISTORY
THESE LAWS WILL BE MYSTERIOUSLY
WRITTEN ON OUR HEARTS AND BRAINS
MEN ON EARTH WILL THEN BE MORE HUMANE

RB WELSH, 12 9 21

TRINITY

YES, GOD HIMSELF IS A TRINITY
WORSHIPED BY ALL THREE
MAJOR RELIGIONS OF THIS REALM
THE HEBREWS CHRISTIANS AND ISLAM

TAKE THE NUMBER NINETY-NINE
WHEN YOU TURN IT UPSIDE DOWN
IT THEN BECOMES A SIXTY-SIX
IT'S STILL NOT EQUAL BECAUSE IT'S FLIPPED

THE ESSENCE OF ALL THREES THE SAME
THEY ARE ALL HOLY BY THEIR NAME
THE SPIRIT IS GOD'S WORKHORSE
THEY ADVOCATE THE MAJOR FORCE

JESUS IS GOD AS MAN
HE'S THERE SO GOD CAN UNDERSTANDING
THE SILLINESS OF HIS CREATION
WHY EVER FORMED IS HIS QUESTION

TO CLAIM THEY'RE EQUAL IS BEYOND ME
LIKE BUDDHA VISHNU HOROS, THERE'S SO MANY
THE UNIVERSE HAS MANY GODS
BAAL IS ONE GOD'S JEALOUS OF

SO LET'S NOT BE RIDICULOUS
THIS GOD IS NOT CALCULUS
CONSTANTINE UNIFIED HIS TRIBES
WITH GODS RELIGION UNIFIED

AT THE COUNCIL OF NICEA
MAKING HIS PRIESTS BELIEVE IT
IF THERE WERE REALLY A TRINITY,
IT WOULD COME FROM ONE OF THE THREE

RB WELSH, 12 11 21

THE RHYTHMIC UNIVERSE

HERE WE ARE LIVING ON A PLANET CALLED EARTH
VICTIMS OF SCHEDULES AND CLOCKS SINCE BIRTH
BUT GOD DOESN'T HAVE TO WORRY ABOUT TIME
FOR ETERNITY NEVER ENDS FOR THE DIVINE

WE ARE TUNED IN LIKE A MACHINE
WE ARE ACCUSTOMED TO A ROUTINE
WE USE EXPERIENCE TO JUDGE WHAT TO DO NEXT
WE HAVE EDUCATION SO RESULTS WILL BE BEST

OUR LIVES SEEM TO BE CONTROLLED BY THE CALENDAR
A STEADY STREAM OF DUTIES TAKING FALLS AND DISASTERS
FROM BEING A BABY, A CHILD, TEENAGER ADULT
TALENT IS THE REGULATOR OF SUCCESSES OR FAULTS

IN VEGAS, SEVEN OR ELEVEN IS THE LUCKY NUMBER
EIGHT HOURS OF SLEEP IS REQUIRED FOR SLUMBER
TEN IS USED FOR THE DECIMAL SYSTEM
BUT TWELVE HAS BEEN PROVED FOR UNIVERSAL RHYTHM

LIKE MACHINES WE PLOD ON FROM DAY TO DAY
UNKNOWING THAT WE ARE CONTROLLED BY OUTER SPACE
THE UNIVERSE IS RHYTHMICALLY ON A COURSE
THE FACE OF THE CLOCK REVEALS THIS FORCE

12 IS THE NUMBER CONTROLLING PLANET EARTH
BY TRAVELING AT THE SPEED OF LIGHT, IT IS AFFIRMED
THAT 12 IS THE NUMBER SCIENTIFICALLY DISCOVERED
AND IS NOW CALLED THE DIVINE NUMBER

PROVED BY BY INVENTORS OF THE PARTICLE ACCELERATOR
GOING ROUND AND ROUND AS A CIRCULAR COLLIDER
ON A RACE TRACK DUG IN A MOUNTAINOUS TUNNEL
AT THE SPEED OF LIGHT, BEAMS COLLIDE, AND 12 IS THE NUMBER

MAN HAS CONQUERED NATURE
A CIRCULAR TUNNEL LIKE A RACETRACK
IN A SWISS MOUNTAIN GOING AT THE SPEED OF LIGHT

THE TIME FOR PUBERTY AVERAGES TWELVE E YEARS
IN GOING FROM ADOLESCENCE TO HOPES AND FEARS

THOUGH IT JUST MAY BE A COINCIDENCE
THAT THERE ARE TWELVE MONTHS IN A YEAR

THE ENGLISH RATHER THAN A DECIMAL SYSTEM
USE TWELVE INCHES IN A FOOT TIME FOR THE PERIOD

WE SAY JESUS WAS BORN IN THE TWELFTH MONTH
THE TIME FOR THE WINTER SOLSTICE BY A VIRGIN
AND HE WAS LEARNED BY THE TIME HE WAS TWELVE
ENLIGHTENING THE PRIESTS IN JERUSALEM

NOW IT'S TIME TO CELEBRATE HIS BIRTH ONCE AGAIN
IT'S BEEN TWENTY DOZEN YEARS SINCE THIS HAPPENED
SO WITH MIRTH AND SONG, WE PRAISE HIS WORKS
HIS LOVE FOR PEACE AND JUSTICE FOR ALL MEN ON EARTH

SO TWELVE IS THE NUMBER FOR UNIVERSAL RHYTHM
NOT TEN AS DETERMINED BY THE DECIMAL SYSTEM

RB WELSH, 12 13 21

ONE AS THREE

IT IS NATURAL FOR GOD TO BE
AS ONE; BUT, SOMETIMES HE IS THREE
TO BECOME JESUS INTO BECOMING MAN
GO THROUGH HIS ORDEALS TO UNDERSTAND

SELECTING THE VIRGIN GIRL MARY
AS THE HOLY SPIRIT, HE SAYS THAT SHE
WILL BEAR A CHILD AND CALL HIM GOD
SINCE SHE IS BETROTHED, THAT DOES SEEM ODD

AND HASN'T KNOWN A MAN, SO HOW
WILL GOD PROVIDE THE SEED TO ENDOW
HER WITH CHILD TO BE CALLED
JESUS THE SON OF GOD?

HE WON'T BE USING MUD AND SPIT
AS HE DID TO MAKE ADAM LEGIT
NOW GOD IS JOSEPH ONCE MORE
GOD MUST HAVE SLEPT HERE JE'T'ADORE

IT SEEMS THAT WE ARE ALL TWO-FACED
FOR I AM ONE TO PLACATE
SO WITH THE UPCOMING BIRTH OF JESUS
I WILL AGREE THAT TRINITY HAS REASON

I HAVE ALWAYS MAINTAINED AND SAY
THAT GOD IS JESUS IN HIS PROTEAN WAY
SO AS TO HOW THIS WILL CORRELATE
WITH A VIRGIN BIRTH, I WILL STATE

FOR ONE AND ESPECIALLY A VIRGIN TO BEAR A CHILD
GOD HIMSELF MUST, WITH THE SEED, PROVIDE
SO GOD IS NOW JOSEPH THE BETROTHED
IN MARY'S WOMB, THE SEED WAS SOWN

FOR GOD TO BE ABLE TO BE THEM BOTH
PERHAPS AS EVEN TO BE THE BETROTHED
FOR JESUS TO BECOME THE HOLY GHOST
SOMEHOW THE SPERM ENTERED THE EGG
IN NINE MONTHS, THERE CAME THE BABE

THE SON IS REBORN ONCE AGAIN
CALLING HIMSELF THE SON OF MAN
HE ONCE WAS IN THE FIERY FURNACE AND VOWED
TO RETURN AGAIN ON THE CLOUDS

GOD COULD HAVE TAKEN A DIRECT ROUTE
IN BECOMING JESUS, THERE IS NO DOUBT
FOR HE CAN ALWAYS WITH HIS POWER
EVEN BECOME YOU OR ME IN ANY ENCOUNTER

IT'S GOD AND MARY AND BABY THAT MAKE THREE
THAT SOUNDS TO ME LIKE A TRINITY
I DON'T KNOW WHAT TO DO WITH THE HOLY SPIRIT
IT MUST BE THE BRAINS THAT FINALLY FIGURED IT

RB WELSH, 12 18 21

CHRISTMAS EVE

IT'S THE NIGHT BEFORE CHRISTMAS
ON THE DAY BEFORE THE BIRTH OF JESUS
PEOPLE ARE GOING BERSERK EVERYWHERE
JESUS WILL BE BORN. EXCITEMENT FILLS THE AIR

IT'S BEEN A LONG TIME, ABOUT NINE MONTHS
SINCE GOD SENT TO MARY A MESSAGE OF LOVE
NOW WE ARE THE ONES TO CELEBRATE
IN SOLICITOUS REVERENCE IN A JOYFUL STATE

IT IS LIKE HEAVEN HAS BEEN BROUGHT TO EARTH
WITH GOD LOOKING ON SILENTLY AS WE GATHER, MIRTH
DO YOU KNOW WHY EVERYONE IS SO EXCITED
WHEREAS GOD IS THE GOD OF THE HEBREWS
JESUS WILL BE TH GOD OF ALL NATIONS RACES AND JEWS

THE HOLY SPIRIT LOOKS DOWN AND SMILES

SINCE ALL NATIONS AND RACES WILL NOW BE RECONCILED
IT'S LIKE AS IF GOD HIMSELF IS REBORN
IT IS NOT LIKE NOW THERE IS ONE MORE
IT'S GOD HIMSELF IN HUMAN FORM

NOW MAN CAN BE A COMPLETE WHOLE
A PERSON OF BODY, BRAIN, AND SOUL
WI TH YOUR HEART CIRCUMCISED AND THE LAW ON YOUR BRAIN
IT'S NOW TO BE LIKE AN EARTHLY HEAVENLY DOMAIN

SO CHRISTMAS IS LIKE A POT OF GOLD
EVERYONE'S EXCITED, BOTH YOUNG AND OLD
A NEW DAY IS DAWNING; IT'S A NEW BEGINNING
SO MERRY CHRISTMAS, CHURCH BELLS ARE RINGING!

RB WELSH, 12 24 21

HAPPY BIRTHDAY JESUS

IT'S DECEMBER TWENTY-FIFTH, AND I CAN SEE GOD
PROUD AS A PEACOCK LOOKING DOWN FROM ABOVE
SAYING TO HIMSELF, "NOW I AM HAPPY MEN WILL ASPIRE
TO BECOME LIKE HIM, THE PROPHESIED MESSIAH"

FROM HIS HUMBLE BEGINNINGS BORN IN A STABLE
SURVIVING, THOUGH HEROD WOULD KILL IF HE WERE ABLE
AND REFUSING TO SUCCUMB TO SIN IN THE WILDERNESS
AFTER BEING BAPTIZED BY THE DOVE WITH FORGIVENESS

LET ALL MEN HAVE HAPPINESS AND JOY
AS THEY EXCHANGE THEIR GIFTS AND TOYS
SING HYMNS OF JOY AND CELEBRATE
GOD HAS COME AMID MEN, SO GIVE PRAISE

THOUGH HE MUST, AS ALL MEN DO DIE
HE WILL HAVE TO BE CRUCIFIED
SAVING THE WORLD FROM ITS FATE
SO THEY CAN LIVE A LIFE FULL OF GRACE

RB WELSH, 12 25 2021

TODAY'S LESSON

HEY, WHAT'S THIS IN OUR SUNDAY SCHOOL LESSON
OUR STOCKING IS FILLED WITH COAL AND DEPRESSION
THE WEEKEND WAS MADE FOR HAPPINESS AND JOY
AND THIS IS THE BIGGEST LET-DOWN EVER EMPLOYED

CHRISTMAS IS SUPPOSED TO BE A SEASON
WE DON'T ALWAYS HAVE TO USE REASON
IT LASTS AT LEAST UNTIL NEW YEAR
TO ME, ALL THIS SEEMS PRETTY WEIRD

FOR THERE'S THE CIRCUMCISION BY A MAN OFF THE STREET
SINCE THIS IS GOD, IT WOULD SEEM TO BE DONE BY A PRIEST
THEN THERE'S THE JOURNEY TO EGYPT FOR THE FLIGHT FROM HEROD
THE ESSENES CLAIMING THIS IS THE CODE WORD FOR QUMRAN

WE ALWAYS THINK ABOUT OUR HAPPINESS
WHEN IN REALITY, JESUS IS HERE TO HELP US PROGRESS
FOR WEEKS WE WERE SIDETRACKED BY THE ADVENT
BUT FINALLY HAD ONE WEEK BEFORE THE CHRISTMAS EVENT

IT SEEMS THAT IF HIS PEOPLE DIDN'T REPENT OF THEIR WAYS
HE WOULD TURN TO THE GENTILES WHO HAD MADE JEWS THEIR SLAVES
NOW EVEN THE NINEVITE GENTILES FROM ANOTHER PLANET, IT SEEMS
COULD NOW, THROUGH JESUS THE CHRIST, BECOME NEW BEINGS

YOU MEAN IT'S LIKE BECOMING LIKE ADAM
NAKED UNASHAMED, RUNNING AROUND IN EDEN
LOVING GOD CHASING EVE AND EATING FROM EVERY TREE
FOR I CAN NOW DISCERN WHAT IS EVIL SINCE I AM FREE

BUT HERE I AM, LORD WAKING UP ON DECEMBER TWENTY-SIXTH
WHEN I READ THE LESSON, I THINK MY MIND'S PLAYING TRICKS
FOR WHAT ON EARTH DOTH IT PROFIT A MAN
TO MAKE NINEVEH REPENT ALL OVER AGAIN

JONAH REBELLED AND JUST DIDN'T CARE
HE JUST COULDN'T FIND ANY MESSAGE THERE
ABOUT ASSYRIANS WHO HAD DRAGGED OFF ISRAEL
THEY MIGHT HAVE JUST DISAPPEARED INTO HELLOR

YES, LET'S FLOUNDER AROUND IN THE RECESSES
OF DARK AGE THEOLOGY, INSTEAD OF ACCESSING
THAT JESUS IS THE KEY TO GETTING INTO HEAVEN
WHICH WOULD BE LOGICAL FOR TODAY'S LESSON

THAT GOD OF THE HEBREWS HAS EXTENDED HIS EMPIRE
TO INCLUDE ALL NATIONS AND RACES WHO DESIRE
TO BE FREE MEN UNDER CHRIST AND HIS CHURCHES
INCLUDING THE HEATHEN NINEVITES OR ANYONE WHO SEARCHES

HOW CAN THE GOD OF THE JEWS
GIVE THEM UP JUST BECAUSE THEY REFUSE
TO WORSHIP HIM AND TURN TO BAAL
LOVE CAN'T BE COMMANDED, SO IT JUST FAILS

INSTEAD OF HAVING PEOPLE ONCE A YEAR WORSHIP
TRAVEL MILES TO ONE TEMPLE WHEN CHURCHES
IN EACH TOWN WOULD REPLACE BAAL ALTARS
THEN THE PEOPLE WOULD BE MORE LIKELY TO EXALT HIM

IF I WERE RICHARD, I WOULD GO ON VACATION
ANYTHING TO AVOID TEACHING THIS LESSON
OR BETTER, JUST STICK TO WHAT IS ON EVERYONE'S MIND
GOD HAS BEEN REBORN AS JESUS THE CHRIST

THE TROUBLE WITH ME IS THAT I WANT TO BEGIN
BEING REBORN OVER AND OVER AGAIN
CELEBRATING WITH SONG IN PRAISE OF THE MESSIAH
CALMING THE WORLD BY SINGING HYMNS BY THE CHOIR

RB WELSH, 12 26 21

UNIVERSAL SALVATION

BEFORE CHRIST, ONLY HEBREWS WERE SAVED
IN GOD'S HEAVEN, SOMEWHERE ORDAINED
GOD HAS COME TO EARTH AS JESUS TO SAVE
THE REST OF MANKIND, EVEN THOUGH THEY'RE DEPRAVED.

ONLY HEBREWS WERE FORMERLY ALLOWED INTO HEAVEN
IF THEY REPENTED FROM ANY TRANSGRESSION
GOD NOW WANTED TO INCLUDE ALL NATIONS AND RACES
EVEN THE ASSYRIANS, THE WORST OF ALL CASES

JESUS IS CALLED THE GOOD NEWS
BECAUSE HE INCLUDED MORE THAN THE JEWS
REPENTANCE IS ALL THAT IT TAKES
AND IT INCLUDES ALL NATIONS AND RACE

MOSES HAD DIED AND WAS BURIED BY GOD
TO REAPPEAR WITH ELIJAH AT THE TRANSFIGURATION
NOW THERE'S A NEW HEAVEN IN OUTER SPACE
SEE REVELATION 21 TO IDENTIFY THIS PLACE

RB WELSH, 12 26 21

WHY HAST THOU

MY GOD MY GOD WHY HAST THOU
FORSAKEN ME HE CRIED ALOUD
AS HE HUNG ON THE CROSS IN THE THROES OF DEATH
IN AGONY HE WAS TAKING HIS LAST BREATH

WAS THIS REALLY THE SON OF GOD
WHO PERFORMED MIRACLES GIVING UP HIS BLOOD
IT SHOULD BETHE BODY OF SATAN HANGING WHO HAS THE GUILT
SUFFERING FOR THE SINS HE ENTICES US TO COMMIT

THERE'S A MESSAGE HERE THAT WE JUST DON'T GET
JESUS WAS BORN AS A MIRACLE FOR OUT BENEFIT
HE WAS TRIED AND CONVICTED FOR HEALING THE BLIND
FEEDING THE POOR, WE THOUGHT HIM DIVINE

HE ASKED GOD TO TAKE THIS CUP FROM HIM
THIS WAS THE PUNISHMENT FOR THOSE WHO SIN

SO I ASK YOU NOW AS WE CELEBRATE HIS BIRTH
SHOULD HE DIE FOR US AS IF WE HAD WORTH?

RB WELSH, 12 29 21

OPPOSITES

THE WORLD IS BUT A MYRIAD OF OPPOSITES.
THAT INCLUDES GOD THOUGH HIS LOVE PREDOMINATES.
FOR WHO DECIDED TO SEND SATAN TO JOB,
OR KILL OFF AT PASSOVER THE EGYPTIAN FIRSTBORN?

YES, IN THIS CONSTELLATION, GOD CREATED THE SUNS,
THEN HE CREATED MAN WITH JEWS AS THE CHOSEN ONES.
THIS WHOLE CREATION IS A SHIMMERING DISC,
MAGNIFICENT IN ITS POLARITIES OPERATIONAL TECHNIQUE.

OTHER GODS IN THE UNIVERSE MADE THEIR OWN MEN,
WHO VISIT US REGULARLY IN UFO FLYING MACHINES.
AIDING IN PROGRESS WITH SIMPLE ELECTRONICS,
HALTING ATOMIC WARS BLASTING SILOS WITH ULTRASONIC.

AS THE SUNS OF THE HEAVENS EXPLODE, CITIZENS GET IN THEIR CRAFTS,
TO FLY TO THE EARTH WITH THEIR GODS WITH GREAT DISPATCH.
GOD IS THEIR GOD UNDER ANOTHER NAME,
NEBUCHADNEZZAR IS GOD'S "SERVANT" WHO REIGNS.

DO WE REALIZE THE BAAL IS BA-EL?
GOD TEMPTED EVE, AND HE ENTICED ISRAEL AS WELL.
ASSYRIA ABSORBED ISRAEL AFTER THE SPLIT,
JUDAH LEARNED NO LESSON WITH THE SAME PUNISHMENT.

IT TOOK JONAH IN A WHALE TO WARN OF THE CONSEQUENCES,
IF ASSYRIA DID NOT SUBMIT TO GOD AND HIS ELEMENTS.
NOW JUDAH IS TO BE SAVED BY THE GOD OF PERSIA,
WHO IS GOD UNDER THE NAME OF AHURA-MAZDA?

NOW WE WONDER WHAT SINS DID THE JEW COMMIT,
FOR GOD TO LET HITLER SEND THEM TO AUSCHWITZ.
AT ANY RATE, THEY ARE NOW FREE AGAIN
IN ISRAEL AGAIN AS THE GARDEN OF EDEN.

RB WELSH, 6 3 22

THE COVENANT

WHY DID GOD HAVE TO BECOME JESUS?
THERE IS BUT ONE SIMPLE REASON.
IT HAS TO DO WITH THE COVENANT
THAT GOD MADE WITH ABRAHAM.

IN THE OLD DAYS, DEALS WERE SEALED WITH A BERIT,
BUT GOD DIDN'T RUN THROUGH IT, SEALING THE COVENANT.
SO GOD FINALLY BECAME JESUS TO BECOME MAN,
TO BE CIRCUMCISED ON THE EIGHTH DAY IN JERUSALEM.

WE WONDER WHY PAUL HAD A FETISH ABOUT THIS,
THAT MAN SHOULD BE CASTRATED IF HE SUBMITS.
THE GREEKS IN THE GYMNASIUM PLAYED IN THE NUDE,
CIRCUMCISION IS HEALTHIER, AND IT SHOULD BE THE RULE.

IT'S NO WONDER PAUL WAS BROUGHT BEFORE THE COUNCIL,
BUT HIS LETTERS ARE PERMANENTLY ENGRAVED AS IF THEY WERE GOSPEL.
GOD PROPHESIED THROUGH THE WORDS OF JEREMIAH AND TO 2 CORINTHIANS,
THAT MEN'S HEARTS WOULD BE CIRCUMCISED, WITH THE LAW WRITTEN ON THE BRAIN.

SO THIS CAN INCLUDE WOMEN AS WELL AS ALL RACES,
EXTRA-TERRESTRIALS HAVE THEIR OWN GOD IN OUTER SPACE.
THE UNIVERSAL HOLY SPIRIT EXUDES THE LIGHT
OF WAVELENGTHS BEYOND HUMAN SIGHT.

BEING IN PROXIMITY FORTY DAYS AND NIGHTS,
MOSES ONLY REFLECTED GOD'S GLOW AND LIGHT.
GOD ORDERED HIM TO MASK HIMSELF SO THAT HE WOULDN'T SCARE
THE PEOPLE WAITING FOR MOSES TO FINALLY REAPPEAR.

THERE WILL BE A REPEAT OF THE FIRST EXODUS,
WHEN GOD AS AHURA-MAZDA AGAIN SAVES US
FROM THE THROES OF BABYLONIA FOR EIGHTY YEARS,
TO RETURN AND REBUILD JUDAH LIKE THE TRAIL OF TEARS.

RB WELSH, 6 4 22

TRUTH

DESPITE ALL THAT THEOLOGIANS SAY
GOD HAS ALL THE HUMAN TRAITS
WHEN HE SELECTED ABRAHAM AND SARAH
IT SEEMS HE MADE A NOTABLE ERROR

AS IT SAYS IN GENESIS 20'1
THEIR FATHER WAS THE SAME ONE
THE FACT THAT THIS WOULD BE A PROBLEM LATER
SARAH SENT HER MARRIED BROTHER TO HAGAR

FACTS HAVE BEEN TWISTED JUST TO DECEIVE
GOD "DID TO HER AS PROMISED" IN THE NRSV
KING JAMES SAYS, "GOD VISITED HER IN HER TENT"
THAT GOD IS ISAAC'S FATHER IS EVIDENT

DID GOD, IN HIS PROTEAN WAY
BECOME ABRAHAM THAT DAY
WHEN HE ENTERED SARAH'S TENT,
TO IMPREGNATE HER FOR THE BLESSED EVENT

THE COVER-UP IS OVER; IT'S NOW EXPOSED
HIS FIRSTBORN SHOULD HAVE BEEN DISCLOSED
IT WOULD HAVE BEEN LIKE ISAAC WAS CRUCIFIED
BUT AT THE LAST MINUTE, HE WAS SAVED FROM SACRIFICE

AT MAMRE IT HAS TO BE WILD SPECULATION·
THE OTHER MEN WERE CHRIST AND THE HOLY SPIRIT
WHAT ROLE THEY PLAYED IS IGNORED
LIKE A TRINITY, THEY WERE JUST ON BOARD

AFTER ALL, THE HOLY SPIRIT INSUFFLATED MARY'S WOMB
THE EGG HAD TO BE FERTILIZED SOMEHOW; IT'S ASSUMED
SO LET'S GET REAL IN THIS CENTURY
AND PRESENT SOME FACTS SENSIBLY

IF ANYTHING, THEOLOGIANS SHOULD BE HONEST
EVEN IF IT TAKES 24 CENTURIES, THEY SHOULD BE TRUSTED
AFTER ALL, WE ARE ADULTS AND TIRED OF BRAINWASHING
IT'S TIME FOR TRUTH SO ADMIT SOME FACTS WITH LOGIC.

RB WELSH, 1 14 22

BOB'S CREED

WHEN GOD SELECTED THIS MAN AND HIS WIFE,
HE JUST HADN'T SEEMED TO REALIZE,
THAT THEY WERE SIBLINGS AND COULDN'T BEAR
CHILDREN WITHOUT DEFORMITIES FOR THE PROMISED HEIR.

HE DIDN'T PERFORM MIRACLES BY HEALING THE BLIND,
FEEDING THE POOR OR COMMUNE WITH BREAD AND WINE.
BUT WAS TAKEN TO THE TEMPLE MOUNT TO BE SACRIFICED
AND BEING GOD'S FIRST SON, IT SHOULD HAVE SUFFICED

SO ONE MISTAKE COMPOUNDS ITSELF INTO ANOTHER,
BY LETTING HAGAR BECOME ISHMAEL'S MOTHER.
THIS BLUNDER CAUSED GOD TO BRING ON THE TEARS,
AND LEAVE THEM IN EGYPT FOR FOUR HUNDRED YEARS.

WHILE HE WENT OFF TO THE EAST AS AHURA-MAZDA
TO SET UP THE RESCUE FROM EXILE BY DARIUS OF PERSIA
ESTHER BECOMES QUEEN SENDING TEMPLE TREASURIES OF GOLD.
CYRUS WILL PROVIDE FUNDS FOR THE TRIP BACK HOME.

YES, I AM THE ONLY CREATOR-GOD OF LIGHT
AS MOSES, WHEN HIS FACE WAS RADIANT, REALIZED

MY WISEMEN WILL COME FROM THE EAST BEARING GIFTS,
TO MY SON JESUS, TO BE BORN OF MARY THE VIRGIN.

THEY CALL ME BUDDHA AND VISHNU IN THE FAR EAST,
THESE WERE THE AXIAL NATIONS, BUT NONE THE LEAST.
IF YOU HAVEN'T NOTICED, IT SEEMS I HAVE SONS ALL OVER,
THERE'S KRISHNA, ARJUNA, AND EGYPTIAN HORUS

THERE'S ONLY ONE GOD, AND THAT IS ME,
THERE'S CERTAINLY NO SUCH THING AS A TRINITY.
THE HOLY SPIRIT RUNS THE UNIVERSE
GODS AND EXTRATERRESTRIALS ABOUND EVEN ON EARTH.

RB WELSH, 1 22 22

SACRIFICE

THAT THERE WAS A RAM INSTEAD SACRIFICED
INSTEAD OF ISAAC, IT WAS A SURPRISE!
TO EVERYONE BUT ABRAHAM, I GUESS
FOR HE WENT RIGHT AWAY WITHOUT ANY PROTEST

DID ABRAHAM KNOW THAT ISAAC WAS GOD'S SON
THAT ISHMAEL WAS HIS FIRSTBORN AND ONLY ONE
SO WITHOUT ARGUMENTS LIKE AT SODOM AND GOMORRAH
HE PACKED UP ISAAC WITH THE WOOD AND WENT TO MORIAH

TELLING HIS SERVANT TO WAIT WITH THE DONKEYS
FOR THEY WOULD BOTH BE BACK, THERE WOULD BE A PROXY
AFTER ALL, THIS WAS GOD'S FIRSTBORN SON
HE WOULD USE FIRSTBORN ANIMALS FROM NOW ON

ABRAHAM HAD CONFIDENCE THAT HE SHOULD SACRIFICE
ISHMAEL INSTEAD, FOR HE WAS THE PROMISED CHILD
SO WHEN WE NOW TAKE COMMUNION EATING FLESH AND BLOOD
IT'S THAT OF ISAAC INSTEAD, OR ADAM MADE OF SPIT AND MUD

RB WELSH, 2 2 22

THIS EARTH

WHEN GOD CREATED MAN AND THIS EARTH
WE WONDER WHY THINGS WENT WRONG FROM ITS BIRTH
AS OTHER STARS WERE CREATED IN THE SKY
THINGS SUDDENLY WENT WRONG THINGS WEN AWRY

AS PRISONS FILLED IN BRITAIN THEY WERE COMPELLED
TO DISPATCHER CRIMINALS TO THE COLONIES AS WELL
A LADY WHO JUST LOOKED AT SILK IN A STORE (Charles Dickens)
WE WAS ARRESTED FOUND GUILTY OF STEALING ONCE MORE

THEN SENT TO AUSTRALIA TO LIVE OUT HER LIFE
SHE FOUND OUT IT WAS FULL OF EVIL AND STRIFE
AS WERE OTHER COLONIES HERE ON THIS EARTH
LEADING TO WAR AND EVIL INSTEAD OF REBIRTH

SO IT IS WITH ALL PLANETS HERE IN THIS UNIVERSE
THEY WERE CREATED GOOD BUT THINGS JUST REVERSED
FOR CRIMINALS CAME IN THEIR FLYING MACHINES
BRINGING EVIL CALLED THE DEVIL TO EARTH IT SEEMS

RB WELSH, 2 3 22

CREATION

THE HOLY SPIRIT WITH THE SPEED OF ITS LIGHT
CREATED HEAVENS OF STARS IN THE VOID OF NIGHT
SENDING MINOR GODS TO THEIR CONSTELLATIONS
SPIRIT'S THE SOURCE OF COSMIC CONSCIOUSNESS

WITH THE SUPER SPEED OF THIS LIGHT
ITS RAYS BEGAN TO SOLIDIFY
STIRRING AS IT WENT ROUND AND ROUND
INTO GRANUALS OF DUST THEN EARTHLY GRIME

THE HOLY SPIRIT IS THE SOURCE
OF STARS AND PLANETS IN THEIR COURSE
WHERE GODS FORMED EXTRA-TERRESTRIAL MEN
TO WORK PROGRESS AND WORSHIPED THEM

WITH THE EXPIRATION OF THESES STARS
MEN MOVED ON IN SPACESHIPS FROM PLACES LIKE MARS
NOW ON EARTH THERE ARE CONSIDERABLY MORE RACES
THAN THOSE OF THE SUMERIAN HAM SHEM AND JAPETH

AFTERLIFE WAS PROVED BY MOSES AND ELIJAH
WHO APPEARED ON TRANSFIGURATION MOUNT WITH THE MESSIAH
SO WE WONDER WHY JESUS HAD TO BE CRUCIFIED
NEVERTHELESS, HE WAS RAISED WITH THE ROBBER THE DAY HE DIED

RB WELSH, 2 4 22

WE

WE ARE ALL THE SONS OF GOD
WE ARE TO BE JESUS TO ONE AND ALL
WE ARE ALL BORN OF VIRGINS
LIKE MARY, EXACTLY THE SAME VERSION

WE ARE MEANT TO CARRY THE CROSS
TO PERFORM MIRACLES FOR THOSE WHO ARE LOST
CURE THE SICK, HEAL THE BLIND
BUT MOST OF ALL, BE KIND

DOES GOD START ALL THESE WARS?
CAUSE DISEASES WE HAVE TO BE VACCINATED FOR
THOUGH ACCIDENT OR LACK OF SKILL
CAUSE MEN TO BE POOR AND HAVE TO STEAL

TODAY YOU'LL BE WITH ME IN PARADISE
IN THE GARDEN OF EDEN WITH THE TREE OF LIFE
WHERE RUNNING AROUND NAKED WILL BE IN STYLE
MEN WILL BE REUNITED WITH THEIR WIVES

NOT HAVING AGAIN TO EAT OF THE APPLE
FOR NOW, OUR COMPUTERS ARE QUITE AMPLE
WE CAN PASS IT ON TO MEN STILL ON EARTH
ANSWERS TO PROBLEMS HAVE SURGED

"YE GODS," THE PSALMIST SAYS
BEING BORN OF ISAAC AND REBECCA'S CLAN
FOR JACOB, WRESTLING WITH GOD FELT VERY ESTRANGED
TO ISRAEL ON A NIGHT WHERE HIS NAME WAS CHANGED

SO IF YOU WANT TO BE BLUNT ABOUT IT ALL
CHANGE YOUR WAYS AND ACT LIKE AS IF YOU ARE GOD.

RB WELSH, 2 1 22

GOD'S LIGHT

IT WAS ON GOD'S MOUNTAIN THAT HE FIRST SHOWED HIS LIGHT,
THEN IT WAS TRANSFERRED TO MOSES. IT WAS SO GLOWING BRIGHT.
NOW WE ARE IN BABYLON TO SOON BE RELEASED,
IT'S THE SAME GOD NAMED AHURA-MAZDA DIRECTING OUR PRIESTS.

USING CYRUS AND DARIUS,
PERSIA CONQUERED BABYLON.
ALLOWING EZRA AND NEHEMIAH
TO FULFILL THE PROPHECY OF JEREMIAH.

GOD'S FINGERPRINTS ARE ALL OVER THIS DRAMATIC RESCUE,
: PERFECT IN TIMING; FULFILLED SO SMOOTH.
THEIR KINGS AND WISE MEN WILL COME FROM THE EAST,
TO LAY GIFTS AT BABY JESUS'S FEET.

THE PEOPLE OF JUDAH WERE RETURNING HOME,
TAKING FIVE MONTHS WITH CATTLE, CAMELS, AND GOLD.
DIRECTED IN MINUTE DETAIL IN METHODS TO BE USED
BY OUR GOD /THEIR GOD, THE TRANSITION WAS SMOOTH.

CAPTURED TEMPLE TREASURES WERE ALL RETURNED,
EXCEPT FOR THE ARK, THAT HAS NEVER EMERGED.
YES, GOD USED HIMSELF AS THE PERSIAN MAZDA
TO DIRECT THEIR ARMIES, LIKE A HEAVENLY RAPTURE.

PERSIA'S GOD AND OUR GOD MUST BE THE SAME,
AND IT'S SAD NEITHER WILL RESCUE UKRAINE.
THEIR SAVIOR, MITHRA, WAS BORN ON A DECEMBER TWENTY-FIFTH,
PERSIANS WORSHIP OUR GOD, ALLAH, BECAUSE OF THE TRINITY MYTH.

RB WELSH, 3 7 22

OUR GOD, THEIR GOD

DO YOU THINK FOR A MINUTE THAT OUR GOD
COULD ORDER OTHER NATIONS, KINGS AND GOD AROUND,
UNLESS HE WERE THE SAME GOD TOO
THAT IS REVERED BY THAT NATION TOO.

OUR GOD IS THE GOD OF ALL THE EARTH,
HE CALLED NEBUCHADNEZZAR HIS "SERVANT" AT FIRST.
NOW THE JUDEANS ARE TO BE RETURNED,
SO GOD ENLISTS CYRUS, HIS "SHEPHERD," TO DO THIS WORK.

IS IT NOT INTERESTING THAT OUR GOD
IS THE SAME AS AHURA-MAZA,
ORDERING KING CYRUS TO INVADE
TO RESCUE THE JUDEANS FROM BABYLONIA.

AHURA-MAZDA IS THEIR GOD OF LIGHT,
LIKE OURS ON SINAI 40 DAYS AND NIGHTS,
TELLING MOSES SINCE HE WAS NOW ALSO AGLOW,
TO PUT ON A MASK SO THE LAW COULD BE BESTOWED.

THE PEOPLE WEREN'T ENSLAVED BUT MERGED IN WELL,
COMPILING THE TALMUD, SEEING THE FEATS OF DANIEL.
THERE WERE SHADRACH, MESHAK AND AKBEDNEGO
AND THE SON OF MAN COMING ON CLOUDS.

CYRUS LOCATES TEMPLE PLANS IN THE LAND OF THE MEDES,
ROUSES EZRA TO AWAKEN THE CHILDREN AND GETS HIM TO LEAD
THEM BACK TO JUDEA WITH A NEW SONG
THEY WON'T BE WORSHIPING BAAL, WHERE ALL WENT WRONG.

HISTORY NEVER REVEALS THIS COINCIDENCE ABOUT THIS THING:
THAT OUR GOD/THEIR GOD USE TIME OF THREE KINGS REIGNS.
IT'S CYRUS, DARIUS, AND ARTAXERXES; BESIDES
AHASUERUS MARRIED ESTHER, A FOREIGN WIFE.

THOUGH EVEN JOSEPH HAD MARRIED THE DAUGHTER OF POTTER,
EZRA INSISTED MEN PUT AWAY WIVES, SONS, AND DAUGHTERS.
CONFORMING TO THE LAW, MEN REPENTED FOR ALL SINS.
THEY WENT TO WORK ON THE WALLS AND THE TEMPLE AGAIN.

THEN IT WAS A SAD DAY WHEN THE SELEUCID KING.
ANTIOCHUS CONQUERED ASSYRIA, ATTACKING THE MACCABEES.
SO THE HEBREWS ARE LOOKING FOR THEIR MESSIAH NOW.
TO SAVE THEM AS DEPICTED IN THE APOCRYPHA.

ONE LIKE THE SON OF MAN IN REVELATION
IT APPEARS AS GOD'S SIGNET RING[1] IN HAGGAI'S PROCLAMATION,
ZERUBBABEL WILL LEAD THE FIRST WAVE BACK TO JERUSALEM
AND BECOME JUDAH'S FIRST KING REBUILDING IT LIKE HEAVEN.

RB WELSH, 3 11 22

IT WAS GOD

GOD WAS JESUS IN THIS SITUATION,
THERE'S BEEN AN INCORRECT INTERPRETATION.
RIGHT BEFORE OUR EYES, IT'S INCOMPREHENSIBLE,
HOW RE-INTERPRETATIONS CAN BECOME SO NONSENSICAL.

IT WAS GOD, HIMSELF, YOU SEE, THAT THEY CRUCIFIED,
FOR ONLY GOD, HIMSELF, COULD BE DEAD AND THEN RISE.
THAT WAS EVIDENT WHEN MARY THOUGHT HE WAS THE GARDENER,
IT WAS THE PROTEAN GOD POSING AS HE DID AS THE JERICHO SOLDIER.

IT WAS GOD AGAIN ON THE ROAD TO EMMAUS,
UNRECOGNIZABLE TILL BREAKING THE BREAD-LIKE JESUS.
GOING THROUGH THE WALL INTO THE UPPER ROOM.
THOMAS HAD TO FEEL THE HOLE IN HIS SIDE, FOR HE DIDN'T KNOW WHOM.

RB WELSH, 4 20 22

GOD:

I'M HERE ON MY MOUNTAIN WITH MOSES; I AM GOD,
TO GIVE HIM MY COMMANDMENTS AND MY LAWS.
THOUGH I AM KNOWN BY MANY NAMES,
I AM THE ONLY ONE JUST THE SAME.
I AM THE FATHER, THE SON, AND THE HOLY SPIRIT,
I AM BUDDHA AND VISHNU AND EVEN MARDUK.
THE HOLY SPIRIT IS SUPREME OF ALL THESE,
FOR IT IS THE ONE YOU CANNOT BLASPHEME.
I CREATED THESE HEAVENS, THIS EARTH, ALL IN IT.
BEGINNING WITH THE NEANDERTHAL MAN,
HEAVENS AND EARTH EVOLVED IN EONS.
SUPPO I'LL HAVE TO BECOME MAN TO UNDERSTAND HIM,
ASSURE HIM THAT WHEN HE DIES, HE'LL GO TO HEAVEN.
NAVAS AND ATOMIC WAR MELTED PLANETS LIKE MARS
MEN IN FLYING MACHINES CAME HERE FROM AFAR,
CALLED THE AXIAL NATIONS, THEY SETTLED IN THE EAST,
BRINGING GIFTS AS WISEMEN TO THE BABY JESUS.
THE HOLY SPIRIT CREATED THE ENTIRE UNIVERSE.
WITH A LIGHT BEYOND MAN'S WAVELENGTH; IT'S SO LUMINOUS;
THE LIGHT OF LOVE BEYOND ALL CALCULATION;
SO INTENSE THIS COSMOS CONSCIOUSNESS BRINGS TRANSFORMATION.
SO A TRINITY IS MORE POWERFUL, STRONGER, AND SAFE,
I AM ONENESS AS ALLAH; MY SUBJECT BOWING TO PRAY.
YOU DIDN'T KNOW THAT I AM ALSO SATAN.
IT'S MY ALTER-EGO LIKE BA-EL OF CANAAN.
ONENESS IS WHOLENESS; THERE IS NO OTHER WAY.
I SELECTED THE HEBREWS AS MY CHOSEN RACE;
THE OTHERS CAME HERE FROM OUTER SPACE.
SO I HAVE BEEN FRUSTRATED IN MANY WAYS,
AT ABOUT EVERY TURN. ABOUT EVERY DAY.

RB WELSH, 3 14 22

ONE GOD

DO YOU WANT TO KNOW WHY I BECAME THE CHRIST?
IT'S TO UNIFY THE WORLD, THE RACES, AND ALL LIVES.
THROUGH CHRIST, ALL MEN CAN BE BORN AGAIN AND FREE,
TO WORSHIP ONLY HIM, THE ONE WHO'S NOW YOUR KING.

THAT WAS GOD UPON THE CROSS.
CRUCIFIED AND GIVING UP THE GHOST.
JESUS CHRIST IS MORE LIBERAL.
NOT SO STRICT AND UNFORGIVABLE.

IT'S ONLY MY BODY THAT WILL DIE,
MY SPIRIT IS STILL ALIVE.
MOHAMMEDANS ARE HALF HEBREWS.
FULFILL MY PROMISE TO ISHMAEL AND BECOME ALLAH TOO.

I KNOW NOW WHERE I MADE A MISTAKE,
IN CHOOSING ONLY ONE AS A CHOSEN RACE.
NOW CHRIST WILL REPRESENT THEM ALL,
UNITE THE WORLD, EAST, AND WEST, LARGE AND SMALL.

THE BAPTISMAL RITUAL SAVED THEM,
THAT'S PRETTY SIMPLE AND FORGIVABLE
IT'S THE LIGHT THAT YOU'LL RECEIVE,
FROM THEN ON, YOU'LL BELIEVE
ABOVE ALL IS THE HOLY SPIRIT,
SOURCE OF ALL BEING AND ITS LIMITS.

MANY PEOPLE RELATE JUST HOW GLORIOUS,
STORIES ABOUT NEAR-DEATH EXPERIENCES.
THEIR SPIRIT JUST POPS OUT AND SEES,
JUST HOW THEIR OPERATION PROCEEDS.

JUST BEFORE THE CALAMITY,
THE SPIRIT JUMPS OUT OF THE BODY,
TO WATCH HIMSELF IN HIS CAR,
PLUNGE OVER THE CLIFF; IT IS BIZARRE.

SO IT WAS GOD WHOM THE JEWS KILLED,
BUT WHEN THEY ASKED, THEY WERE FORGIVEN.
NOW IT IS OUR HEART THAT IS CIRCUMCISED,
THE LAW IS WRITTEN ON OUR MINDS.

SO IF I WERE A FORTUNE TELLER,
I WOULD PREDICT ETERNAL LIFE BY THE SAVIOR,
IN THE FORM OF NOT A BODY BUT AN IKON,
THIS, YOU CAN ABOUT RELY ON.

SO NOW IT IS JESUS CHRIST AS KING,
THAT IS BASICALLY WHAT SAINT PAUL IS SAYING.,
BUT ONE CAN BE CRUCIFIED, HIS BODY DEAD,
BUT HIS SPIRIT IS STILL ALIVE AND WELL.

RB WELSH, 3 31 22

SUBSTITUTE

YOU DON'T REALLY THINK THAT A MAN IN HIS RIGHT MIND
WOULD CAUSE HIS OWN SON TO COMMIT SUICIDE.
THEN TELL THE WORLD THAT WHOEVER BELIEVED
WOULD BE SAVED FROM HELL FOR ETERNITY.

IT WASN'T A JESUS-LIKE THING FOR A MAN TO SAY,
GET THIRTY PIECES AND GIVE ME AWAY.
OR SELL YOUR CLOAKS AND BUY SWORDS,
BUT GOD WOULD DO THIS AND CHANGE PLACES FOR THE ONE HE ADORES.

NO, IT WOULD BE BETTER IF THE MAN GO AND HANG HIMSELF AS THE LOSS,
THEN HAVE HIS OWN SON COMMITTED TO THE CROSS.
SO GOD, IN HIS OWN INIMITABLE WAY,
HE PICKED UP THE CROSS AND TOOK HIS PLACE.

GOD WAS JESUS IN THIS SITUATION,
THERE HAVE BEEN INCORRECT INTERPRETATIONS.
RIGHT BEFORE OUR EYES, IT'S INCOMPREHENSIBLE,
HOW RE-INTERPRETATIONS CAN BECOME SO NONSENSICAL.

RB WELSH, 4 20 22

GROUNDS FOR INCRIMINATION

WHAT DID JESUS EVER DO? IS THERE SOMETHING I'VE MISSED?
FOR TO EVER GET ON THE ROMANS MOST WANTED LIST?
HE MAY HAVE CREATED AN UPROAR AMONGST JEWS,
HE IS ARGUING WITH THE PHARISEES WITH PARABLES AND HIS VIEWS.

IT WAS WHEN HE ADVISED THEM TO PAY THE ROMAN TAX,
BUT THEY WERE NEVER THREATENING THEIR POWER OR LEADING AN ATTACK.
I KNOW HE WAS ON A DEFINITE MISSION,
TO BE TRIED AND CRUCIFIED FOR MAN'S SINS.

ONE NEVER KNOWS WHAT MAN BELIEVES,
HE SITS AROUND WITH THE ATTITUDE OF "JUST WAIT AND SEE."
CAN THE COURTS TRY A MAN WHO HEALS THE BLIND?
FEEDING THE POOR IS WHAT KIND OF CRIME?

ON WHAT GROUNDS FOR HEALING THE CENTURIANS SERVANT?
CAN HE BE TRIED IN COURT AND CONVICTED?
THERE WERE ZEALOTS LIKE THE MACCABEES
WHO WON INDEPENDENCE FROM THE GREEKS

BUT THIS HISTORY LIES IN THE APOCRYPHA AS A GREAT EVENT,
SO THE CRUCIFIXION OF JESUS WILL TAKE PRECEDENCE.
JESUS HAD THE CHARACTERISTICS OF GOD HIMSELF AND IGNORED,
ORDERING HIS DISCIPLES TO SELL THEIR CLOAKS AND BUY SWORDS.

IT WAS HIS MESSIANIC MISSION TO COME TO JERUSALEM AND DIE,
SO YOU COULD BE SAVED IF YOU BELIEVED HE SURVIVED.
BUT CHECK AND SEE IF IT'S NOT GOD WHO HAS DIED.
AND THAT THE SPIRIT OF JESUS THE CHRIST HAS SURVIVED.

AMEN,
RB WELSH, 4 11 22

A TRINITY

THE HOLY SPIRIT IS THE GOD ABOVE GOD
A TRINITY WOULD INCLUDE MOHAMMED.
THE HOLY TRINITY THAT MAN HAS CONTRIVED,'
DOES NOT COME FROM ABOVE, IT IS A LIE.

THE TRINITY WE WORSHIP WAS INVENTED BY MAN,
AT THE COUNCIL OF NIVEA BY CONSTANTINE.
HE WANTED TO UNIFY HIS WHOLE EMPIRE,
SO HE CONCOCTED THIS THEORY WITH ANASTASIA'S ADVICE.

THE HOLY SPIRIT DECIDED TO CREATE THE UNIVERSE,
WITH THE SPEED OF LIGHT ATOMS SUDDENLY BURST.
FORMING ANNUALS INTO SOLIDS OVERRULED BY GODS,
FORMING MEN TO INHABIT WITH NATURE'S REWARDS.

THE EARTH IS STILL SPINNING IN ITS ORBIT,
TAKING ON RACES OF DYING PLANETS.
OUR GOD MAKING MEN CALLED ISRAELIS,
THOSE IN UFOS ARE EXTRA-TERRESTRIALS.

THEY ARE BRILLIANT AND SMART LOOKING LIKE A GECKO,
THEY HAVE AN ACCENT LIKE THOSE FROM AUSTRALIA.
THEY ARE LIGHT-YEARS AHEAD OF US IN FLYING MACHINES,
HELPING US INVENT ELECTRONICS, ROCKETS AND VACCINES.

THEY'VE BEEN AIDING MAN WITH PERSISTENCE,
BUT IT'S TOP SECRET, GOVERNMENT DENY THEIR EXISTENCE.
FLOATING STONES THROUGH THE AIR, BUILDING PYRAMIDS AND STONEHENGE.
PROVING TO GOVERNMENTS AND MEN OF THEIR EXISTENCE.

IF YOU DON'T THINK GOD IS AHURA-MAZSDA THEN,
WHERE IS THE LOGIC WHERE IS THE SENSE?
FOR MAZDA GLOWS AND GOD IS THE LIGHT,
JUST ASK MOSES FOR HE WORE A MASK TO PREVENT ISRAELI FRIGHT.

GOD IS ABOUT TO FREE JUDAH FROM CAPTIVITY;
ONLY THE PERSIANS ARE MENTIONED IN THIS ACTIVITY.
TAKING PLACE DURING REIGNS OF THREE PERSIAN KINGS.
THOUGH GOD PREDICTED IT, HE IS NOT MENTIONED IN THEIR RETURNING.

WHEN GOD INVENTED MAN HE DIDN'T SAY HE WAS ANGELIC,
GOD TEMPTS HIM AS SATAN; MOST ARE PSYCHO-PATHETIC,
TEMPTING GOD BACK WITH SMOKE, DRINK AND SEX.
WONDERING WHY JESUS DOESN'T HEAL THEM AS THEY EXPECT.

RB WELSH, 4 7 22

JOHN THE BAPTIST

WHY WAS JOHN THE BAPTIST ARRESTED AND PUT INTO PRISON?
IT SEEMS THAT HE ACCUSED HEROD OF INCEST AS THE REASON.
BUT HIS COUSIN, JESUS, HAD PROCLAIMED TO ALL,
HE HAD COME TO "FREE THE PRISONERS AND OPEN THEIR CELL DOORS."

DID HE COME TO SAVE US FROM OUR ADDICTION TO SIN?
OUR CRAZE FOR ALCOHOL, SEX AND DRUGS BINGE.
OR DID HE COME JUST TO SAVE OUR SOULS?
ERASING ALL TEMPTATIONS SHOULD BE HIS GOAL.

THE CHURCH IS ONLY INTERESTED IN THOSE WHO RECEIVED
JESUS, AS HIS SAVIOR, ACCEPTED CHURCH DOGMA AS DECREED.
NOW HERE HE IS IN JERUSALEM AT LAST,
FOR HE LIVED AND WORKED IN GALILEE FOR MANY YEARS PAST.

CONCLUDING WITH ANNOUNCING HE WAS THE EXPECTED MESSIAH,
PERFORMING MIRACLES AROUND THE SEA OF GALILEE, BUT NOT IN JUDAH.
WHILE HIS COUSIN, JOHN, WAS BAPTIZING, SAVING SOULS FROM ALL SIN.
SO WITH HIS FOLLOWING, JESUS LED THEM DOWN TO JERUSALEM.

TO CELEBRATE THE FEAST OF THE PASSOVER OF THE ANGEL OF DEATH,
FREEING ALL HEBREWS FROM SLAVERY AND NOW PRISONERS OF SIN.
IT TOOK THE DEATH OF THE FIRSTBORN, AND NOW IT IS SAID,
THAT JESUS IS THE SON OF GOD, SO CRUCIFY HIM AS REVENGE.

OF THE NATION OF THOUSANDS OF JEWS ATTENDING THIS FESTIVAL
WHILE JOHN THE BAPTIST HAS NOT BEEN ONE "FREED AS A PRISONER."
FOR HE, TOO, BE SACRIFICED JUST TO PLEASE SALOME, THE DANCER,
BY BEING BEHEADED WITH HIS HEAD ON A PLATTER.

JOHN'S HERITAGE IS PURE FROM A FAMILY OF PRIESTS,
WHILE THAT OF JESUS INCLUDES EVERY SIN, YOU CAN THINK.

SO THIS WHOLE WEEKEND TURNS OUT TO BE
ONE OF CHAOTIC HELL, WITH NO PRISONERS FREED.
AND TWO MESSIAHS CRUCIFIED WITH THE ROMANS STILL HERE.
SO, WHERE IS THE PROMISE? WHERE IS MY SHRINK?

RB WELSH, 4 27 22

THE FIG TREE

WOULD YOU JUST SPONTANEOUSLY,
JUST UP AND KILL A FIG TREE?
WHEN OTHERS ARE PRODUCING NEARBY,
TO FILL YOUR HUNGER PANGS AND SATISFY.

I DON'T THINK THIS WAS ANYONE BUT GOD
FOR JESUS, I'M SURE, NEVER WOULD.
ESPECIALLY WHEN IT'S IN A GROVE,
AND NOT JUST STANDING ALL ALONE.

THIS STORY WAS INSERTED INTENTIONALLY,
WITH NO CONNECTION THAT I COULD SEE.

WAS THIS A JUDGMENT AGAINST US ALL,
IF WE DON'T ACCEPT HIM OR FOLLOW THE LAW?
JESUS ALWAYS CURES OR HEALS,
THIS IS A GOD-LIKE ACT, I FEEL.

IT'S LIKE ONE WITH A DOUBLE PERSONALITY,
BOTH GOOD AND BAD ALTERNATELY.
DOES THIS REPRESENT ONE ON THE CROSS,
CONVICTED OF BEING KING OF THE UNIVERSE?

SMITTEN DOWN JUST BECAUSE
IT DISAGREES WITH GOD'S LAW.
THIS IS SO UN-JESUS-LIKE,
IT MUST BE GOD IN HIS WRATH TO SPITE.

THE JEWS ARE WAITING FOR JESUS
TO GET RID THEM OF THE ROMANS FOR THEIR FREEDOM.
THE FIG TREE GIVES THEM THE PERFECT EXAMPLE,
OF HOW HE WILL FREE THEM FROM THEIR SHACKLES.

HE HEALED THE SICK, FED THE POOR, AND HEALED THE BLIND.
WE LAY DOWN PALM LEAVES, CHEERING THAT HE ARRIVES.
THIS IS OUR SALVATION FROM THIS TYRANNY,
HE'S OUR SAVIOR; WE SHALL BE FREE!

BUT THAT'S NOT THE WAY IT TURNED OUT,
IT'S FOR OUR SINS IS WHAT IT'S ALL ABOUT.
BUT, I WAS SAVED WHEN BAPTIZED.
SO WAS JESUS, SO I'M SURPRISED.

HEBREWS ARE SAVED DESPITE THEIR TRANSGRESSIONS,
FOR WE SAW MOSES AND ELIJAH AT TRANSFIGURATION.
IF GENTILES DON'T BELIEVE AND OBEY,
THEY'LL BE LIKE THE FIG TREE, TO THEIR DISMAY.

RB WELSH, 5 13 22

CIRCUMCISION

PAUL WISHES HE COULD REMOVE HIS CIRCUMCISION,
NOW THAT HE'S BECOME A BONE-FIDE CHRISTIAN.
THE SPIRIT OF CHRIST SUPERSEDES GOD'S LAW, (REV 3:2-26).
AS HE WRITES TO THE GALATIANS RECEIVING THE CALL.

SO YOU CAN JUST FORGET THE COMMANDMENTS
FOR TO BE HIS DISCIPLE, YOU MUST HATE YOUR PARENT. (LK 14:26)
MOSES, PAUL SAID, WORE A MASK BECAUSE OF GOD'S WANING LIGHT. (2 COR 3)
YOUR EARTH SHALL BE CONVENANT FOR THE LAW CIRCUMCISED YOUR HEART. (JER 31:31)

RB WELSH, 5 14 22

THE WORD IS GOD

IF JESUS IS THE WORD IN THE BEGINNING. (JN 1:1)
THEN GOD IS JESUS, A HUMAN BEING.
FOR GOD CAN BE ANYTHING IN HIS PROTEAN WAY
A BURNING BUSH, A SOLDIER, OR EVEN JONAH'S WHALE.

GOD CAN BE THE GARDNER TO MARY AT THE TOMB; OR
THE BREAKER OF BREAD OR TO THE DISCIPLES IN THE ROOM
WHERE THOMAS MUST STICK HIS HAND IN HIS SIDE,
BEFORE GOD, AS JESUS, CAN BE RECOGNIZED.

IT'S LIKE JESUS WAS THE BABE BROUGHT IN BY THE STORK;
BUT IT'S REALLY GOD HIMSELF, IN HUMAN FORM.
THE SURPRISE BABY WAS LEFT ON THE FRONT PORCH,
BELIEVE IN HIM FOR YOUR ETERNAL REWARD.

ALL THAT'S REQUIRED IS YOUR BELIEF,
OUR SINS ARE FORGIVEN FOR CONSIDERATION SO CHEAP.
YOU WILL SEE THE LIGHT, EAT THE BREAD, DRINK THE WINE,
WITH JESUS HIMSELF, ON THE OTHER SIDE.

I DON'T THINK THAT ALL OF MY SINS CAN BE CONFESSED,
FOR I TRIED AND SUCCEEDED TO HAVE THEM REPRESSED.
TOO, I HAVE DEMENTIA, SO THE BELL SAVES ME,
INDEED, IT'S NOT POSSIBLE THAT I COULD GO TO HELL.

JESUS IS THE LOGOS, THE WORD IN JOHN ONE,
BUT IN 3:16 TURNS OUT TO BE GOD'S SON.
SO THE ONLY CONCLUSION THERE EVER CAN BE,
IS THAT GOD IS JESUS; IT'S CLEAR AS A BELL TO ME.

RB WELSH, 7 1 22

COMMUNION

IT IS SAID THAT JESUS, ON THE NIGHT HE WAS BETRAYED,
TOOK AND DRANK FROM THE CUP KNOWN AS THE HOLY GRAIL.
SAYING THIS IS MY BODY, THIS IS MY BLOOD.
THOUGH FORBIDDEN BY GOD IN A COVENANT WITH NOAH. (GEN 9:4)

I AM SURE THAT SAINT PAUL KNEW WELL OF THIS,
BUT HE HAD TO GET THE CORINTHIANS TO CONVERT TO JESUS.
PAUL'S LETTERS WERE WRITTEN RIGHT AFTER JESUS DIED,
AND IT WAS UP TO EIGHTY YEARS LATER THAT GOSPELS WERE DEVISED,

PAUL SAID IT CAME TO HIM RIGHT OUT OF THE BLUE,
EXACTLY JUST WHAT HE HAD TO DO.
TO GET THE CORINTHIANS TO SWITCH,
TO CHRISTIANITY FROM DIONYSUS.

THEIR CEREMONY INVOLVED EATING FLESH AND DRINKING BLOOD,
OF DANCING AND SINGING ON THE MOUNTAIN TO DIONYSUS.
THOUGH JESUS SAID HE WOULD NOT PARTAKE OF THE VINE,
PAUL CONCOCTED THIS CEREMONY OF THE BREAD AND THE WINE.

SUGGESTING TO THEM THAT THEY SHOULD SUBSTITUTE,
CHRISTIANITY FOR THIS CEREMONY OF CARNAL DISREPUTE.
SO TO THE CORINTHIANS, GOING INTO GREAT DETAIL,
PAUL OUTLINED THE PROCEDURE VERY WELL. (1 COR 11:23)

HIS LETTER TO THE CORINTHIANS WAS WRITTEN TWENTY YEARS BEFORE,
THE FIRST GOSPEL OF MARK IS BIBLICAL, OUT OF ORDER, OF COURSE.
EVEN THOUGH THERE COULD NOT BE ANY HOLY GRAIL,
THE KNIGHTS TEMPLAR HAVE POSSESSION OF IT, IT'S SAID.

SO THIS IS THE SACRAMENT OF THE EUCHARIST IT IS PROCLAIMED,
HAPPENS ONCE EVERY MONTH TO CONSUME HIS BODY AND BLOOD.
THOUGH GOD FORBADE THIS IN A COVENANT WITH NOAH, (GEN 9:4)
AS PAUL WELL KNOWS, HAVING STUDIED WITH GAMALIEL.

INTINCTION WAS THE ONE I WAS NOT TOO FOND OF THE WORST,
AND ALWAYS S THE CRUMBS I GAVE TO THE BIRDS.
"FOR THIS IS HIS BODY BROKEN FOR YOU."
OR THIS IS HIS BLOOD SHED FOR YOU TOO.

JESUS KNOWS THAT JUST ONCE A MONTH,
IT IS NOT EVEN QUITE ENOUGH,
FOR I HAVE TO PRAY CONSTANTLY,
TO GET THINGS DONE, HIS AND MY WAY.

WE ARE A TEAM, AND HE'S THE QUARTERBACK,
TELLING ME WHAT TO DO, NOT TO BE SLACK.
BARGING AHEAD, LETTING HIM LEAD,
FOR I AM A DUMMY, IN WAR OR PEACE.

RB WELSH, 5 16 22

THE LOST ARK

IT SEEMS THAT GOD'S SERVANT NEBUCHADNEZZAR
TOOK OFF WITH ALL OF THE TEMPLE TREASURES,
BUT ON ALL THE LISTS OF GOLDEN VESSELS RETURNED,
NOT ONE MENTION OF GOD'S ARK IS LEARNED.

NOW THAT IS GOD'S ARK OF THE COVENANT
CONTAMINATING THE LAW AND GOD HIMSELF.
IF IT ISN'T COMING BACK WITH THE ONES WHO WERE BANISHED,
ALL WE CAN SAY IS THAT IT SIMPLY HAS VANISHED.

THE PREVIOUS JOURNEY TOOK THEM 40 YEARS
TO RECEIVE THE LAW TO WHICH NOT EVEN GOD ADHERED
FOR THEY PLUNDERED AND MURDERED TO RECOVER THE LAND
THAT GOD HAD PROMISED TO ABRAHAM.

IT LOOKS LIKE THE ARK SHOULD BE LEADING AGAIN,
LIKE IT DID RETURN TO THE PROMISED LAND.
BUT SINCE SOLOMON PLACED IT IN THE HOLY OF HOLIES,
ONLY THE HIGH PRIEST WAS ALLOWED THERE FOR GOD'S GLORY.

GOD WAS BA-EL BRINGING ON THE DEPORTATION,
HE WAS AHURA-MAZDA BRINGING BACK THE NATION.
THE LORD GOD IS GOD, AND THERE IS NO OTHER,
HE MAKES MAN HAPPY; HE CAUSES HIM TO SUFFER.

RB WELSH, 6 24 22

CHRIST'S SPIRIT (PAUL TO GALATIANS)

WHAT PAUL IS TRYING TO TELL THE GALATIANS,
IS THAT THEY ARE NOT FIRST REQUIRED TO BE JEWS BEFORE CHRISTIANS.
IT IS THE SPIRIT OF CHRIST THAT POSSESSES THE MAN,
THEN THE LAW WILL TAKE CARE OF ITSELF, PERCHANCE.

THIS DOESN'T MEAN HE CAN NOW BE TATTOOED,
OR THAT PORK IS NO LONGER RESTRICTED FOOD.
IT'S A MATTER OF CONSCIENCE IN EVERY CASE.
IT INCLUDES EVERY PERSON OF EVERY RACE.

THE COVENANT WITH GOD CAN NOW BE BYPASSED,
THEY HAD A GOOD START, BUT NOW THEY HAVE LAPSED.
PAUL WISHES HE COULD REMOVE HIS CIRCUMCISION,
NOW THAT HE'S BECOME A BONE'-FIFE CHRISTIAN.

AFTER GOING THROUGH THE EYE OF THE NEEDLE WITH QUMRAN'S ESSENES,
HE GRADUATED AS A CAMEL, NICKNAMED THE WICKED PRIEST.
THAT HE GRADUATED AT ALL IS A SURPRISE.,
FOR THE ESSENES ARE NOT FOR CHRIST.

THEY ARE GOD-CENTERED, NOT GOING AMISS,
BUT PAUL HAD FALLEN ON HIS HEAD WATCHING AN ECLIPSE.
ONE DOESN'T "SEE" A LIGHT, FOR IT'S BEYOND MAN'S WAVELENGTH.'
HE JUST FEELS THE RAY OR BEAM DRIVING INTO HIS BRAIN.

PAUL CLAIMS THE SPIRIT OF CHRIST SUPERSEDES GOD'S LAW, (GAL 3:2-26)
AS HE WRITES TO THE GALATIANS RECEIVING THE CALL.
SO YOU CAN JUST FORGET THE LAW AND COMMANDMENTS,
FOR TO BE HIS DISCIPLE, YOU MUST HATE YOUR PARENTS. (LK 14:26)

THE MOST CONFUSING PART OF HIS WHOLE LETTER,
IT IS THE ANALOGY OF HAGAR AND SARAH.
HAGAR IS KNOWN AS BEING THOSE FROM SINAI AND THE LAW,
WHILE THOSE OF SARAH ARE THOSE IN JERUSALEM OF HEAVEN ABOVE.

IT WAS EMBARRASSING WHEN PAUL CHALLENGED PETER,
ABOUT EATING WITH GENTILES AFTER ENVISIONING FORBIDDEN FOOD ON THE SHEET.
THIS, YOU MIGHT SAY, IS A NEW LAW,
THE SPIRIT OF CHRIST ALLOWS THIS "FAUX PAS."

ONE HAS TO BE A GENIUS TO FIGURE OUT WHAT HE SAYS,
THOUGH JESUS LOVES CHILDREN, PAUL "BECAME A MAN."
THIS DOUBLE-TALK MUST BE CONFUSING TO THEM,
BUT NOW IT'S THE GOSPEL, SO JUST SAY, "AMEN."

RB WELSH, 5 28 22

OPPOSITES

THE WORLD IS BUT A MYRIAD OF OPPOSITES.
THAT INCLUDES GOD THOUGH HIS LOVE PREDOMINATES.
FOR WHO DECIDED TO SEND SATAN TO JOB,
OR KILL OFF AT PASSOVER THE EGYPTIAN FIRSTBORN?

YES, IN THIS CONSTELLATION, GOD CREATED THE SUNS,
THEN HE CREATED MAN WITH JEWS AS THE CHOSEN ONES.
THIS WHOLE CREATION IS A SHIMMERING DISC,
MAGNIFICENT IN ITS POLARITIES OPERATIONAL TECHNIQUE.

OTHER GODS IN THE UNIVERSE MADE THEIR OWN MEN,
WHO VISIT US REGULARLY IN UFO FLYING MACHINES.
AIDING IN PROGRESS WITH SIMPLE ELECTRONICS,
HALTING ATOMIC WARS BLASTING SILOS WITH ULTRASONIC.

AS THE SUNS OF THE HEAVENS EXPLODE, CITIZENS GET IN THEIR CRAFTS,
TO FLY TO THE EARTH WITH THEIR GODS WITH GREAT DISPATCH.
GOD IS THEIR GOD UNDER ANOTHER NAME,
NEBUCHADNEZZAR IS GOD'S "SERVANT" WHO REIGNS.

DO WE REALIZE THE BAAL IS REALLY BA-EL?
GOD TEMPTED EVE, AND HE TEMPTED ISRAEL AS WELL.
ASSYRIA ABSORBED ISRAEL AFTER THE SPLIT,
JUDAH LEARNED NO LESSON WITH THE SAME PUNISHMENT.

IT TOOK JONAH IN A WHALE TO WARN OF THE CONSEQUENCES,
IF ASSYRIA DID NOT SUBMIT TO GOD AND HIS ELEMENTS.
NOW JUDAH IS TO BE SAVED BY THE GOD OF PERSIA,
WHO IS GOD UNDER THE NAME OF AHURA-MAZDA?

NOW WE WONDER WHAT SINS DID THE JEW COMMIT,
FOR GOD TO LET HITLER SEND THEM TO AUSCHWITZ.
AT ANY RATE, THEY ARE NOW ACCESSIBLE AGAIN
IN ISRAEL AGAIN AS THE GARDEN OF EDEN.

RB WELSH, 6 3 2022

REBIRTH

EXILE TO BABYLON IS JEWISH CRUCIFIXION,
THE RETURN TO JUDAH IS BEING RAISED TO HEAVEN.
THIS RETURN IS THE SAME AS REBIRTH AGAIN,
SALVATION FROM THE BONDAGE OF SIN.

WITH GOD AS JESUS, ONLY ONE MAN DIED,
BUT JUDAH IN THE EXILE WAS CRUCIFIED,
THEY DESCENDED INTO THE HELL OF BABYLON,
TO BE RAISED ONCE MORE TO JERUSALEM.

THE HEBREWS ARE GOD'S LABORATORY.
FROM CREATION, THEY ARE QUITE A STORY,
GOD'S GIANT FLOOD LET HIM BEGIN AGAIN,
BUT MOTHER NATURE LED TO THE FAMINE.

FROM THE HELL OF SLAVERY DUE TO SARAH'S SIN
OF SENDING ABRAHAM INTO HAGAR FOR THE PROMISE
TO REBIRTH IN THE EXODUS TO SINAI,
THE SAME THING IS HAPPENING TO YOU AND ME.

INSTEAD OF CRUCIFYING THE WHOLE NATION,
JESUS AS KING WAS THEIR SALVATION.
SO WHY SHOULD MEN DISCRIMINATE? WE'RE EQUALS,
EXCEPT WHEN WE LOOK AT EXTRA-TERRESTRIALS.

THAT WE ARE THE ONLY HUMANS IN THE UNIVERSE
IS PRESUMPTUOUS OR WORSE,

RB WELSH, 6 11 22

SALVATION

THE PREACHERS TELL US THAT JESUS CHRIST
IS THE ONE OF THE THREE TO EMPHASIZE.
SO WHY DID PETER AND JOHN RETURN AND REBAPTIZE
SAMARITANS WHO WERE BAPTIZED BY JESUS CHRIST. (ACTS 8:15,16)

WE ALREADY KNOW THAT THE HOLY SPIRIT IS SUPREME,
FOR COSMIC CONSCIOUSNESS TO BE ACHIEVED.
FOR ONE MAY TAKE THE NAME OF JESUS OR GOD IN VAIN,
BUT ASSUMING THAT OF THE SPIRIT; NO FORGIVENESS IS OBTAINED. (MK 3:28)

JUST THAT TO ME, IT SEEMS,
MAKES THE HOLY SPIRIT SUPREME.
THAT MAKES THE TRINITY OF NICEA,
JUST ANOTHER ONE OF MAN'S PANACEAS.

WHEN THE JUDEANS WERE RESCUED FROM BABYLONIA,
AND RETURNED TO JERUSALEM BY THE KING OF PERSIA,
THEY FOUND THE ONES REMAINING HAD FOREIGN WIVES,
BUT ESTHER HAD MARRIED ASAHEURUS TO SAVE JEWISH LIVES.

COMMON SENSE IS WHAT WE ALWAYS EXPECT,
BUT IRONY OF LIFE IS WHAT WE ALWAYS GET.

RB WELSH, 6 15 22

IN EXILE

WHY WOULD WE, IN OUR WEAKNESS, WISH TO RETURN
TO OUR HOMELAND IN ISRAEL, THAT HAS BEEN BURNED?
WE ARE NOW SETTLED DOWN AS A NEW GENERATION
TO FACE THE FUTURE WITHOUT ALL THIS HUMILIATION.

NO ONE SAID ANYTHING ABOUT SCHOOL,
WE CAN'T READ THE COMMANDMENTS, SO WE ARE FOOLS.
THERE WAS ONLY ONE TEMPLE IN WHICH TO PRAY,
AND IT WAS IN THE CENTER OF THE NATION, FAR AWAY.

MEN CAN EASILY BE TEMPTED, WE KNOW,
IT'S IN MAN'S NATURE, AS EVE DID SHOW.
GOD INSTILLED IT IN MAN AT THE CREATION,
BAAL IS REALLY BA-EL, THE GOD OF OUR NATION.

THERE WON'T BE LOVE TILL WE'RE TAKEN TO HEAVEN,
ALL THIS FUSS ABOUT SACRIFICE IN THE TEMPLE FOR REDEMPTION,
IT IS JUST ROUTINE AND IS MEANINGLESS,
SO I'LL STAY HERE IN BABYLON, WORSHIPING DANIEL INSTEAD.

LIKE THE SON OF MAN, HE CAME IB ON THE CLOUDS,
SURVIVING A FIERY FURNACE, WE THINK HE'S ENDOWED
WITH THE STATUS OF THE PROMISED MESSIAH;
WHO WILL CIRCUMCISE OUR HEARTS, PROPHESIED JEREMIAH?

RB WELSH, 6 16 22

MESSIANIC SECRET

THIS WAS SOMETHING NEVER PROPHESIED.
THAT JESUS WOULD GO TO JERUSALEM TO COMMIT SUICIDE.
FOR HE WAS TO LEAVE GALILEE AFTER CURING MEN
AND ORDER THEM NOT TO TELL HOW IT HAPPENED.

THE ACT OF BEING TRIED BY THE ROMAN COURT FOR BLASPHEMY,
AND AS KING OF THE JEWS, HIS DEATH GOES DOWN IN INFAMY.
FOR THIS WAS THE OBJECT OF HIS MESSIANIC SECRET,
THAT HE WOULD BE CRUCIFIED YET RISE FOR OUR SALVATION.

ALL MAN HAS TO DO IS BELIEVE IN THIS
AND HE WILL BE SAVED IN ETERNAL BLISS.
BUT FIRST, CURE ISRAEL FROM THE WHIP OF THE ROMANS,
FOR THIS IS HARD TO BELIEVE IF YOU WANT TO KNOW IT.

WE KNOW YOU CAN PERFORM THE IMPOSSIBLE,
THE HEALING, THE CURING, THE FEEDING OF THOUSANDS.
BUT ONLY GOD HIMSELF COULD RISE FROM BEING DEAD,
THOUGH WE SAW MOSES AND ELIJAH, YOUR BLOOD WASN'T SHED.

AND IT IS TRUE; THE THIEF BELIEVED, NEXT TO YOU, OKAY?
WE HEARD YOU SAY, "HE WOULD BE IN PARADISE TODAY."
WE KNOW THAT MARY WOULDN'T RECOGNIZE GOD,
ESPECIALLY SINCE SHE THOUGHT YOU WERE THE GARDENER,
ALL THIS IS GETTING TO SEEM ODDER AND ODDER.

IF THAT WAS YOU, WHY DID THE MEN ON THE ROAD TO EMMAUS,
NOT RECOGNIZING YOU UNTIL BREAKING THE BREAD IS CURIOUS.
BUT THE STRAW WAS WHEN THOMAS COULDN'T RECOGNIZE YOU,
IT'S BECAUSE YOU ARE GOD, NOT THE JESUS WE KNEW.

RB WELSH, 7 16 22

THE WORD

JUST THINK, GOD, AND I CREATED THIS SPECK OF EARTH,
IN THE VASTNESS AND FAR-REACHING SPACE OF THE UNIVERSE.
WITH THE LAWS OF OPPOSITES CONTROLLING ITS OPERATION,
THE RULERS WILL NECESSARILY BE GOD AND SATAN.

IN THE PROMISED LAND, THERE'LL BE BAAL AND BA-EL,
AS IN LIFE, MAN IS CONFRONTED WITH HEAVEN AND HELL.
THE GOD OF STRICTNESS AND LAWS,
HAS TURNED IT ALL OVER TO JESUS, HIS SON.

IT WAS GOD THEY CRUCIFIED. DEAD AND BURIED,
THEN WHEN FOUND ALIVE, HE HAD LOST HIS IDENTITY.
A GARDENER TO MARY, THOMAS FELT THE SWORD HOLE IN HIS SIDE
IT WAS GOD WHO WAS DEAD, NOT HIS SON WHO WAS ALIVE.

IN HIS PROTEAN WAY, GOD HAD APPEARED
AS A BUSH, A SOLDIER, A WHALE, OR SPIRIT WIND.
ON A MISSION TO SODOM OR AS ABRAHAM IN SARAH'S TENT,
IT'S LIKE NIETZSCHE SAID, "WE KILLED HIM," CRUCIFIED AND DEAD.

JESUS, THE CHRIST, THE LOGOS, GOD'S SON,
IS ALIVE AND WELL, IS KING, HE IS ONE,
GOD IS ALLAH OF ISLAM, NOT IN THE TRINITY
AS VOTED ON BY THE COUNCIL OF NICEA.

JESUS, THE LOGOS, CREATED HEAVEN AND EARTH,
THOUGH BOTH WILL PASS AWAY, HIS WORDS,
THE LOGOS, WILL LIVE FOREVER AS HE PROCLAIMED.
HUMANITY WILL DEPART IN THEIR SAUCERS TO ESCAPE.

I AM HERE AT PENTECOST TO BAPTIZE
WITH WIND AND FIRE, AS JOHN PROPHESIED.
TRANSFIGURED AS SAVED FOR ALL WILL BELIEVE,
IN THE HOLY SPIRIT, GOD, AND ME.

RB WELSH, 7 20 22

LAZARUS

BELIEF IN RESURRECTION REVOLVES AROUND THIS EVENT:
THAT JESUS COULD RAISE MEN FROM THE DEAD.
LAZARUS HAD BEEN FOUR DAYS IN THE TOMB FOR,
BUT WAS RESURRECTED AS IF REBORN FROM THE WOMB.

THIS SEEMS TO BE THE CRUX OF THE JESUS STORY.
THAT LIFE IS EVERLASTING, AS SHOWN BY CALGARY.
WE COULD HAVE ASKED LAZARUS WHAT TO EXPECT,
WHEN A MAN DIES, WHAT IS IT LIKE IN HEAVEN?

WHAT IS THE TEMPERATURE? DOES IT EVER RAIN?
ARE THERE FISH IN THE BROOK? DO I HAVE TO SHAVE?
NO, ALL THAT WE KNOW IS THAT HE'S STILL ALIVE,
ALL WE HAVE TO DO IS BELIEVE TO SURVIVE.

ALL THIS SHOWS IS THAT MAN SURVIVES,
THAT HE LIVES FOREVER AND NEVER DIES.
SO WHY, THEN DOES JESUS GO TO JERUSALEM,
TO BE TRIED AND KILLED, THEN GO TO HEAVEN?

MARTHA, I'M SURE, WOULD ASK WHAT IT'S LIKE,
WHEN ONE DIES, WHAT TO EXPECT ON THE OTHER SIDE?
MARY WOULD NOT CARE JUST SO LONG AS SHE
COULD BE WITH JESUS, WHATEVER HE SHOULD BE.

FOR ALL WE KNOW, HE WENT TO OBLIVION,
FOR HE DIDN'T SAY WHAT IT'S LIKE IN HEAVEN.
THIS MAKES JESUS' DEATH SEMI-CLIMATIC,
SUICIDAL AT BEST; PSYCHOSOMATIC.

THIS ONLY HELPS PROVE THE THEORY OF RE-INCARNATION,
IN MY PREVIOUS LIFE, I WAS CLEOPATRA OR CARL SAGAN.
GOD IS REBORN AS JESUS, FOR SURE.
THE CHRIST IS ONE WE CAN LOVE AND ADORE.

SO THIS IS WHY GOD-JESUS WENT TO HIS TRIAL,
TO DECLARE HE IS NOT GOD FOR HIS SURVIVAL.
TO DENY THAT HE IS "KING OF THE JEWS,"
THAT HE WOULDN'T TRY TO OVERTHROW THE ROMAN RULE.

BUT JESUS DOES NOTHING ON HIS OWN BEHALF,
HE INTENDED ALL ALONG TO BE COMMITTED TO DEATH.
ONLY TO PROVE TO MAN THAT THERE'S ETERNAL LIFE,
THOUGH MEN THOUGHT THEY WERE SAVED WHEN BAPTIZED.

WHAT IS THE POINT OF HIS COMING AGAIN ON THE CLOUDS?
MEN SPEAKING IN TONGUES, BAPTIZING WITH WIND AND FIRE?
ETERNITY IS LONG, EVEN THOUGH THERE'S NO WAR OR CRIME.
TRANSFIGURATION PROVED THE AFTERLIFE, SO WHY BE CRUCIFIED?

LET'S HAVE A HEAVEN RIGHT HERE ON EARTH.
WITH NO DIVISIONS, RACE PROBLEMS TO AVERT.
LET'S HAVE PERPETUAL PEACE, THE THRILL OF LIGHT.
WITH NATIONS AND MEN WITH THE SPIRIT OF CHRIST.

BY THE TIME THESE GOSPELS ARE WRITTEN, THE TEMPLE'S DESTROYED.
GOD'S ARK DISAPPEARED, THE LAW'S NULL AND VOID.
THE SPIRIT OF CHRIST, ACCORDING TO SAINT PAUL,
IT HAS REPLACED GOD'S LAW, AND GOD IS NOW ISLAM'S ALLAH.

RB WELSH, 7 22 22

THE HOLY SPIRIT

THE HOLY SPIRIT IS SUPREME.
IT'S THE HOLIEST OF THE THREE.
THEY SAY, FATHER, SON, AND HOLY GHOST,
THE SPIRIT COMES IN LAST WHEN IT SHOULD BE THE FIRST.

IT IS THE SOURCE OF GOD'S POWER,
THE SPIRIT IS THAT UNSEEN QUALITY THAT SURROUNDS US.
THE FLUID MOVEMENT OF THE STARS,
YOUR PSYCHIC SENSE CREATES LOVE OR HARM.

HOW DOES ONE GET A WARNING CHILL
OR SUDDENLY BECOME VERY THRILLED,
IF IT WEREN'T FOR THIS SAME SPIRIT,
THAT GUIDES US EVERY HOUR, EVERY MINUTE.

WE'D BE DROWNING IN PANIC EVERY DAY, EVERY HOUR,
WE WOULD SUCCUMB TO EVERY DESIRE.
WE COULDN'T SEE BEYOND OUR NOSE,
WITH PSYCHIC ABILITY TO COMPOSE.

BUT THE WIDOW HAD IN HER HOME AN EVIL SPIRIT,
SEVEN MORE RETURNED WHEN SHE FINALLY GOT RID OF IT.
FOR GOD CLAIMS HE'S THE SOURCE OF GOOD AND EVIL, (IS 45:7)
EVEN PLACING ONE INTO THE HEART OF KING SAUL.

WHAT GOD DID TO JOB DOESN'T MAKE SENSE,
MAKING IT ALL UP LATER IS NO RECOMPENSE.
HE KNEW ALL ALONG THAT ADAM AND EVE,
WOULD EAT THE APPLE OF THE FORBIDDEN TREE.

THE HOLY SPIRIT IS THE SOURCE OF A BEAM OF LIGHT,
ITS RAY JUST MOVING NOTHINGNESS OF SPACE INTO THE FLIGHT,
CREATING THE STARS AND PLANETS OF THE UNIVERSE,
MAKING BIG BANG AND STRING THEORIES ABSURD.

THE SPIRIT WAS ORIGINAL; IT WAS NOT THOUGHT UP.
IT DOESN'T HAVE TO BE PLUGGED IN OR EVEN WOUND UP.
IT'S NOT DEPENDENT ON GOD OR CHRIST.
THE SPIRIT'S THE BEGINNING, THE MIDDLE AND LAST.

ONE MAY SAY IT'S THE GOD ABOVE ALL GODS.
FOR THERE'S AT LEAST ONE MORE; IT'S OF THE EXTRATERRESTRIALS.
THAT GOD CREATED MEN WHO APPEAR LIKE GEIKO GREMLINS,
FLITTING ABOUT IN SAUCERS FROM ANOTHER DIMENSION.

OURS WILL HAVE US SPEAKING IN TONGUES WHEN JESUS RETURNS,
BAPTIZING THEM WITH THE HOLY SPIRIT AND FIRE AS HUMANKIND LEARNS,
THAT THESE ARE THE ONES WHO SEE ITS LIGHT,
DRIVING INTO THEIR BRAIN AND LEADING THEM TO CHRIST.

WHY DID PETER AND JOHN HAVE TO RETURN TO SAMARIA?
TO REBAPTIZE WITH THE HOLY SPIRIT IN THE AREA,
SAYING THEY HAD ONLY RECEIVED THE RIGHTS,
FROM BEING BAPTIZED ONLY BY JESUS CHRIST. (ACTS 8:15-16)

THE SUPERIORITY OF THE SPIRIT, TO PROVE IT AGAIN,
YOU MAY BE FORGIVEN FOR TAKING JESUS' NAME IN VAIN,
OR EVEN GOD THE FATHER, BUT NOT THE HOLY SPIRIT.
SO CLAIM THOMAS 44, MARK 3:29, MT 12:31, AND LK IN 12:10.

THIS INDICATES THAT THE HOLY SPIRIT IS SUPREME IN ANY TRINITY.
THAT THEY ARE NOT EQUAL BY ANY MEANS IN DIVINITY.
BUT WE'LL KEEP ON BELIEVING IN THE SAME OLD VEIN,
AND KEEP ON REPEATING THE SAME OLD REFRAINS.

WHY DO YOU THINK THERE ARE SO MANY RELIGIOUS DIVISIONS?
IT'S BECAUSE THERE'S NO CHURCH OF THE HOLY SPIRIT.
WHAT IF JESUS CAME AGAIN? HE WOULD BE MOBBED,
WELL, HE'S HERE RIGHT NOW; HIS OWN SPIRIT'S ON THE JOB.

SO THAT'S SOMETHING GOD'S SPIRIT IS, IS A BEAM OF LIGHT,
TO TURN OUR LIVES AROUND. TO MAKE THEM RIGHT.
TO HELP US IN ANY DIRECTION THAT WE TAKE.
TO KEEP US FROM MAKING ANY MISTAKES.

WE ALWAYS SAY THAT GOD IS ONE,
SO HOW MANY DO WE NEED TO GET THINGS DONE?
HE IS A SPIRIT, AND HE IS HOLY,
JESUS IS IN HEAVEN. I NEED ONE GOD ONLY.

RB WELSH, 7 26 22

FAITH

LET US ASSUME THAT WE WISH FOR HEAVEN
WE THINK IT'S A PLACE THAT MUST BE UNLEAVENED
\LIKE EXORCISING FROM EGYPT TO ISRAEL
IT'S PARADISE LIKE A GARDEN OF EDEN IN HEAVEN

THE FRUIT OF THE TREE OF FAITH WE MUST EAT
COMING LIKE A LIGHT OF LOVE AND PEACE
IT'S A GIFT THAT MAN OPENS TO READILY ACCEPT
IT'S GOD CALL GIVING FAITH FREELY IN SPITE THAT MAN IS INEPT

THE DISCIPLES WERE CALLED AND JUST THREW DOWN THEIR POLES
FOLLOWING JESUS AS DISCIPLES TILL HE ACCOMPLISHED HIS GOAL
HE PURPOSELY HAD HIS TRIAL AND CRUCIFIXION FOR ALL SIN
FAITH WILL TELL YOU IT'S THE ONLY WAY HE COULD SAVE YOUR SKIN

FOR FAITH ONE CAN'T JUST SAY "I BELIEVE"
THAT'S NOT THE FORMULA IT MUST BE RECEIVED
IT'S A GIFT FROM THE CHRIST THE ONE WHO DIED
ALONG WITH YOUR SINS THROWN IN HELL FOR ALL TIME

HE TOLD THE SINFUL ROBBER BY HIS SIDE
"TODAY YOU WILL BE WITH ME IN PARADISE"
SALVATION IS INSTANT, NOT IN THREE DAYS
HEAVEN IS OPEN TO THOSE WHO ACCEPT FAITH

RB WELSH, 7 30 21

THE GRAIN OF WHEAT

A GRAIN OF WHEAT MUST FIRST FALL TO EARTH AND DIE,
BEFORE IT CAN LIVE, THAT'S WHY I WILL BE CRUCIFIED.
NO ONE PROMISED A HEAVEN ON EARTH,
IT'S BEEN A LONG FIGHT FOR MAN SINCE HIS BIRTH.

THERE'S SICKNESS AND WAR, STARVATION AND DRUGS.
SOME SELF-INFLICTED OR NEGLIGENCE WITH SEEMINGLY NO CAUSE.
ALL MEN, IN SOME WAY, MUST SUFFER BEFORE DEATH,
THE CRUCIFIXION OF GOD LEADS THE WAY TO HEAVEN AND SUCCESS.

AS FOR ME, I HAD TO DO A LOT OF SUFFERING BEFORE I DIED,
THE SINS OF THE WORLD SEEMED TO BE PILED A MILE HIGH.
IF YOU ARE SUFFERING RIGHT NOW, BE OF GOOD HEART,
WHEN IT'S ALL OVER, YOU'LL BE RAISED TO HEAVEN FOR A START.

WHEN I WAS ON EARTH, I CURED JUST A FEW,
THEY WERE TOLD NOT TO TELL, BUT THEY SPREAD THE NEWS.
IT WAS A MESSIANIC SECRET THAT I WAS THE CHRIST,
ALL PREVIOUS SINS WERE CANCELED WHEN YOU WERE BAPTIZED.

NOW THERE IS AN OPPORTUNITY TO BE REBORN.
BECOME NEW BEINGS WITH THIS REFORM.
IF YOUR CONSCIENCE IS BOTHERING YOU ABOUT ANYTHING.
REPLACE IT WITH GOOD AND FORGIVENESS IS AUTOMATIC.

IF CONFESSION SEEMS TO HELP EASE THE PAIN
I SHOULD CONFESS THAT I TOO SHOULD EXPLAIN
THAT I TOLD MY DISCIPLES TO JUST "TAKE" A COLT,
THEN TO BUY SWORDS BY SELLING THEIR CLOAKS.

I EVEN STRUCK A FIG TREE DEAD ONE TIME
AND RUINED A GENTILE'S HERD OF SWINE,
BY PLACING THE DEMONIAC DEMONS INTO HIS PIGS
AND RUNNING THEM OVER THE CLIFF INTO THE SEA.

SO I AM GOING TO JERUSALEM TO DIE FOR ME AND YOU,
AND AS THE KING INSTEAD OF THE WHOLE NATION OF JEWS.
ALL THIS YOU CAN BELIEVE AND SPREAD THE WORD
THAT GOD IS IN ME, AND THERE'S NO OTHER IN THE WORLD.

RB WELSH, 7 30 22

REBIRTH

WHAT DOES IT MEAN "TO BE REBORN??
LIKE LAMB'S WOOL, YOUR SINS ARE SHORN.
YOU HAVE RE-ENTERED THE VIRGIN'S WOMB,
A CHRIST-LIKE PERSON, YOU'RE BORN ANEW.

THE SPIRIT'S RAY OR BEAM OF LIGHT,
STRUCK DOWN THE SINNERS' PREVIOUS LIFE.
HE AT ONCE WAS BORN ANEW,
AND THAT'S WHAT HAPPENED TO YOU.

THAT'S NOW STILL YOU, THE SAME OLD SELF,
YOUR PREVIOUS LIFE DESCENDED INTO HELL.
YOU ARE SAVED, FOR YOU'RE REBORN,
IT'S YOUR OLD LIFE THAT'S DEAD AND GONE.

GOD, HIMSELF HAS BEEN REBORN,
AS JESUS CHRIST, HE IS ADORED.
HE IS NOT HIS SAME OLD SELF,
GOD IS JESUS, REBORN AS WELL.

GOD WAS THE ONE CRUCIFIED,
JESUS CHRIST HAS SURVIVED.
HIS SPIRIT SUPERSEDES GOD'S LAWS,
ONLY GOD'S LIGHT SURVIVED THE CROSS.

JESUS THE CHRIST HAS TAKEN OVER,
IT'S LIKE THE JEWISH PASSOVER,
HE GUIDES YOU NOW THAT GOD IS DEAD.
WE KILLED HIM, AS NIETZSCHE SAID.

RB WELSH, 8 5 22

PORTENT OF ISRAEL

OUT OF THE COSMOS IN THIS CONSTELLATION, (REV 12:1-12)
A GREAT PORTENT APPEARED HERE IN HEAVEN.
FOR STANDING THERE UPON THE MOON,
A BEAUTIFUL LADY, MAKING ONE SWOON.

ALL CLOTHED WITH THE SUN, WEARING A CROWN OF STARS,
SHE MUST HAVE COME FROM SOMEWHERE AFAR.
MICHEL IS THERE TO PUMMEL THE DRAGON,
WHOSE SEVEN FIERY MOUTHS SEEK THIS VULNERABLE WOMAN.

SHE IS PREGNANT WITH CHILD, LIKE A NATION BESIEGED,
WITH THE DRAGON'S DEVOURING HEADS AS HER ENEMIES.
GLANCING BEHIND HER WITH FOREBODINGS OF DREAD,
SHE WISHED THAT SOMEHOW SHE WERE ELSEWHERE INSTEAD.

IN ITS QUEST OF DEVOURING JESUS' ISRAEL BEING REBORN,
THE DRAGON WAS NOW DROOLING, ITS FANGS FILLED WITH SCORN.
WAR IN HEAVEN WITH MICHAEL AND HIS ANGELS OUTBREAKS,
THROWING SATAN AND ITS DEMONS INTO EARTHQUAKES.
THOUGH THE DRAGON HAD PURSUED HER, ITS TENACITY UNBELIEVABLE,
THE WOMAN WAS BORNE ALOFT ON THE WINGS OF AN EAGLE.

JESUS HAD PROCLAIMED, "ONE MUST BE REBORN
TO ENTER INTO HEAVEN," THOUGH ALL ARE STUBBORN.
THE DRAGON FINALLY WENT OFF TO MAKE A WAR OF JIHAD,
WITH THE SHEPHERDING OF THE PROMISE BY CHRIST THE ISRAELI, (REV 12:5)
SURROUNDING NATIONS OF ISLAM UNITE TO THROW THEM INTO THE SEA.
ON ALL FAITHFUL SERVANTS KEEPING THE COMMANDMENTS OF GOD. (REV 12:12-17)

RB WELSH, 8 7 22

THE PEARLY GATES

WHY SHOULD I THINK HEAVEN'S SO GREAT?
JUST BECAUSE IT HAS PEARLY GATES.
WITH JEWELED WALLS AND STREETS OF GOLD.
TO BE ACCEPTABLE IN HEAVEN, ALL OF OURS HAD TO BE SOLD.

THEN GIVE ALL OUR MONEY AND SELL ALL WE HAD,
TO GIVE TO THE POOR AND BE SCARCELY CLAD.
AS I RECALL, IT IS GOD WHO LIKES JEWELS,
AS WE CONQUERED CANAAN

THIS IS FAR FROM BEING JUST A MUSTARD SEED,
GOD EVEN ORDERED TAKING GOLD AND SILVER JEWELS
FROM EGYPTIANS, BUT IN MAKING A GOLDEN CALF,
TO WORSHIP, FOR THEY THOUGHT GOD DESERTED THEM AGAIN.

AND FOR GIVING COMMANDMENT NOT TO KILL OR EVEN AVENGE,
GOD SET THE ISRAELITE TEETH ON EDGE,
RECLAIMING ALL CANAAN AS THE LAND OF ABRAHAM,
HE IS CONTRADICTING MOST OF ALL OF HIS LAWS AND COMMANDS.

WHAT AGE CAN I BE WHEN OR IF I GO TO HEAVEN WHEN I DIE?
WILL L BE AT MY PRIME OR JUST A BABE THAT JUST CRIES?
ARE WE JUST STATUES THAT BOW AND PRAY ALL DAY?
OR DO WE WORK AND INVENT OR HAVE GAMES TO PLAY?

I GET BORED QUICKLY, AND I NEED SOMETHING TO DO.
ARE THERE DANCING AND SINGING GAMES AND SPORTS
I KNOW THERE'S NO WAR, NO DEBATES IN POLITICS.
THAT WAS A PERFECT HELL; ALL THOSE ATAVISTS

IF THERE'S A WORLD WAR ON EARTH, WILL YOU STILL BE ALIVE?
YOU CAN'T EAT GOLD AND JEWELS; HOW CAN YOU SURVIVE?
SOMEWHERE THERE MUST BE A GARDEN OF EDEN.
OR WILL WE JUST STARVE OR LIVE LIKE EPICUREANS?

GOD ONCE FAVORED ABEL'S BURNT OFFERING OF A LAMB,
WITHOUT PRAISE-ONE OF CAIN'S GRAINS BEFORE THE WHEAT SEASON BEGAN.
I DIDN'T OBSERVE ANY FARMS OR RANCHES AROUND,
SO WHAT DO WE EAT, WHAT IS TILLED IN THE GROUND?

THE PRIESTS SAID, "YES, ARE GODS."
AS SONS OF ISAAC, THEY WERE NOT WRONG.
FOR HE WAS GOD'S FIRST SON
HE WAS BORN AS THE CHILD OF ABRAHAM.

AS I LOOKED AT MYSELF, I WONDERED AND BEGAN TO THINK
FOR IT WAS ASHES TO ASHES, I WAS DUST, I BEGAN TO SHRINK.
I TURNED INTO AN IKON, A DOT IN THE SKY.
AN IMMORTAL BEING, A SPIRIT JUST FLITTING BY.

AS JUST ANOTHER SOUL IN GOD'S HEAVEN ABOVE,
LOOKING AROUND AT THE UNIVERSE AND OBSERVE
THAT EARTH IS JUST ANOTHER PLANET FILLED WITH MEN,
WHO SUFFER FOR NOTHING BUT TO REPEAT IT AGAIN.
TO LITERALLY BE REBORN WITH WAR AND THE SAME PESTILENCE,
TILL HE GETS IT RIGHT AS GOD PREDESTINED MEN.

AS YOU CAN SEE, THE EARTH IS FILLING UP
AND IT SEEMS WE NEVER LEARN MUCH.
JOHN'S HEAVEN SHOULD BE OUR ULTIMATE GOAL,
WE HAVE TO BELIEVE THIS WITH BODY AND SOUL.

RB WELSH, 8 18 22

THE BIRTHRIGHT

IN BIBLICAL TERMS, ESAU SACRIFICED
FOR A BOWL OF POTAGE, HIS BIRTHRIGHT.
I CANNOT SELL MINE NOR YOU YOURS,
A BIRTHRIGHT IS SOMETHING THAT SIMPLY OCCURS.

IT CAN'T BE BOUGHT; IT CAN'T BE SOLD,
IT'S JUST A LEGACY, A HERITAGE, AND IT'S YOURS.
YOU CAN'T EVEN GIVE A BIRTHRIGHT AWAY,
SO ESAU DIDN'T KNOW IT, BUT THE POTTAGE WAS FREE.

ONE CAN ONLY INHERIT A BIRTHRIGHT,
JACOB WOULD HAVE TO WAIT TILL ESAU DIED.
THIS IS A POSITION THAT CANNOT BE SOLD,
WE CAN TAKE IT UP WITH THE SUPREME COURT.

THIS CHANGES EVERYTHING FOR ALL GENERATIONS,
BESIDES, A BOWL OF SOUP IS INSUFFICIENT CONSIDERATION.
IT SEEMS LIKE THIS REMINDS ME OF WHEN GOD
BREACHED HIS SIDE OF THE ABRAHAMIC COVENANT

RB WELSH, 9 16 22

LOVE

WHAT IS THIS THING THAT WE CALL LOVE?
WE ARE COMMANDED TO LOVE GOD,
CAN ONE BUY IT AT THE STORE?
OR IS IT NATURAL WHEN ONE ADORES?

THERE ARE SOME DIFFERENT VARIETIES,
LIKE WHEN JUST FRIENDS IN SOCIETY,
THEN WHEN ONE LOVES HIS FAMILY,
OR LOVING GOD AS AGAPE.

WHAT IS UNREQUITED LOVE?
LOVE THAT IS NOT RECIPROCATED.
IS THAT WHAT GOD GETS FROM US?
A LOT OF WORDS, BUT MEANINGLESS.

JUST TAKE, FOR INSTANCE, THE APOSTLES CREED
THERE'S NOT ONE WORD OF LOVE, ONLY BELIEF.
IS BEAUTY REQUIRED OR JUST RESPECT?
JUST WHAT APPEALS WHAT IS THE ELEMENT?

PHILOSOPHERS SPEND DAY AND NIGHT,
TRYING TO GET THE DEFINITION RIGHT.
LOVE SEEMS TO COME IN DEGREES,
HOT OR COLD, IT MAY EVEN FREEZE.

JUST WHERE IT COMES FROM, NO ONE KNOWS,
SOMETIMES ONE FEELS LIKE SHE'S BEEN SNOWED.
DOES SATAN EVER MAKE US THINK
THAT HIS WAY IS LOVE OR JUST A MISTAKE?

LOVE OR LUST, WE OUGHT TO KNOW,
ACTING LIKE KIDS FOR A MOMENT'S GLOW.
MAYBE WE'LL FIGURE IT OUT SOMEDAY,
THAT IT IS LOVE THAT LIGHTS THE WAY.

RB WELSH, 8 21 22

ATON

ONCE UPON A TIME, I WAS AN EGYPTIAN GOD,
IT WAS THE TIME OF EXILE, AND MY NAME WAS ATON.
THE SYMBOL OF ONENESS LIKE AHURA-MAZDA,
HE WAS THEIR SUN GOD DURING THE HEBREW DISASTER.

ALL OTHER GODS OF EGYPT WERE REMOVED OR DEFACED,
THERE IS NO DIFFERENCE; THE LISTS ARE REPLACED.
HIS NAME IS ATON, AND THOUGH HE WAS ONE,
HIS REIGN, UNFORTUNATELY, WAS ONLY ONE TERM.

SO GOD WENT TO SINAI TO PREPARE THE WAY
FOR THE CHILDREN OF ISRAEL TO LEARN TO OBEY,
BY PRESENTING THEM WITH HIS LAWS ON STONE,
FOR JACOB HAD DECEIVED ESAU AND SHOULD HAVE ATONED.

THE CHILDREN WERE RETURNED TO THE PROMISED LAND
WHERE DESPITE MY LAWS, THEY WORSHIPED ME AS BA-EL.
THOUGH, AS PUNISHMENT, I SPLIT THE NATION IN TWO,
THEY CONTINUED TO SIN, SO THEY BOTH WERE REMOVED.

THE ASSYRIANS CAPTURED JACOB'S ISRAEL TO NINEVEH,
WHERE I ORDERED JONAH TO MAKE THEM REPENT.
I HAD TO CHASE HIM DOWN IN MY CHARIOT OF WHEELS,
THAT EVEN GOES UNDERWATER LIKE THE EXTRATERRESTRIALS.

THE OTHER NATION OF JUDAH, A SINNER COHABITATING WITH TAMAR,
I BANISHED TO BABYLON, BUT RESCUE THEM WITH CYRUS AND MAZDA.
HAVING PROMISED THE SON OF MAN COMING ON CLOUDS,
WE SAW HIS MIRACLES IN THE LION'S DEN AND FIERY FURNACE.

MANY MIRACLES OCCURRED DURING THE TIME OF THE MACCABEES,
BUT THEIR FEATS WERE SO GREAT WE REMOVED THEM FROM HISTORY.
MY TEMPLE AND ARK ARE REMOVED FOREVER,
MY ONENESS IS IN CHRIST WHO NOW IS YOUR TREASURE.

RB WELSH, 9 17 22

MOSES

MOSES RECEIVED GOD'S ETERNAL LIGHT
WHILE BEING WITH HIM ON MOUNT SINAI

GOD IS MORE THAN JUST "I AM."
HE IS ALSO THE "SON OF MAN."

MOSES JUST RAISED HIS STAFF
SAVING ALL OF ISRAEL WITH THIS ACT

IT IS UNNECESSARY TO JUST BELIEVE
THAT JESUS DIED FOR THE SINFUL LIFE, YOU LIVED,
FOR MOSES WITH ELIJAH JUST APPEARED
ON TRANSFIGURATION MOUNT AFTER BEING DEAD A 1000 YEARS.

THOUGH MOSES HAD STRUCK A ROCK
AND WAS ACCUSED OF BEING GOD
SO HE DIED FOR NOT HEEDING GOD'S COMMAND,
OVERLOOKING THE PROMISED LAND

TO BE SAVED WOULD BE PLENTY, BUT WHAT ABOUT NOW?
WE ARE SICK, AND WE'RE HUNGRY; A HURRICANE HOWLS.
THE COUNTRY IS BANKRUPT AND WITHOUT REASON,
WE EXCEEDED THE DEBT LIMIT OF 29 TRILLION.

MEN ARE SAVED WHO BELIEVE, BUT WHAT ABOUT FOOLS?
LIARS, DECEIVERS, MEN WHO DELUDE,
PRINTING FAKE BALLOTS TO GET FAVORABLE WINS,
FILLING THEIR POCKETS WITH SIN CONCOCTED FOR ELECTIONS.

WE HAVE TO BE SAVED FROM OURSELVES,
FOR WE ARE SURELY GOING TO HELL
IN EITHER CASE, WE'LL BE THE ILLEGAL ALIENS,
SLAVES WITHOUT EITHER GOD OR JESUS TO SAVE US.

RB WELSH, 9 30 22

COMMANDER IN CHIEF

GOD CREATED THE HEAVENS, AND THE MAN GAVE BIRTH
BUT MAN DISOBEYED, SO HE FLOODED THE EARTH
AFTER THE RACES DESCENDED TO INTERMARRY,
POLLUTING HUMANITY THAT BECAME JUST ORDINARY.

THE FLOODING BROUGHT OCEAN WATERS TO THE NOW-DEAD SEA,
THE PROMISED LAND TURNED INTO A DESERT OF TRAGEDY.
SARAH HAD ABRAHAM GO INTO HAGAR, HER HANDMAIDEN OF HELL,
WITH THE FIRSTBORN CHILD RECEIVING THE PROMISE AS WELL.

IF GOD WERE THE C COMMANDER IN CHIEF OF AN ARMY UNIT
HE WOULD BE DEMOTED, FOR HE BLEW IT.
IN THE SELECTION OF ABRAM AND SAYRE AS THE CHOSEN RACE
AND THE CIRCUMCISION COVENANT IN WHICH HE DIDN'T PARTICIPATE.

FOR THIS COUPLE, WHO WERE COUSINS TO HAVE A PROMISED CHILD,
THEY WOULD BE AS NUTTY AS LOT, WHO WAS DEFILED
THERE WAS INBREEDING IN THE LAND OF UR
WHERE THE CHOSEN RACE WAS RAISED AND MATURED.

IT WAS ONLY WHEN GOD, HIMSELF FATHERED ISAAC,
THAT THE RACE WAS SAVED FROM FURTHER STIGMATIC
"YE ARE GODS," THE PSALMIST SAYS OF SUCCEEDING GENERATIONS,
JUST BEFORE BECOMING ENSLAVED IN THE EGYPT OF SALVATION.

WHEN THE FAMINES ARE AT THEIR WORST, GOD DISAPPEARS,
NOT JUST TEMPORARILY BUT FOR FOUR HUNDRED YEARS.
THIS FAMINE IS DESERTION IN ANY ARMY'S BOOK.
CRUCIFIED DEAD AND BURIED, BUT SAVES THEM FOR GOOD,

IT WAS NOT THE ONLY TIME GOD WAS ABSENT FROM THEM,
THERE WAS AUSCHWITZ WITHOUT A GOD FOR SALVATION AGAIN.
BUT THERE WAS A SAVIOR TO LEAD THIS RAGGED BAND,
A MESSIAH NAMED MOSES WENT BACK TO THE PROMISED LAND.

TO RE-ASSURE HE WOULDN'T DESERT HIS PEOPLE OF REVERENCE,
GOD SEALED HIMSELF UP IN THE ARK OF THE COVENANT.
TO BE RELEASED TO BECOME SON OF MAN
WHEN THE TEMPLE TREASURIES WERE TAKEN TO BABYLON.

WHEN THE ARK WAS OPENED, GOD BECAME THE SON OF MAN,
A SPIRIT COMING ON CLOUDS RESURRECTED AGAIN,
SAVING HIS PEOPLE FROM BABYLON,
IN THE FIERY FURNACE AND LION'S DEN.

NOW GOD IS THE SPIRIT OF ALL HUMANKIND,
FOREVER PRESENT AS THE DIVINE MIND,
FOREVER EMBRACING MAN'S NEEDS AND WANTS,
GUIDING MANKIND WITH HOLY THOUGHTS.

MAN CAN LEAVE GOD; TRY TO LIVE ON HIS OWN,
BUT IT'S LIKE AFLOAT ON THE OCEAN WITHOUT A LIFEBOAT.
MOSES AND ELIJAH WERE SEEN AGAIN, ALL ALIVE
ON TRANSFIGURATION MOUNT, SO MAN NEVER DIES.

RB WELSH, 9 29 22

ZARUBBABBLE

IN THE LINE OF ASCENSION TO THE MESSIANIC KING,
THERE IS NO MENTION OF ZARUBABBLE WEARING GOD'S SIGNET RING,
THOUGH THAT WAS FORETOLD BY THE PROPHET HAGGAI, (REV 2:23)
IN THE LEGACY OF JESUS THROUGHOUT THE DAVIDIC LINE,

ALONG WITH DANIEL, LIKE THE SON OF MAN,
ZARUBABBLE WAS A CAPTIVE IN BABYLON.
AT LEAST THERE WAS ONE IN THE DAVID LINE
WHO WAS NOT A SEX PERVERT BUT DIGNIFIED?

WITH THE HELP OF DARIUS AND CYRUS THE GREAT,
ZARRUBABLE LED THE JEWS IN THEIR ESCAPE
TO REBUILD GOD'S TEMPLE IN JERUSALEM OF JUDEA,
AND SEND THOSE WHO HAD MARRIED FOREIGN WIVES TO SAMARIA.

NEVER PERFORMING MIRACLES OF HEALING
OR GETTING 5,000 FOLLOWERS BY FEEDING,
ZARRABABEL'S MIRACLE WAS GETTING 42,000 REBORN
AS NEW BEINGS TO BUILD GOD'S TEMPLE AGAIN.

RB WELSH, 9 23 22

HATE ONE'S PARENTS?

OF ALL THE VIRGINS IN THE WORLD, GOD HAD TO PICK MARY
THOUGH ALREADY BETROTHED, SHE WASN'T CONTRARY.
THIS ACCEPTANCE SEEMS ODD, FOR SHE CONSENTED AT WILL
WITH ALL THE SCAMS OUT THERE, SHE FELT NO GUILT.

NO ONE ELSE IN THE VILLAGE KNEW HOW FAR THIS HAD GONE.
UNLESS IT WAS HER COUSIN ELIZBETH, THE MOTHER OF JOHN.
JOSEPH, HER BETROTHED, DECIDED TO PUT HER AWAY,
TILL AN ANGEL OF THE LORD TOLD HIM TO STAY

DO YOU THINK JESUS HATED GOD AND MARY
FOR HE HAD A MESSAGE OF LOVE, AND THIS IS SO CONTRARY.
TO SAY, "TO BE MY DISCIPLE, YOU MUST HATE YOUR PARENTS."
IT IS ALSO CONTRADICTORY TO GOD'S FIFTH COMMANDMENT.

DOES JESUS EVEN KNOW THAT HE IS GOD'S SON?
THE NEIGHBORS JUST NEED AN EXPLANATION.
THOUGH GOD SAYS THAT HE IS WELL PLEASED WITH HIS BAPTISMAL,
JESUS SAYS WE MUST HATE OUR PARENTS TO BE HIS DISCIPLES.

SO JESUS IS SAYING, THAT IN COMPARISON TO HIM,
EVERYTHING AND EVERYONE ELSE IS INFERIOR AND NIL.
HE JUST DIDN'T INCLUDE THE HOLY SPIRIT,
NUMBER ONE IN THE UNIVERSE, THAT HE ADMITS

DID JESUS HATE HIS OWN PARENTS, GOD AND MARY?
WAS IT BECAUSE THEY WERE NOT MARRIED
THAT MADE HIM ILLEGITIMATE, YOU KNOW,
THIS DOUBLE-IDENTITY CRISIS GETS WORSE AS HE GROWS.

WHEN JESUS PREACHED ABOUT HIS FATHER, DID THE PEOPLE KNOW
HE WAS TALKING ABOUT GOD, NOT THE CARPENTER, JOSEPH
THE GOSPEL OF MARK, WHICH WAS WRITTEN FIRST
JESUS IS KNOWN AS THE SON OF MARY, AS HE DESERVES.

THEN MATTHEW PROCEEDED TO FILL IN THE BLANKS
WITH A TRIP TO JERUSALEM TO PAY THE TAX,
HERE JESUS IS REFERRED TO AS THE CARPENTER'S SON,
IT IS A FAMILY AFFAIR WHEN JESUS GETS LOST

I'VE BEEN A PRACTICING PSYCHIATRIST FOR THE LAST FIFTY YEARS
AND MY DIAGNOSIS IS THAT OF AN OUTBURST FROM FEAR,

IT DOESN'T FIT IN WITH HIS OTHER STATEMENTS, AND I'LL REMIND YOU,
TO FOLLOW HIM LOVE ALL MANKIND

THE PROBLEM IS THE PROPHECY OF ISAIAH.
THEOLOGIAN DECIDED TO SAY SHE WAS A YOUNG MAIDEN.
ACTUALLY, CONCEPTION OCCURRED WITH THE HOLY SPIRIT'S INSUFFLATION.
JOSEPH AND MARY WERE ACTUALLY BETROTHED
IN A CEREMONY DESCRIBED IN THE DEAD SEA SCROLLS.

I AM SURPRISED THAT THEOLOGIANS HAVEN'T SCRATCHED THIS,
FOR IT'S SO UNLIKE JESUS TO INCLUDE ANYTHING AMISS.

JESUS WAS IMBIBED WITH A DUO-FATHERLY LIFE,
THE EGYPT THEY FLEW TO DURING HEROD'S FORAY
IT WAS QUMRAN, ONLY TWENTY MILES AWAY.
THERE HE BECAME LEARNED ABOUT ISRAEL'S HISTORY,
SO THE TEMPLE DISCUSSIONS WITH PRIESTS ARE NO MYSTERY.

SO, WITH TWO SETS OF FATHERS PLUS A HOLY SPIRIT THROWN IN,
YOU CAN EASILY SEE WHERE DUO-PERSONALITIES SYMPTOMS SET IN.
HE HAS ESTABLISHED HIMSELF NOW AS A TRUE GOD.
SO TO HATE HIS PARENTS, THEN, DOESN'T SEEM SO ODD AT ALL.

R B WELSH, 10 1 22

FAVORITE BIBLICAL CHARACTER

I WONDER WHY GIDEON GETS NO PRESS
AS A PROPHET AND JUDGE, I AM IMPRESSED
IT'S WHEN GOD APPEARS AS A HUMAN AGAIN
LIKE HE DID AT MAMRE WITH ABRAHAM

A BATTLE WAS IMMINENT WITH GIDEON AS THE LEADER
WITH ONLY 32 THOUSAND BUT MANY ARE TOO FEARFUL
TO FIGHT OFF THE MIDIANITES WHO STOLE CATTLE AND GRAIN
EVERY YEAR AT THE HARVEST, LEAVING NOTHING FOR THEM

GOD APPEARED AS AN ANGEL SITTING UNDER AN OAK TREE
GIDEON SAID TO IT, "IF YOU ARE GOD, JUST PROVE IT TO ME"
I AM SURPRISED HE DIDN'T TELL GIDEON TO FALL ON HIS FACE
BUT IN BRINGING FORTH FIRE FROM A ROCK, ALL DOUBT WAS ERASED

LIKE THE BURNING BUSH OR THE SOLDIER AT JERICHO
GOD AS AN ANGEL, APPEARED AS A HUMAN-LIKE JESUS
BUT CALMLY, THE ANGEL BROUGHT FIRE FROM A ROCK
THEN GIDEON SAID, " TELL ME WHAT TO DO. LET ME START"

I WANT YOU TO LEAD TROOPS AGAINST THE MIDIANITES
BUT FIRST, REMOVE THE ALTARS OF BAAL DURING THE NIGHT
FOR I AM THE LORD, AND THEY SHOULD WORSHIP ONLY ME
AND I WILL SAVE THEIR GRAIN AND LIVESTOCK; THEY WILL BE FREE

SO DURING THE NIGHT, A GROUP TORE DOWN THE ALTAR OF BAAL
GROUND PIECES OF ASHERAH AND BURNED THEM AS WELL
THE TOWNSPEOPLE WERE FURIOUS WHEN THEY WENT TO PRAY
ON LEARNING IT WAS GIDEON, THEY SWORE TO KILL HIM THAT DAY

GIDEON'S FATHER TOLD THE CROWD THAT BAAL COULD TAKE CARE OF HIMSELF
SO THEY RETURNED TO THE LORD TO FIGHT THE MIDIANITES AND REPEL

WITH THAT, GIDEON ROUNDED UP A 300 THOUSAND MAN ARMY
TO EXTERMINATE THE MIDIANITE RAID, THAT OCCURRED ANNUALLY
REDUCING THE HEBREWS TO POVERTY
NOW GOD WAS GOING TO INTERVENE FOR THEM

DO YOU MEAN GIDEON CHALLENGED GOD WITH ANOTHER TEST OF THIS
NOT ONLY ONCE BUT TWICE WITH A PIECE OF FLEECE
YOU SHALL NOT TEST THE LORD YOUR GOD DT 6:16
BUT MY FAVORITE CHARACTER GIDEON JUST DID

THE MIDIANITES WAITED EACH YEAR TILL HEBREW ANIMALS WERE FAT
THAT THE GRAIN WAS TAKEN IN, AND THEN THEY WOULD ATTACK
GOD DECLARED THAT THE HEBREW ARMY WAS MUCH TOO LARGE
SO WITH A TEST OF JUST FEAR OR LAPPING WATER LIKE DOGS

THE ISRAELITE ARMY WAS REDUCED TO ONLY THREE HUNDRED SOLDIERS
ARMED WITH ONLY TRUMPETS AND JUGS OVER LIGHTED CANDLES
THEY BLEW THE HORNS AND BROKE THE JUGS OVER THE FLASHING LIGHTS
THE MIDIANITES PANICKED AND WERE SLAUGHTERED DURING THE NIGHT

GIDEON WAS THE HERO FOR SAVING THE TRIBE OF MANASSEH
AND WAS MADE JUDGE AND PROPHET FOR THEM FOREVER
A FREE BIBLE IS AN EXAMPLE OF GIDEON'S FAME
IS IN EVERY HOTEL ROOM BEARING GIDEON'S NAME

RB WELSH, 4 13 21

QUMRAN

ON THE CLIFFS OVERLOOKING THE RIVER JORDAN
IS A COMMUNITY OF GOD FEARING SCHOLARS.
THEY ARE KNOWN TO ALL AS THE ESSENES,
SAVING SCRIPTURES CALLED THE DEAD SEA SCROLLS.

WHEN HEROD WAS THREATENING ALL JEWISH CHILDREN,
JOSEPH AND MARY HURRIED TO AVOID ANY JESUS EXTINCTION.
ONLY FIFTEEN MILES TO QUMRAN INSTEAD OF 300 TO EGYPT
WITH NEWLY DELIVERED CHILD, I CAN'T BELIEVE IT.

WHAT IF GOD IN THE EXODUS HAD ONLY TAKEN THIS ROUTE,
THEY WOULDN'T HAVE THE LAW, BUT THEY WOULD BE ON MORIAH.
WE CAN NEVER WONDER ABOUT THE THINKING OF GOD.
HE KNOWS WHAT HE WANTS TO BE THE BEST FOR ALL.

JESUS WAS KNOWN AS THE TEACHER OF RIGHTEOUSNESS TO THE PEOPLE.
HE WAS A CAMEL IN SCHOOL, GOING THROUGH THE EYE OF THE NEEDLE.
THE CATHOLICS RECEIVED AUTHORITY TO CHECK ALL THE VERSES,
TO ELIMINATE IN CASE THEY DISAGREED WITH CATHOLIC VERSIONS.

WHEN SAUL WAS KNOCKED OFF HIS HORSE AND BLINDED BY AN ECLIPSE,
HE WARNED TO "LOOK THROUGH A GLASS DARKLY" TO AVOID RISK.
HE WAS ON HIS WAY TO QUMRAN INSTEAD OF DAMASCUS.
FOR THAT WAS OUT OF HIS JURISDICTION IN BEING SO FRACTIOUS.

SOMEHOW IT'S ALWAYS 400 YEARS,
THE TIME GOD WAS ABSENT WHILE JEWS WERE SLAVES IN EGYPT
OR WHEN THEY WERE TAKEN TO BABYLONIA, THEY WERE IN EXILE 400 YEARS.
THEN CHURCH FATHERS REMOVED MACCABEAN APOCRYPHA OF 400 YEARS.

AND JUST WHERE IS THE HOLY SPIRIT ALL OF THESE YEARS?
UNTIL INSUFFLATING MARY'S WOMB, IT JUST DOESN'T APPEAR.
FOR BEING THE GOD ABOVE GOD IT'S UNREASONABLE,
TO BE ABSENT IN THE OLD TESTAMENT, IT'S JUST INCONCEIVABLE.

RB WELSH, 5 31 23

WHY ANOTHER GOD

WHY DID GOD DUPLICATE HIMSELF?
AFTER CENTURIES WITH THE CHOSEN, GOD NEEDED HELP.
THERE WERE MORE AND MORE GODS ALL AROUND.
IN ROME AND GREECE, IN EGYPT, THEY ABOUND.

IN HIS PROTEAN WAY HE MADE A MIMIC OF HIMSELF,
JUST TO JAZZ IT UP HE GOT A VIRGIN TO HELP.
FOR IT MAKES IT MORE DRAMATIC TO DO THE IMPOSSIBLE,
THEN IF IT'S PROPHESIED, IT BECOMES PHENOMENAL!

SO GOD AS JESUS HIMSELF, IS DIVERSIFYING TO RELATE
TO ALL THESE RACES COMING IN FROM OUTER SPACE.
WITH THE INCREASED POPULATION, GOD NEEDED HELP,
CAN YOU IMAGINE DOING THIS ALL BY YOURSELF?

BUT JESUS DIDN'T NEED A PAUL TO HELP.
THE APOSTLES COULD DO IT ALL BY THEMSELVES.
SOME THOUGHT THAT JESUS WAS REPLACING GOD
WHEN THE IDEA WAS TO BE AN ASSOCIATE, THAT'S ALL.

GOD HAD PRACTICED THIS SYSTEM IN BABYLONIA,
HE HAD ZERUBBABEL GET THEM BACK FROM EXILE TO JUDAH.
NOW IT WOULD BE LIKE GOING ON VACATION,
UNLESS JESUS SURPRISED THEM WITH NEWS ABOUT HEAVEN.

AS A MAN, NOT AS SPIRIT, GOD CAN REASON WITH THEM,
GIVING THEM PARABLES HELPS MAKES THEM THINK.
ONCE THEY'RE BAPTIZED, THEY'LL BE SAVED FROM THEIR SINS.
THEY WON'T HAVE TO CONFESS, FOR I KNOW WHAT THEY DID.

MOST COME HERE AND LEAVE, AS EXTRATERRESTRIALS,
SOME STAY AND ADJUST, BRINGING PROGRESS TO ALL.
WHY DID JESUS DIE AS SALVATION FOR YOUR SINS?
WHEN YOUR BAPTISM IS ENOUGH TO GET IN?

ANYHOW, HE WENT AHEAD AND WAS EXECUTED.
THOUGH GOD HAD POWER TO SAVE AS REPUTED,
HE WANTED TO PROVE HE COULD STILL BE ALIVE,
BUT NO ONE COULD RECOGNIZE HIM AFTER HE DIED.

EVERYTHING WORKED OUT THOUGH, AS IT WAS PLANNED,
THE JEWS STILL WORSHIP GOD, THEY UNDERSTAND.
LEAVING ALL OTHER NATIONS AND RACES,
TO WORSHIP GOD, WHO'S NOW JESUS IN HIS PLACE.

RB WELSH, 5 15 23

THE GREAT EXPERIMENT

GOD GAVE THEM ALL THE EVER ASKED FOR,
BUT EVERYTHING TURNED INTO DISASTER.
IT SEEMED THEY COULDN'T STAND SUCCESS,
EACH ADVANCE TURNED INTO A GREAT BIG MESS.

AFTER FINALLY GETTING RESCUED FROM BEING SLAVES,
THE ISRAELITES BEGAN WORSHIPPING BAAL.
TO WORSHIP IN GOD'S HOUSE WAS A LONG TREK,
ALL THE WAY TO SHILOH AND BACK.

ALTARS AND TEMPLES MADE FOR BAAL
WERE RIGHT OUT THE DOOR IN THE TOWN SQUARE.
THERE WERE ALSO TEMPLE PROSTITUTES,
SO GOD GOT MAD; DIVIDING THE NATION IN TWO.

GOD GAVE THEM JUDGES, PROPHETS AND THEN KINGS,
THREATENING HE WOULD NOW SEND THEM PACKING.
THE NATIONS, EPHRAIM, AND JUDAH, WERE BOTH CAPTURED
BY ASSYRIA THEN BABYLON, BUT NOAH CONVERTED NINEVEH.

EZEKIEL PROPHESIED THAT ISRAEL WOULD RETURN,
BUT THE ASSYRIANS SWALLOWED THEM UP AND DISPERSED.
JUDAH SAW THIS AND SIMPLY DIDN'T LEARN, WHEN
BABYLON TOOK THEM CAPTIVE FOR A COMPLETE GENERATION.

GOD SEEMS TO BE WORKING AT CROSS-PURPOSES IN TIME,
HE CAN'T SEEM TO KEEP HIS SUBJECTS IN LINE,
GOD NOW HAS THREE PEOPLES SPREADING THE GOOD NEWS,
JESUS PREACHED TO GALILEANS, SAMARIANS AND JEWS.

PAUL SAYS HE SPENT THREE YEARS ON THE MOUNTAIN OF GOD,
BUT INSTEAD OF THE MOUNT INN ARABIA, IT WAS AT QUMRAN,
HE WAS STUDYING GOD'S WORD, JESUS AND HE.
TO GRADUATE AS CAMELS, "THRU THE EYE OF A NEEDLE."

ISRAEL, IT SEEMS, WAS SIMPLY ABSORBED
INTO THE LAND OF THE GOD ANUNNAKI, AND DISPERSED.
WHILE JUDAH WAS LATER TAKEN TO BABYLON,
WHERE DANIEL SEEMED TO BE THE SON OF MAN.

GOD FINALLY RETURNED THEM AS HEBREWS TO JUDAH,
WHERE THEY HAVE LEARNED TO WORSHIP THE ONLY GOD.
THEY ARE TIRED OF FOREVER BEING CHASTISED,
FOR WORSHIPING OTHER GODS NOT AUTHORIZED.

THEN WHEN JESUS AND THE HOLY SPIRIT CAME ALONG,
THE JEWS DECLINED THE INVITATION TO JOIN,
SAYING, "WE HAVE LEARNED OUR LESSON AT LAST,
DON'T TEMPT US, WE REMEMBER THE PAST."

TO ME, IT IS TRUE THAT GOD IS JESUS.
GOD APPEARS ALL THE TIME, EVEN AS ONE OF US,
WHILE STILL REMAINING HIMSELF AS GOD,
AS IT IS WRITTEN IN THE GOSPEL OF MARK.

FOR JESUS WAS IN REALITY, NEVER BORN.
MATHEW WROTE THIS FICTION IN CE 60, WHEN HE CAME ALONG.
ALL GOSPEL STORIES ARE BASED ON Q, THOMAS AND MARK,
THE HOLY SPIRIT FIRST APPEARS IN LUKE, BUT WAS THERE FROM THE START.

THE HOLY SPIRIT IS SUPREME,
CREATING THE UNIVERSE, READ ACTS 8:15-17.
YOU MAY BE FORGIVEN FOR TAKING THE LORD'S NAME IN VAIN,
BUT YOU WILL NOT BE FORGIVEN FOR DOING SO WITH THE SPIRIT'S NAME (MT 12:3 1-32)

THE MORE TIMES YOU SAY THAT JESUS IS KING,
THE MORE LIKELY PEOPLE WILL THEN BELIEVE.
GOD WAS JESUS ON EARTH FOR 32 YEARS,
WHO RETURNS AT PENTECOST ANNUALLY.

RB WELSH, 1 4 23

WONDER

AFTER GOING THROUGH THE YEARS OF LIFE AFTER A MIRACULOUS BIRTH,
KING HEROD'S MURDER OF ALL BABIES WHO COULD BE KING OF THIS EARTH.
THE TRAUMATIC ESCAPE TO EGYPT OR QUMRAN TO AVOID DEATH,
WE WONDER HOW OR WHY WE SHOULD MAKE HIM THE OBJECT OF AFFECTION.

IS THAT ALL IT TAKES TO BE QUALIFIED?
TO BE HEAD OF A CHURCH AS DEIFIED?
WE WERE TOLD MANY TIMES THAT GOD IS ONE.
THAT DOESN'T MEAN WE NOW WORSHIP HIS SON.

DOES THAT MEAN THAT GOD WILL SOON DIE?
THAT THERE'S NOW ANOTHER ON WHOM WE'LL RELY.
IT COULD BE JOHN WHO WAS THERE SAVING MEN OF THEIR SINS.
IMMERSING THEM IN THE JORDAN WITH CLEANSING BAPTISM.

I THINK BY NOW WE SHOULD HAVE LEARNED OUR LESSON.
NOT TO WORSHIP MORE BAALS AFTER DANIEL'S SUCCESSION.
MOTHER ALWAYS SAID WHEN I NAGGED HER TO LET ME GO,
"HOW MAY TIMES HAVE I TOLD YOU, I SAID NO".

BUT JESUS WAS CRUCIFIED AS PAYMENT FOR MY SINS,
AND I'LL GO TO HEAVEN FOR ETERNITY IF I BELIEVE THIS.
SO WE OUGHT TO FORM A CHURCH AND WORSHIP HIM,
BECAUSE IT WAS HIS MESSIANIC MISSION FOR HIM TO DO THIS.

THOUGH HE COULD CURE OUR BIRTH DEFECTS AND ALL ILLS,
FEED US BY THE THOUSANDS WITH A LOAF AND A FISH,
HE DIDN'T DIE TO GIVE THE PEOPLE A BETTER LIFE,
WITHOUT THIEVERY, DECEPTION, WARS, OR STRIFE.

REMEMBER, HE IS THE CORNERSTONE OF THE TEMPLE DESTROYED.
GOD AND THE ARK FROM THE HOLY OF HOLIES, DISAPPEARED.
WE ARE NOW ORDERED TO WORSHIP THE SPIRIT OF CHRIST,
WHO SUPPLANTS THE LAWS ISSUED ON MOUNT SINAI (ROM 8:2-4)

IT WAS TO ALL THE DISCIPLES THAT JOHN PROPHESIED,'
HE WILL BAPTIZE YOU WITH THE HOLY SPIRIT AND FIRE. (LK 3:16)
LIKE A GUST OF WIND AND SPEAKING IN TONGUES,
AT THE PENTECOST YOU HAVE NEW BEINGS BECOME.

RB WELSH, 5 3 23

SAVIORS

WHY DOES JESUS HAVE TO BE BAPTIZED?
IF GOD IS JESUS WE WONDER WHY.
ACTUALLY, JESUS IS BAPTIZED BY
THE HOLY SPIRIT AS THE DOVE SYMBOLIZED.

IT'S THE SPIRIT'S VOICE COMING OUT OF THE CLOUD,
"THIS IS MY SON OF WHOM I AM PROUD."
WELL THEN, WHERE DID JOHN EVER GET THE IDEA
THAT HE SHOULD BAPTIZE ALL THE SINNERS IN JUDEA?

JOHN'S FATHER WAS A PRIEST IN A LINE OF AARON.
HIS WIFE WAS TOO OLD TO BEAR A CHILD AND WAS BARREN. (LK 1:5-2:20)
LIKE ISAAC, JOHN WAS BORN AS A CHILD OF GOD, (GEN 21:1)
WHO VISITED ELIZABETH LIKE HE DID SARAH.

ZECHARIAH WAS MUTED FOR HE MUST HAVE KNOWN,
THAT SHE WAS PREGNANT BY THE ANGEL GABRIEL AS TOLD,
TO MARY ABOUT JESUS AND HER PREGNANCY,
THEY WERE BOTH SAVIORS, JESUS AND HE. ("JESUS DYNASTY," JAMES TABOR)

JESUS BAPTIZED NO ONE DURING HIS LIFE,
HE COMES AT THE PENTECOST AS JOHN PROPHESIED,
TO BAPTIZE ALL MEN WITH THE HOLY SPIRIT AND FIRE,
AS PETER AND JOHN WENT TO SAMARIA AS INSPIRED. (ACTS 8: 15-17)

JOHN WAS CRUCIFIED BECAUSE OF A WHIM,
HAVING HIS HEAD CHOPPED OFF WAS HEROD'S SIN.
GOD NEVER VISITED OR EVEN SAVED,
HIS OWN COUSIN, WHO WAS IN JAIL.

WHEN WILL WE EVER GET OUR ACT TOGETHER?
CHURCH FATHERS HAVE NO IDEA OF TRUTH, SO THEY ARE IN ERROR.
IT'S NO WONDER DENOMINATIONS AND SPLITS OCCUR,
GOD HAS A PROBLEM AND IT'S HIS CREATION ON EARTH.

RB WELSH, 5 3 23

THOMAS

I HAD ALWAYS THOUGHT THAT PETER WAS THE ROCK
CHRIST WOULD BUILD HIS CHURCH, BUT HE WAS NOT.
AS IT TURNS OUT IT'S JAMES THE JUST
A BROTHER OF JESUS IN WHOM HE CAN TRUST.

UPON PETER I WILL BUILD MY CHURCH, JESUS SAID,
BUT AFTER THE "DENIAL" HE MADE JAMES THE HEAD
OF THE JERUSALEM CHURCH; PETER TO CONVERT HEBREWS.
PAUL TO THE GENTILES AND TO CHRISTIANIZE YOU.

PETER EVENTUALLY RECRUITED THE JEWS TO THE WAY
THIS WAS CHRISTIANITY AS IT WAS CALLED IN ITS DAY.
THIS IS DESCRIBED IN THE GOSPEL OF THOMAS DIDYMUS
THAT THE LEADER OF THE JERUSALEM CHURCH IS JAMES THE JUST (THOM 12)

FOR PETER HAD SUDDENLY PANICKED AND LOST FACE,
THE ROCK HAS CRUMBLED DOWN TO THE SIZE OF A GRAIN.
HE AND JOHN BAPTIZED SAMARITANS IN THE HOLY SPIRIT. (ACTS 8:15)
ALL DISCIPLES AND SAUL ARE ON A CHRISTIAN MISSION.

SO WHAT DO WE DO AS DISCIPLES OF CHRIST?
DO WE STRAIGHTEN OUT ALL THE ERRORS WE RECITE?
OR ARE WE ABLE TO SEE THE LIGHT
IN ITS SERIOUS WAY OF BEING DIVINE?

RB WELSH, 4 22 23

TEASE

JESUS IS GETTING BACK AT SIMON PETER
WHO DENIED HIM THREE TIMES LAST EASTER.
SO HE ASKS HIM THREE TIMES SINCE HE WANTS TO TEASE,
IF PETER LOVES HIM AND WILL FEED HIS SHEEP.

IN DENYING JESUS PETER PROVED HE WAS WEAK,
NOW HE HAS TO FEED HIS SHEEP.
PETER MUST BE QUITE EMBARRASSED,
FOR JESUS KNEW, SO NOW IS HARASSED.

THE OTHERS ARE SITTING AROUND IN RANGE,
SNICKERING AT THIS EXCHANGE.
BUT THEY KNEW THAT THEY TOO WOULD RISE,
WHEN THEY TOO GAVE UP THE GHOST AND DIED.

FOR THEY HAD BEEN LOYAL ALL THE TIME
AND TOO, COULD HAVE BEEN CRUCIFIED.
PETER HAD EVEN DENIED.
THAT HE WOULD EVEN EVER DENY.

SO THAT JUST COMPOUNDED THE FELONY.
THAT HE COULD POSSIBLY LOSE HIS FIDELITY.
PETER IS TORTURED BY THIS TEST,
AND IS SOON IN COMPLETE DISTRESS.

FEED HIS SHEEP MEANS SPREAD THE WORD.
AS A DISCIPLE PETER HAS LEARNED.
HE WILL BE RESPONSIBLE INDEED,
TO SPREAD THE WORD OF CHRISTIANITY.

RB WELSH, 4 20 23

CREATION

MR. AND MRS. GOD WERE SITTING IN THEIR PORCH.
GOD SAYS, "IT'S SO QUIET IN THE UNIVERSE, I'M A LITTLE BORED"
SO HE DECIDED WHAT THEY MUST DO TO MAKE A MAN
TO BE LIKE THEM AND GIVE SOME FAMILY LIFE A PLAN.

FIRST WE'LL HAVE TO CREATE THE EARTH
THEN MAKE THEM OUT OF SPIT AND DIRT
PUT THEM ALONE IN A GARDEN
WATCH WHAT THEY DO TO KEEP FROM BOREDOM.

GOD SAYS," THEY'RE ALREADY SMART, SO IT SEEMS TO ME,
I THINK I'LL PLANT A KNOWLEDGE TREE,
THEN PROHIBIT EATING OF ITS FRUIT
THEN THEY'LL BE OBEDIENT TO MY RULES."

THEN THEY'LL BE MY TINKER TOYS
MAKING NATIONS OF GIRLS AND BOYS
I CAN HAVE A CHOSEN RACE
TO WORSHIP ME LIKE MINUETS.

I'LL GIVE THEM LAWS ON HOW TO LIVE,
TO GIVE GRAIN AND ANIMAL OFFERINGS.
HELP THEM FIGHT ALL THEIR WARS,
SO THEY'LL PERPETUALLY ME ADORE."

MAN'S LIFE WILL IMPROVE UNTIL
IT POPS BECAUSE THE EXCESSES IN SIN.
MAN AT LEAST CAN SAVE HIS SOUL
TO LIVE HERE IN HEAVEN WITH STREETS OF GOLD.

THERE ARE PLENTY OF PLANETS WITH ATMOSPHERES,
TAKE YOUR SAUCER TO THERE IF YOU WANT TO BREATHE.
MRS. GOD AND I WILL GIVE UP THIS LIFE
MAN AS A CREATION IS A DISASTER I FIND.

HE'S LOVING SIN AND MAKING WAR
HE FAKES WORDS TO ADORE.
OF ALL CREATION MAN IS THE BIGGEST
DISAPPOINTMENT BECAUSE HE'S A BIGOT

EVEN A CRUCIFIXION IS NOT HORRIBLE ENOUGH
TO SAVE, FOR THE SINNING GOING ON IS TOO MUCH.,
BUT IF WE ARE BAPTIZED WITH THE DOVE AND HOLY SPIRIT
OUR SINS ARE CLEANSED FOR HEAVEN TO INHERIT. (ACTS 8:15-17)

RB WELSH 4 27 23

TRUTH

YOU KNOW HOW IT IS FOR YOU TO BELIEVE,
BE TOLD IT IS TRUE BY THE AUTHORITIES.
NOT ONCE BUT TWICE AND SO MANY TIMES,
AGAIN AND AGAIN TILL IT'S GLUED IN YOUR MIND.

THAT'S WHAT YOU'RE TOLD ABOUT THE TRINITY,
THAT THE GOD OF ONE IS REALLY THREE.
IT'S GOD, THE SON AND THE HOLY SPIRIT,
VOTED ON BY THE COUNCIL AT NICEA.

IT IS SAID THAT CONSTANTINE SAW A CROSS IN THE SKY,
BUT HE CONFESSED TO EUSEBIUS THAT HE HAD LIED, GIBBON," RISE AND FALL,
ROMAN EMPIRE."
TO UNIFY CONQUERED NATIONS, TO WORSHIP IN UNISON
AND GET HIS PRIESTS TO VOTE THAT THREE IS ONENESS.

AN ANGEL HAD ONLY COME TO HIM IN A DREAM,
CHANGING ALL OF THE CHURCH'S HISTORY.
NOT EVEN KNOWING THE HOLY SPIRIT IS SUPREME,
IT BEING THE GREATEST OF ALL THE THREE.

IF ONE ASKS HE'LL BE FORGIVEN FOR TAKING GOD'S NAME,
OR THAT OF JESUS WHEN ONE'S MAD, IN VAIN,
BUT NOT IF TAKING THE NAME OF THE HOLY SPIRIT,
FOR IF IN DOING SO, HE'LL NOT BE FORGIVEN. THOM 44, LK, 12:10, MT 12:31, MK3:28

LOOK IN ACTS, CHAPTER 8, 15 TO 17 WHERE PETER AND JOHN
REBAPTIZED SAMARITANS IN THE HOLY SPIRIT AGAIN,
FOR WHEN THEY WERE BAPTIZED FOR THE FIRST TIME,
IT WAS ONLY IN THE NAME OF JESUS CHRIST.

WHEN WORLDS MEET THEIR FATE WITH SUPER-NOVAS,
THEIR RACES ESCAPE IN THEIR FLYING SAUCERS.
COMING TO PLANET EARTH AS IN THE AXIAL AGE,
BRINGING THEIR GODS FOR WORSHIPPING SAGES.

THE REASON WHY YOU'RE NOT INFORMED OF ALL THIS,
IS THAT CHURCH FATHERS WOULD LOSE CONTROL OF YOUR BLISS.
MY THOUGHTS ARE NOT YOUR THOUGHTS, SAITH THE LORD, (IS 55-8)
BUT OUR GOAL IS TO EVER BE AT ONENESS AND IN ACCORD. (ROM 12:3-13)

IT MUST BE CONCLUDED AFTER ALL THIS
THAT THE HOLY SPIRIT IS SUPERIOR TO GOD AND JESUS.
OUR CHURCH IS ONLY PRESBYTERIAN
TO JESUS CHRIST, THE CORNERSTONE.

RB WELSH, 4 19 23

ACKNOWLEDGEMENTS

To my daughter, Katherine Welsh Nelson, and my son, George Wilhelm Welsh, without whose encouragement and assistance, this collection of poetry would never have been published.